PENGUIN

INDIGENOUS HEALING

RUPERT ROSS is a retired assistant Crown Attorney for the District of Kenora, Ontario. Starting in 1985, he conducted criminal prosecutions for more than twenty remote Ojibway and Cree First Nations communities in northwestern Ontario. His first book, *Dancing with a Ghost*, started his exploration of aboriginal visions of existence and became a bestseller. His second book, *Returning to the Teachings*, was also a bestseller and examined the aboriginal preference for the "peacemaker justice" he observed during a three-year secondment with Justice Canada. Both books were shortlisted for the Gordon Montour Award for the best Canadian non-fiction book on social issues, and are presently used in universities and colleges across North America. Following his retirement, Ross was awarded the prestigious 2011 National Prosecution Award for Humanitarianism, and the Ontario Crown Attorneys Association has created an award named after him. He continues to live just north of Kenora with his wife, Val.

ALSO BY RUPERT ROSS

Dancing with a Ghost:
Exploring Aboriginal Reality

Returning to the Teachings:
Exploring Aboriginal Justice

INDIGENOUS
HEALING

EXPLORING TRADITIONAL PATHS

RUPERT ROSS

PENGUIN

an imprint of Penguin Canada Books Inc., a Penguin Random House Company

Published by the Penguin Group
Penguin Canada Books Inc., 90 Eglinton Avenue East, Suite 700, Toronto, Ontario, Canada M4P 2Y3

Penguin Group (USA) LLC, 375 Hudson Street, New York, New York 10014, U.S.A.
Penguin Books Ltd, 80 Strand, London WC2R 0RL, England
Penguin Ireland, 25 St Stephen's Green, Dublin 2, Ireland (a division of Penguin Books Ltd)
Penguin Group (Australia), 707 Collins Street, Melbourne, Victoria 3008, Australia
(a division of Pearson Australia Group Pty Ltd)
Penguin Books India Pvt Ltd, 11 Community Centre, Panchsheel Park, New Delhi – 110 017, India
Penguin Group (NZ), 67 Apollo Drive, Rosedale, Auckland 0632, New Zealand
(a division of Pearson New Zealand Ltd)
Penguin Books (South Africa) (Pty) Ltd, 24 Sturdee Avenue, Rosebank,
Johannesburg 2196, South Africa

Penguin Books Ltd, Registered Offices: 80 Strand, London WC2R 0RL, England

First published 2014

6 7 8 9 10 (WEB)

Copyright © Rupert Ross, 2014

Manufactured in Canada.

LIBRARY AND ARCHIVES CANADA CATALOGUING IN PUBLICATION

Ross, Rupert, 1946–, author
Indigenous healing : exploring traditional paths / Rupert Ross.

Includes bibliographical references and index.
ISBN 978-0-14-319110-0 (pbk.)

1. Social justice—Canada. 2. Indian ethics—Canada. 3. Native
philosophy—Canada. 4. Native peoples—Canada—Social conditions.
5. Native peoples—Legal status, laws, etc.—Canada. I. Title.

E78.C2R6858 2014   303.3'7208997071   C2014-901128-8

eBook ISBN 978-0-14-319197-1

Visit the Penguin Canada website at www.penguin.ca

Special and corporate bulk purchase rates available; please see
www.penguin.ca/corporatesales or call 1-800-810-3104, ext. 2477.

To Val—my partner, wife and co-adventurer,
with all my love, respect and gratitude

Much of what used to be described as "healing" is now viewed as "decolonization therapy."

—HOLLOW WATER FIRST NATION, MANITOBA, 2002

Contents

Introduction

Some time ago, I attended a justice conference with a large group of Crown attorneys, police officers and aboriginal people. I remember an Anishinaabe (Ojibway) Elder telling us a story before he opened the conference with a traditional prayer. He told us that before the white man came to Turtle Island, his people had their own way of praying. It involved turning their heads skyward, searching the heavens with eyes wide open and raising their arms in a gesture of greeting and friendship. He told us that they had prayed that way for centuries and it seemed to work, because everybody had a pretty good life here on Mother Earth.

Then the white man came, and he had a different way of praying. Instead of turning his head skyward, he turned his head down. Instead of holding his arms out, he pulled them in tight and clasped his hands in a tipi shape below his chin. And instead of keeping his eyes open, he held them firmly closed for the whole prayer.

When the Indians saw that, they decided to give it a try. So that's what they did—they prayed, head down, hands clasped and eyes closed.

When they finished their prayer and looked up, however, all their land was gone! So that's why, he told us, they went back to praying in their own way.

When the Elder told us that story, he changed everything in the room. We had been three groups of people with a history of not getting along all that well together. Police often hold Crown attorneys in rather low regard, either because we tell them they don't have enough evidence or because we simply fail to prove their charges in court. Sometimes, Crown attorneys can come down on police for things like breaches of Charter rights that make the evidence they brought us inadmissible in court. And it's fair to say that aboriginal people have many good reasons to be wary of both groups. At any rate, you could feel the polite tension in that room—until, that is, the Elder told us that story.

We all laughed, and we all laughed together. It was just such a beautiful, respectful way to break the ice at the very start of the conference. It set a common-ground tone that took all of us through the next two days in relative comfort with one another. We all became better listeners because of it, and better able to work together on the serious topics we were there to discuss.

I tell this story now with the same hope: that it will help to set a tone of being together in a state of mutual respect. If we can all laugh at the same thing, then anything is possible.

IT'S BEEN A LONG TIME since the publication of my first two books, *Dancing with a Ghost: Exploring Aboriginal Reality* in 1992 and *Returning to the Teachings: Exploring Aboriginal Justice* in 1995. I have been largely silent since then, with the exception of several unpublished papers I've written that have been making the rounds. My attention and energies have, instead, been focused on my wife, Val; on our three growing children; and on the pressing demands of being a criminal prosecutor in the remote, fly-in First Nations of northwestern Ontario. Now, after twenty-six years, I've finally said goodbye to the courts and the formal justice system, and our children have grown and moved away. This is supposed to be my quiet time, when my focus rests on Val, on our travels together (especially back into the bush) and on our children and (at the moment) one grandson.

So why am I writing this book?

In fact, there are many reasons, but I want to share two in particular at the outset. Both came from a Calgary conference that was called some years ago to discuss the creation of the Truth and Reconciliation Commission (TRC), a body established as a result of aboriginal lawsuits against churches and governments for their operation of the residential schools. Much discussion took place at the conference of the commission's determination to investigate that system and chronicle the impact across the decades. At the end of those discussions, the microphone was offered to people who had attended residential schools and wanted to comment on how they saw the reconciliation process unfolding. Two aboriginal people, a woman and a man, said things that have stayed with me ever since.

The first speaker was an aboriginal Grandmother. She said that she wished the TRC every success in helping to tell the full story of residential schools. Then she surprised me, because she didn't mention the need to educate non-aboriginal Canadians about that system. Instead, she focused on aboriginal children. Specifically, she said she felt they needed to understand how their parents and grandparents had been changed by those schools. "Maybe then," she said softly, "they can learn to forgive us for failing them so badly."

I have heard the same sentiment many times since then, and from many different people. The most recent was an aboriginal woman who spoke on the radio about a weekend gathering of female Elders and youth, and how surprised the Elders were to learn how little the youngest generation knew of residential schools. She too made a plea for that kind of education to begin.

So that is one reason for writing: to help tell the story of residential schools to the people who need to hear it if they are ever going to forge healthy relations with their own parents, grandparents and communities. I know I'm not the only one to tell that story, or even the best one to do it, but I've been told, and I believe, that every voice counts. My hope is that aboriginal and non-aboriginal people will find value in what I write here.

The second person who came to that TRC microphone was an older aboriginal man, an obvious "graduate" of residential school (now known as a "survivor" to distinguish the experience of imprisonment within residential schools from simply being a student in the country's regular schools). He told the assembly that he had just one question he needed the TRC to answer for him: "Why can't I cry?" He explained that even when he knew things were sad, he could not cry. At that time, I had just begun my exploration of what western psychology calls *emotional intelligence*. Much of the discussion centres on what a child needs to be able to develop the emotional skill sets necessary to become an emotionally mature adult. I was particularly interested in learning about what happens to children who grow up in states of emotional numbness, with no one wanting to hear how they feel and no one able to guide them into nuanced awareness of the many feelings that course through them. That, as I was beginning to understand, was what children experienced in residential schools. When that man asked, "Why can't I cry?" he seemed to be speaking on behalf of generations of aboriginal children who had no choice but to grow up intentionally numbing themselves, both within residential schools and after leaving them. Lacking those emotional skill sets as adults, many do not know how to respond to the normal frustrations of life except by continuing that numbness or, particularly when alcohol or drugs are involved, exploding into anger and violence.

That story of intentional numbing also needs to be told because the combination of childhood trauma and emotional numbing is, in my view, one of the most important legacies of residential school. As I have come to understand it, this explains why the destructive forces begun within residential schools still plague so many aboriginal families today, even when the last school shut its doors forty years ago. Parents cannot teach what they never learned, and they cannot demonstrate what they have never experienced. The numbness and later difficulties in life may, in fact, be even more intense today than they were originally, if only because the stockpile of traumatic experiences has been building in the generations since.

So that is the second reason I am writing: once we gain some understanding of how psychologically damaging the residential school system was to those who attended, we must then explore why it remains such a powerfully destructive force today. Aboriginal children need to know about the history of their families, and non-aboriginal Canadians need to know about the true history of our country. I don't think Canada understands, and I think we ought to.

That being said, I also want to write about the hugely inspiring things I have encountered within traditional culture, and about the determination of so many leading aboriginal people to restore traditional visions to prominence in the modern world. Non-aboriginal Canada needs to see this determination as well, and to gain some understanding of how those visions can play an important role in Canada today. This cultural revival is being promoted as not only the best way to restore health within aboriginal families and communities, but also as simply a better way to live. As much as I have been saddened by the extraordinary violence and despair I have witnessed in so many aboriginal communities, I have also been blessed to meet some of the most inspiring and powerful teachers within the larger aboriginal community. All of them focus on learning about, and sharing, traditional visions of humankind and our best way to live on Mother Earth. I have seen first-hand their determination to bring their original histories to full flower in the modern world. I have been told that there are now over a thousand aboriginal people holding Ph.D.s in Canada, and I know something of what they've been taught and where they want to go. I want to share some of those stories, too.

In the last two years before my retirement in 2011, I was lucky enough to be given a temporary placement with the First Nations and Inuit Health Branch of Health Canada, working on community healing programs. Our primary task was to supply the TRC with health support workers to take care of the often elderly people who came forward at the hearings to share their stories of life within residential school. I spent time with some of the four hundred–odd people who filled the role of healer, most of them aboriginal, and I learned a great deal about how they saw healing in the modern context. After years of working with lawyers and judges, seeing the pain brought out by the courts, the time that I spent with the healers was very special; I will always be grateful to them for sharing so readily with me. I also witnessed the renewal of the National Native Alcohol and Drug Addiction Program (NNADAP) and travelled across Canada to hear how aboriginal people understood the high degree of substance abuse in their communities, as well as to work with them on redefining the kinds of healing processes that might be most effective. In this role, I met one Mohawk woman who is determined to restore emotional skill sets to her people, and I experienced her excitement as I sat in on her training sessions.

The more I learned about those kinds of healing activities, the more I saw that they shared a larger goal: they all wanted to anchor aboriginal life in traditional cultural visions once again. That experience affected me deeply. I believe that the rest of Canada needs to learn about these visions, about how aboriginal people see them as being a part of the modern world, and about the determination of so many people to bring them back to life.

For this reason, I have included many quotations from other

authors as I go along. I think it is important for non-aboriginal Canadians to understand how many aboriginal people have become well educated in the western world yet remain determined to restore traditional visions. I have also quoted many non-aboriginal psychologists, academics and other researchers, primarily to demonstrate the degree to which they have come to agreement on such realities as the devastating impact of residential schools. Many of the authors whose work I have quoted are listed at the back of the book, with brief descriptions of their careers and writings. I encourage everyone to begin looking at work such as theirs. The body of literature that speaks to aboriginal life and history in Canada is growing rapidly, and I suspect it will change Canada's sense of its own history as time goes on.

Most of this book will focus on how aboriginal people see a healthy future, not the sadness of their colonized past. I acknowledge that I like what I have learned about traditional visions. To me, they are sane, exhilarating and productive. My only concern lies in how well I can give voice to them in English, because they come out of a different paradigm, a different way of understanding how humankind fits into the life of Mother Earth. I suspect that many of the ways of articulating that vision simply cannot be replicated in English, but that's all I've got to work with. I'll have to fall back on something I was told by a Mohawk woman who recently invited me to make a presentation at her community's annual Justice Day: "I think you have a very positive way of relating and talking to both First Nations and non–First Nations, which is a rare gift indeed." I hope she is right, and that I can convey even a small sense of my appreciation of the beautiful balances struck within traditional visions.

In that regard, I want to pass along something I heard from a Cree Grandmother, Maria Linklater, who was speaking to a group of aboriginal youngsters from across Canada, telling them stories about the ups and downs in her life. We were all sitting outside in a circle under a tree, with warm prairie sunshine dappling through the leaves. She spoke of the times in her life when the sadness was so engulfing that it seemed as if there were only darkness all around her, but then something bright or cheerful always came along to bring her back into balance. She spoke of times when the unfairness of situations was so hurtful that she wanted to strike out in anger, but something generous or compassionate always came along to bring her back into balance once more. Then she paused, as if an idea had just occurred to her. She slapped her thigh, chuckled out loud and said something I've never forgotten: "You know, I think I finally figured out what it means to live a good life." That declaration really caught my attention, because "a good life" is a serious concept within aboriginal traditions, and because Elders seldom tell others what they should think, say or do. "Maybe," Maria told us, "you know you're living a good life when you get to my age, and you look back maybe five years or so, and you find yourself saying, 'Boy, I sure didn't know too much ... way back then!'"

As the years go by, I continue to unravel what she told us, finding new significance in her words. For one thing, I love the idea that "a good life" does not demand amassing a stockpile of answers, but rather encountering deeper questions as you struggle along. As a result, I no longer worry about finding myself saying "I don't know" far more frequently than I used to.

But her Teaching suggested something else, as well: if I acknowledge that every five years or so I'll probably change my advice to myself, why would I try to give anyone else advice along the way? Instead, all I can do is tell my stories as best I can. If they happen to touch someone in a positive way, that's wonderful. If they don't, well, they don't, but it's all I can offer.

And that's the spirit in which I write, as a co-explorer, knowing that I'll probably see things differently as time passes and my questions get deeper still. I must be patient and remember the fragility of what I think I know. We have a duty to offer our own stories, however, just in case something we say does touch someone else in a positive way. Stories of struggle can be especially important, because we all struggle. In the same way, stories of how we have overcome our challenges might help inspire others to believe that they too can overcome. I have witnessed the extremes of aboriginal life, from the most awful to the most awe-inspiring. I have been told that the uniqueness of my experiences within the aboriginal world imposes a special duty to share my stories as best I can.

I should also mention that I have capitalized three words throughout the book: Grandmother, Teachings and (with a couple of exceptions) Elder. All three words prompt deep feelings of respect and appreciation in me, feelings I want to honour whenever I write about them.

Finally, I remember what I was told at the end of a week-long session with some of the most highly educated aboriginal people in North America. One man turned toward me and said, "Okay, get out there and write about what you've learned." When I looked a little puzzled by the responsibility he was giving me, his amused response was this: "You don't think you were invited here just for your own good, do you?"

PART ONE

STUMBLING INTO A WORLD OF RIGHT RELATIONS

CHAPTER 1

LEARNING TO SEE RELATIONALLY

In the eighteen years since *Returning to the Teachings* was first published, my learning has never ended. Each new experience has given old experiences a new shape and my sense of exploration has never diminished. While much of my learning has been conscious work, perhaps the most important parts just emerged over time, showing up first as "that's an interesting thought" and then gradually revealing much wider applications than I'd ever imagined.

For that, I have to thank Murdena Marshall, an Elder from the Eskasoni First Nation on Cape Breton Island, who invested much of her time in me during my first visit to her community in 1992. I had just been seconded to the Aboriginal Justice Directorate, a new division of the federal Department of Justice, and my job was to explore the aboriginal assertion that, for them, justice was primarily a healing activity, not one of vengeance or retribution. My plan at the time was to go to the various First Nations engaged in healing to try to understand what their version of counselling looked like, whether it was working and, if so, why. Her response took me a little by surprise. Over the course of several conversations, she made it clear that gaining an understanding of aboriginal healing programs required much more than just visiting them and examining what they did. In her view, I first had to gain a deeper appreciation of how aboriginal people saw Creation and the position of humankind within it. For those kinds of explorations, she suggested I would be wise to seek out Elders, philosophers and teachers and spend time learning from them. If I felt comfortable with the idea, it would also be good to participate in traditions such as the sweat lodge and letting-go ceremonies. I will be forever grateful for that guidance. As I sat with aboriginal philosophers and teachers, it became clear that the aboriginal preference for healing is not a preference at all, but rather a necessary manifestation of a world view that is fundamentally at odds with the Cartesian, Newtonian and Darwinian world view in which I grew up.

World views are hard to talk about. You have to substantially escape your own to even begin to hear what is being said about another. For instance, I remember being told at an aboriginal justice conference that western and aboriginal scientists might approach the study of a plant in very different ways. The western scientist, we were told, would probably focus primarily on understanding and naming all the parts and properties of the plant; figuring out its root, stem and leaf patterns; examining how it takes in water, sunlight and nutrients; determining how it reproduces and its life expectancy; and so forth. The aboriginal scientist, by contrast, would likely focus on understanding what role that plant plays in the meadow. She would examine how it holds soil when the rains come; what plants flourish close to it; what birds, animals and insects are attracted to it; how it is useful to them; what kinds of conditions it needs to remain healthy—that sort of thing. It's not that the two scientists would pay no attention to the concerns of the other, just that their emphases would be different; they would see the plant in different ways.

Remember that I was told this story at an aboriginal justice conference. Afterwards, I was asked how aboriginal people could possibly accept my justice system, given such different ways of seeing. I was confused. I honestly saw no connection between that story and justice, but I recalled Murdena's encouragement to keep my horizons wide and open. I had already opened a special shelf in my memory and labelled it "Indian puzzles," using it to store the many things I had seen or experienced but couldn't understand. So, I stuffed that plant-in-the-meadow story up there as well, hoping that one day I might figure out the connection. I'd already decided that I had no choice but to wait, eyes and ears open, to see if understanding came to me further down the road.

I discovered the same phenomenon virtually everywhere I went. There were dozens of times when I was left in confusion by responses that seemed disconnected from what had prompted them, but I'll mention just a few other instances at this point.

One of them took place during a coffee break at a cross-cultural conference with Anishinaabe people on the shores of Lake of the Woods, just outside Kenora, Ontario. An Elder, Alex Skead, came up to me and, out of the blue, said, "You're a lawyer, so maybe you can answer a question for me." I knew that Alex had done a pipe ceremony for Pierre Trudeau when he was prime minister, and that he didn't ask frivolous questions, so I was all ears. "Why is it that all of your people seem to think that law comes from books?" He looked directly at me, but I knew enough to keep silent. "That's not the way my people understand it," he continued. He then turned toward a window and pointed out at the water, rocks and dense bush surrounding us. "*That's* where law comes from!" he announced grandly. Now I was totally lost. All I could think of was Charles Darwin's law of the jungle, which describes us as living in dog-eat-dog anarchy. Wasn't that exactly what our laws were designed to control? I didn't say that, of course, because I'd often heard Alex giving his Teachings, and he always spoke of values like respect, love, caring, sharing and humility. How did he get those values from the bush? Which one of us was missing something, and why did I think it was me? Without hesitation, I stored that conversation with my other Indian puzzles, right beside the plant-in-the-meadow story.

But there were even more confusing conversations. At the opening of an aboriginal justice conference in the mountains of Alberta, a large shell filled with smouldering sweetgrass was brought around. Each of us wafted the fragrant smoke over his head, eyes, ears, mouth, chest and thighs, asking for its assistance to think, see, hear, speak and feel only in healthy and respectful ways during our time together. This smudging is a common way for serious discussions or events to begin. The discussion leader then spoke about language differences, explaining that aboriginal languages were not so much noun-centred as they were verb-centred, trying to emphasize not the *thing* aspect of Creation but rather the pattern, flow and function aspect. Once again I felt lost, wondering what this had to do with justice systems. He then held out the shell and told us that in aboriginal languages it would be "called" differently at various times. It could be a sacred vessel at one point in time, a vessel holding candy at another, or a vessel receiving cigarette butts at some other time. It all depended on its relationship to the speaker and to the occasion. To call it, as European languages did, by one name for all occasions was seen as a "poorer" way to speak of the world. When Indian eyes look upon Creation, he told us, they see a much more fluid, transforming and interconnecting reality than Newton ever did, with his linear, billiard-ball chains of cause and effect.

Then he asked the question directly: Given those differences, how could I expect aboriginal people to happily join in all the things done by the western justice system? Once again, I had no answer, because I couldn't see how the story connected to such a question. Up it went onto the Indian puzzles shelf.

The final event I'll mention here was a time when I was told that western and aboriginal cultures hold opposite views about the importance of human beings in Creation. The Bible puts humans right at the top, set on earth to rule all the fish in the sea and everything else out there. Aboriginal Teachings present an opposite hierarchy. Mother Earth, with her lifeblood, the waters, plays the most important role in Creation. Without the soil and water, there would be no plant realm. Without the plants, there would be no animal realm, and without all of them, there would be no us. Within this reverse hierarchy, human creatures are understood to be the least essential and the most dependent. No longer masters of Creation, we are its humble servants instead.

In fact, I was given that Teaching many times, and for years I failed to see why it was important enough that I be told about it. Why, I silently asked myself, should seeing Creation in a way that puts broccoli on a higher plane than my best buddies lead to different visions of justice? I felt that my Indian puzzles shelf was starting to creak and groan under the load.

Then, one beautiful August day several years later, a very small event hit me in a very large way. I encountered an Anishinaabe Grandmother hitchhiking in northwestern Ontario and I gave her a lift. Knowing that a lot of the old people gathered blueberries at that time of year to raise a little cash, I asked her how the blueberry crop was that summer. She immediately replied, "Oh, I was at the garbage dump last night, and there were sixteen bears out there!" That's all she said, apparently satisfied that it was a complete answer to my question. Fortunately, I had lived in the North long enough to understand her answer: bears thrive on blueberries, and a bumper crop means all the bears are back in the blueberry patches sporting huge purple grins. A failed crop, however, causes hungry bears to converge on the nearest dumps in search of food.

But it was the automatic way she answered that stuck out to me.

I could feel all the Teachings I had jammed onto my Indian puzzles shelf doing little two-steps around each other, as if they were finally organizing around a theme. I had asked about one thing, but I had received an answer that seemed to refer to something separate instead.

It started coming: things weren't separate to her at all, not the way they were to me. Instead, all things acted within complex webs of relationships. Whatever happened with one rippled out to touch and affect all others. If you talked about one, you were talking about all, and any point in their relationship would do. To her, the real essence of Creation lay in what was going on *between* things. That's where her attention went, to all the relationships that bind things together so strongly that a question about blueberries gets an answer about bears.

Relationships. Why had I not seen it before? After all, every sweat lodge I had ever attended was called to a close by everyone declaring, "All my relations!"—referring not just to aunties and grandfathers but to all the rocks, trees, animals and waters that are known as "relations" to aboriginal people.

As time went by, Teachings started sliding down off my Indian puzzles shelf and fitting together in ways I hadn't seen before. The plant-in-the-meadow Teaching, for instance, told me that the well-educated aboriginal eye sees not the plant in isolation, but, instead, the vast web of relationships connecting it with everything else that makes up the meadow. If you look at it that way, the meadow is, in its essence, less a collection of things than a complex web of ever-modifying relationships. When I applied this eye to justice, I suddenly saw the aboriginal people's complaint: you could not deal with offenders alone. They were the product of all their relationships, and a true justice system would have to bring in the other parties to those many relationships if there were to be any hope of turning him around. Victims were part of a similar circle;

once touched by a crime, they brought new dynamics into all their relationships as well. To return to the plant-in-the-meadow story, it is clear that if the plant becomes ill, that is because the other contributors to the meadow must have changed their relationships with it in some way. You can't simply heal the plant and send it back into an unchanged meadow.

Relationships. They are what make, direct, unmake, damage and reward us. You can't know me without knowing something of my relationships.

The naming of the shell showed the same emphasis. You don't simply look at something and put a name on it. Instead, the relationship between it, the person using it and the occasion of its use shapes the way it must be named at any point in time. Change any part of the dynamic and you must also change how it is known—if, that is, your eye has been trained to look between, among and around, not simply at.

I also began to see how Alex Skead could find values like respect and sharing when he looked out the window. When he pointed to the bush as the source of law, he was not directing me toward individual things, but to relationships. What he saw, and what his Teachings helped me see, was a totality defined primarily by healthy, sustaining and symbiotic relationships between all the things out there. Bears live off fish, who need frogs, who eat insects, who need algae that live in water and so forth. But these are not so much linear chains of dependency as they are interwoven, beneficial relationships of such complexity that no one can truly know what will happen if one element changes its contribution to— its relationship with—the mix. All we can say is that all elements are necessary to one another, to us, and to the relationships that sustain us. In the language of the Elders, they are all sacred. This fundamental law, taken from seeing the symbiotic dynamism of the natural order, was not Darwin's thing-centred law of violent competition, but the law of respect. Each entity makes essential and unique contributions to every other thing, and in that way to the maintenance of a healthy whole. Every contribution, whether it seems positive or negative to us, touches all and plays a role within the whole. It is patterned forces, not the matter they push around, that are the true essence of Creation. Aboriginal Teachings suggest we direct the bulk of our attention toward those patterned forces if we wish to maintain ourselves—and our world—in health.

Alex's message about the justice system was wholly aligned with the plant-in-the-meadow story but took it a step further. The eye cannot focus simply on the single acts of the offender. Instead, it must look at all the relationships that engaged him, and the values upon which those relationships were built. In committing his crime, the offender saw himself as a solitary being and felt indifferent to his impact on others. Didn't he need to be shown his connection with others, his reliance on them and his duty to create respectful relationships with them instead? A system that fails to teach such things to people cannot, in the aboriginal view, be appropriately called a justice system at all.

Finally, the reverse hierarchy of Creation came tumbling off the Indian puzzles shelf. If your way of knowing focuses on separate things, you will likely turn your attention to their individual properties and powers. If you do that, it is likely that humans will naturally stand out as deserving the top ranking, given our unique powers of communication, movement, toolmaking and the like. From that lofty vantage point, it would be only natural for us to maintain our separation from everything else, and to look down on everything else as well. After all, what lessons could the natural world have for us except those that Darwin saw, the lessons of dog eat dog and survival of the fittest? If, by contrast, your way of knowing focuses on relationships rather than individual people, it will be natural to see that the relationships between human, animal, plant and earth/water aspects of Creation are fundamentally those of dependency. Once you do that, everything changes. We become, in our own eyes, dependent on the health of everything else. Our obligation then must be to promote accommodation with, rather than to seek dominance over, all things. A justice system must work to restore accommodation where relationships have been broken, not promote further alienation between people.

ONCE I SAW THE IMPORTANCE of relationships, many other memories came back to me. I remembered one long day at court in a remote First Nation where we were assisted by an Elder who was giving us a community perspective. One of our last cases involved a spousal assault. The accused pleaded guilty, and when it came time for sentencing, the Elder asked the judge where the man's wife was, advising us that she should be in the courtroom. I recall jumping all over him, insisting that the court was definitely not looking at her behaviour, that it was only the husband's behaviour that we were dealing with, and that putting an obligation on her to attend was a further act of violence toward her. The judge did the same, and the Elder sat down, looking confused and perplexed. Once I began to see the aboriginal focus on relationships and on the obligation of a justice system to bring accommodation and respect back into them, I began to feel very embarrassed. The Elder had thought we were all there for the same reason—to assist the couple in bringing health back into their relationship—while we were there only to punish the man for his use of violence toward his spouse. In our system, the focus was entirely on the offender; in the Elder's system, both parties to the relationship would receive the benefit of our counselling. He had obviously not learned that our justice system seldom takes a counselling role of any sort, except to warn an offender that if he continues in the same behaviour, we'll be even harsher the next time.

I also recalled one of my first encounters with an aboriginal Elder. Her name was Mary Anne Anderson, and she lived in the remote First Nation of Big Trout Lake in northwestern Ontario. She was a member of the band council, and she began the meeting by asking me, through the interpreter, why it was that all my justice system did was take away her people's money, or take her people out to jail, leaving her community with "the problem." I answered that it was our hope that punishing people through either fines or jail time would cause them to think twice about repeating that behaviour in the future. She thought about that, then responded, "So your system is built on terror, then." I answered that we called our approach general and specific deterrence but that, yes, it was meant to scare people away from committing crimes. She responded by declaring that almost all the crimes in her community were committed by people who were drunk at the time and that "you can't scare an ill person into becoming healthy." Sensing that I was running out of answers, I turned the tables and asked her what her community used to do to people who had caused injury of some sort. She snorted then, and stated in a tone that suggested it was almost beneath her to have to reply to such a silly question, "We didn't do anything *to* them. We counselled them instead!"

I was given a similar response many years later while speaking to a Cree Grandmother from northern Quebec. We were talking about family violence, and she told me about the first time the community had asked the judge to adjourn a family violence case so they could begin trying to bring the couple into healthier ways of relating. The judge agreed, and they began their work. Because they were new at healing, however, they didn't watch the husband closely enough. He went back to his wife and assaulted her again. When the court returned and saw the new charge, the judge declared that the community had been given their chance to heal and it hadn't worked, so both cases were now back in the court system. The Cree

Grandmother asked me how that could happen. "After all," she told me, "your jail system hasn't worked after four hundred years, but you never think about shutting it down!" She went on to tell me how she saw the dynamics: "We know you put them in jail to protect the women and children, but to protect us in your way, you would have to keep them there forever. Since you don't, we'd like to try our way instead."

When I asked what their way was, she told me that in their understanding anyone who can act in these ways toward others has somehow learned, perhaps while growing up, that relationships are based on values like anger, power, fear, jealousy and so on. She asked me what values people built relationships upon "inside those jails of yours." I took it as a rhetorical question and just nodded. She then expressed her fear that going to jail might make it even harder for her community to teach those men when they came back how to live in relationships built on values like trust, openness, respect and sharing instead.

For the first time, I had an explanation for why so many people who were abused as children grow up to abuse children themselves. I had always wondered, since they knew first-hand the pain of being a helpless victim, how they could later inflict exactly the same pain on others. Under the relational lens, my perspective changed: they were simply operating within the same kind of relationship they knew from their childhood, the only kind they knew of, a relationship based on manipulation, fear, lies and using others for self-gratification. The only difference was that, as adults, they now held the position of power in that relationship.

The Grandmother's words also helped me understand why so many offenders who had been exposed to powerful healing programs were ultimately moved into a stage of explosive remorse: they had never forgotten the pain of their own victimization. In fact, it seems that a part of them recalled that childhood pain even as they victimized others, giving rise to intense guilt and self-loathing. Not knowing how to relate in any other way, however, meant that they'd abuse again, and that their guilt and self-loathing would grow exponentially.

WRITING ABOUT THESE EVENTS in this way may give the impression that suddenly a light came on and everything became clear to me. That was certainly not the case. Bit by bit and case by case, I found myself asking more frequently what things might look like if I viewed them relationally. My first real use of the relational lens was, naturally, in my work as a prosecutor. Frankly, what I found surprised me, because it slowly became evident that this ancient, traditional vision of who we are as human beings showed the way to a much more enlightened justice system than the one we currently rely upon.

CHAPTER 2

SEEING JUSTICE RELATIONALLY

A s I have come to understand it, "seeing relationally" means looking at how the crime came out of all of the offender's relationships, and in turn affected the relationships surrounding both the offender and the victim, including those with their families and friends, and their places in the community. Seeing relationally invites people to fashion processes where those relationships can be fully explored and, eventually, altered for the better.

I recall, for instance, a case in which a young man who was walking down the street saw a bottle of rum sitting on a table just inside a partly open patio door. He slipped inside, grabbed the rum and took off, never seeing the middle-aged couple who lived there. He bragged about what he'd done afterwards, and that brought about his arrest. In his eyes, all he did was steal that bottle, worth little more than twenty dollars. Big deal. As the court saw it, while he had indeed invaded the couple's privacy, it had been only for a moment, the crime had involved no physical confrontation, and the financial loss to the victims had been minimal.

For the victims, however, this was not just a minor property crime. Every noise in the night now caused them to bolt upright in bed. Their home was no longer a place of comfort and security, but a vulnerable place, open to threat. When we brought the youth together with the homeowners, they expressed their sense of injury, leading him to exclaim, "Geez, I never thought about it that way." And we often don't. Looked at relationally, however, it becomes obvious that the crime had significantly injured the victims' relationship with their home. Being relational in nature, that injury remained long after the court would have closed their property-centred case. As the Elder Mary Anne Anderson phrased it when we spoke about life before western justice, the court would have "left them with the problem": their damaged relationship with their home. Bringing the offender and victims together in a non-adversarial process began to open up that reality to all of them.

Questions began to emerge for me. When victims complain that the court has never really heard them, is it because neither the court nor the offender has ever defined the crime in the same way that victims experience it—as causing an enduring injury to central relationships in their lives? Are victims even able to articulate their experience of injury in that way, or has our thing-centred way of looking at the world kept us from recognizing that it is our capacity for building healthy relationships that is really injured by crime?

In another case, a woman was walking down the street when an angry, muttering stranger suddenly veered toward her, grabbed her purse and ran. She was not hurt and got her purse back, recovering everything except the cash, but she no longer felt safe on the streets of her own community. She worried that every man coming her way might turn out to be another attacker. Under the relational lens, the real damage was done to her relationship with the streets of her neighbourhood. The crime was not just a brief, one-time event, but something that would continue to affect her way of relating to her community long into the future. When victim and offender were brought together in a "case conference," and she told him about her fear, everything changed. The offender began to understand what he had really done to her, and he expressed sincere regret. He explained that he had just sold his car and deposited the cheque, then went home only to find that his girlfriend had decided to break up with him. He went out drinking, one drink led to another and when he went to the ATM for more drinking money he discovered that the cheque for his car had bounced and he was flat broke. That was his state when he encountered the victim walking down the street: broke, car-less, deserted and drunk, he just grabbed that woman's purse, rifled through it to find some cash and carried on drinking. When she heard this and saw how real his apology was, she lost her fear of him; he became just another human being. She later found her fear of strangers on the streets had also diminished. The victim–offender conferencing process had gone a long way toward restoring her relationship with the streets of her town.

But these were relatively minor crimes. The relational lens is even more powerful when applied to far more serious offences. It was sexual assault cases that really showed me the power of thinking about things relationally. I particularly remember a healing circle in the Hollow Water First Nation in Manitoba, for a woman who had been sexually abused. Two women who were members of the healing team described how their rapes many years earlier had changed everything in their lives. One said she still felt so dirty that whenever her grandchildren crawled onto her lap she had to shoo them away; those children had no idea why their grandmother "didn't want them," and she couldn't tell them. The crime had severely affected her capacity to engage in warm and embracing relationships with other human beings, even her own grandchildren. The other woman said that after fourteen years, the sight of her own body still made her feel so dirty that whenever she went into someone's bathroom, she opened the medicine cabinet and turned the mirror to the wall so she wouldn't see her own reflection. Her rape had poisoned her relationship with her own body. "Maybe," she wondered aloud, "that's why I stay so fat, take such poor care of my body, because I can't stand living in it."

Those kinds of experiences caused me to start defining crimes differently, as events that have immediate and enduring impacts on all victims' ability to maintain or develop healthy relationships, whether with their towns, their neighbourhoods, their homes, their friends and loved ones, their bodies, their sense of self or any combination of those essential aspects of a healthy life.

An Inuit Grandmother expressed this perspective during a sentencing for an offender who had sexually touched her granddaughter twice while he was a visitor in their small Nunavut community. He had come up behind the little girl and pressed his groin into her back, once in the church while she was playing piano, and once in the school while she was working on a shop project. What the Grandmother told the sentencing court was this: "We have to help her try and rebuild the trust that he destroyed: the trust that she had in the church, the trust that she had in the school system, and the trust that she had with adults." All of that was relational, reciting the trust that his actions had broken. Interestingly, she also spoke about how sorry she now was for the offender. Her community had seen that he had been given a special gift, the ability to relate well with children, and they had valued his help in counselling suicidal youngsters. However, he had "abused his gift" by what he had done, and now the court was going to forbid him from using it in the future, because he would not be allowed to be alone with children. That, she told us, is what happens when you don't respect the gifts you are given.

Once I began to look at things relationally, and to think of crimes as primarily relational events, I found myself reviewing my own justice system and discovering that it wasn't nearly as sophisticated as I had always thought.

For one thing, the western system shows an almost fanatical determination to focus on acts alone. Those acts must be carefully alleged and subsequently proven in court beyond a reasonable doubt. Those same acts then largely determine the court's response, because we believe that the punishment must fit the crime. In traditional culture, however, the violent act is important primarily as a signal of disharmonies within the offender's relational life. Once the act is understood, the spotlight shines elsewhere, on those disharmonies, because that is where change must happen if the community is to be made safer.

I remember one day asking Charlie Fisher, Ontario's first full-time aboriginal justice of the peace, how his home community would have handled violence in traditional times. His answer surprised me. Offender and victim would each be assigned an Elder, whose job was to "restore people to peace and harmony" by counselling them. Those Elders, Charlie told me, seldom talked about the violence itself. Instead, they focused on what it meant to live in harmony, and why everyone had a duty to live in that way. Every once in a while the Elders would come together to indicate whether they had achieved this goal yet. When both Elders placed their pipes in the circle together, that meant they were satisfied. As far as the community was concerned, this would mark the end of the justice process. Whether the people involved offered apologies or restitution or compensation of some kind was entirely up to them.

When Charlie told me that there was likely no discussion of the offence, I was at a loss for words. How could anyone call that a justice system, when it seldom even discussed the harmful activity? Was this what Mary Anne Anderson was talking about in Big Trout Lake when she said they didn't do anything *to* the offender, but counselled him instead? What kind of counselling were they both talking about? The answer, as the Cree Grandmother from Quebec expressed it, involved teaching people that healthy relationships were built on values like respect, caring, sharing and humility, not fear, anger and manipulation. It was the absence of those values that made relationships abusive, and caused the criminal acts that are so much the focus of the western system.

The western criminal justice system also seems to believe that individuals can simply choose to alter their behaviour. We regularly ship troubled youngsters off to treatment facilities, for instance, hoping that a few more skills will enable them to make better choices. When they go right back to making poor choices within days of returning home, we scratch our heads and wonder, Did they just get poor treatment, or not enough treatment, or, worse yet, is this just a truly bad kid? The relational analysis, by contrast, begins with the proposition that the tide of unhealthy relations swirling around individuals is, in many cases, simply too powerful to resist, no matter how skilled and determined an individual person (especially a youngster) might be. Each person can be seen as the plant in the meadow: if it is ill, then there must be something no longer working supportively within all the relationships that normally sustain it. If progress is to be made, all of those relationships must be brought into the process so that everyone can see the need to make better choices, and be given help in making them together.

In short, thinking relationally has drawn me toward a proposition that still sounds strange to me: perhaps the thing that we feel gives us true justice is not really about "stuff" at all, whether it is the criminal act, the physical loss or injury, the work done or dollars paid in compensation, or even the years served in jail in an attempt to somehow atone for what was done. If our lives are made precious by the relationships that nourish us, and if crime is understood as a disruption of those relationships, it may be that justice involves three relational goals: having offenders come to understand, on an emotional level, the relational damage that their crimes have created in others; looking at the relational disharmonies in the offender's life that spawned the crime; and searching for ways to move both parties out of the relational disfigurement that has bound them together in fear, guilt and anger from the moment of the crime.

I HAVE SINCE RECOGNIZED that it is far from easy to maintain that relational lens against the powerful western insistence on a non-relational world. In fact, it is even difficult for aboriginal organizations to remain faithful to the relational understanding.

I recall, for instance, one aboriginal organization that conducted victim–offender conferences in remote First Nations. Those conferences were established so both parties could explore the relational dimensions of the crime. At one point, I heard that the organization had just hired an aboriginal man I knew, someone who had great experience in aboriginal family healing. Because his work had always involved maintaining a focus on bringing relational disharmonies back into balance, I was quite excited to hear that he had been chosen. I felt that the organization itself really needed him to restore that kind of focus, given that they seemed to be slipping into the western emphasis on whether the offender should pay restitution, do free work for the victim or just do free work for the community. He told me that he was being sent to a major university as part of his training, apparently to study mediation. That worried me a little. When he got back I made a point of asking him how his training had gone. He answered that, on the first day of the course, he and the other students were told to "leave your values at the door and go for win-win." I couldn't believe it. This man had extensive experience restoring people to good relations, yet he was being told to follow win-win western mediation—and it was an aboriginal agency that had sent him there! He chose to leave that organization after a few months and went back to family healing. I still shake my head.

After exploring restorative justice approaches for several years, I was left with no doubt that bringing a relational perspective to criminal events offered a much wider range of productive responses than those presented by the western justice system. In fact, I quite enjoyed being involved in those processes and seeing all the good that came out of them so frequently.

At the same time, I carried a nagging sense that seeing relationally was just the beginning of something much larger in the aboriginal world. I felt convinced that, although I was going in the right direction, I was a long way from understanding the aboriginal vision of who we are within Creation.

So, while I knew that seeing relationally was just the start of something much deeper, I also knew that I'd have to be patient. In time, I believed, greater clarity might begin to emerge.

CHAPTER 3

MOVING INTO RIGHT RELATIONS

THE EMBEDDED INDIGENOUS SOUL

I remember when I first moved beyond the notion of a relational lens and started to gain a stronger sense of the underlying aboriginal vision in which those relations played such a prominent role. In my reading, I came across a few sentences attributed to Jennie Leading Cloud, a Lakota woman from the Rosebud Reservation in South Dakota:

> We Indians think of the earth and the whole universe as a never-ending circle, and in this circle man is just another animal. The buffalo and the coyote are our brothers; the birds, our cousins. Even the tiniest ant, even a louse, even the smallest flower you can find—they are all relatives. We end our prayers with the words *mitakuyo oyasin*—"all my relations"—and that includes everything that grows, crawls, runs, creeps, hops and flies on this continent. White people see man as nature's master and conqueror, but Indians, who are close to nature, know better.[1]

I had heard such ideas before, but something about the way she put her words together gave me pause. Just another animal?

A true relative to everything that grows, crawls, runs, creeps, hops and flies? Something started to turn in my head about the kind of relationships that indigenous people saw themselves as actors within.

Then I had the good fortune to listen to an aboriginal man from northern Manitoba who came to share traditional Teachings with the children of one of the more traumatized communities of my region. He gave his Teachings in the school gymnasium, repeating them for three different age groups. I recall vividly the way he spoke with the girls in each group, telling them about their special power, as women, to give new life. That new life is given in the moment when their waters break, sluicing a new being into the world. He then expanded the discussion, pointing out that women have "special connections" with water everywhere. Each woman's menstrual cycle, for instance, is known as her "moon time," referencing the fact that Grandmother Moon follows similar cycles, growing to fullness thirteen times a year. She also controls the tides in all the oceans upon Mother Earth, and those tides, in turn, control the washing of shorelines and the provision of food in tidal pools. He told them that there are even species of clams in some deserts that respond to the full moon, opening up when its light shines upon them. He told them that because of their special connections with water, women carry a sacred responsibility to ensure the purity of water for all creatures and for all future generations.

At that point, as he talked about responsibilities, I guessed that he would lose the support of his audience. After all, most of the children came from broken families where intoxication and violence were the norm, and they were notoriously free to run around at all hours doing exactly as they pleased. I could not have been more wrong, and I think I now know why: no one had ever told those children they were a part of, and important to, anything at all, much less something as huge and magical as the universe. If they had responsibilities, that meant they had an identity as an important part of something grand. Their lives then had meaning within that larger whole, something they had never been told before.

The boys, in turn, were given many stories about their connection with fire, and their responsibility to ensure that its power is only used for the good of the community. The Teachings offered an alternative to the disconnection those children lived within every day. It was exactly what they needed to hear.

And there was something about the kind of connection he spoke about that seemed to stay with me, even though I couldn't put it into words at that point.

My moment of real crystallization came when I encountered the writings of a man I had met on several occasions and admired deeply. His name was Dr. Joe Couture, and he was a Cree-Métis psychologist, Elder and educator from northern Alberta. Although he has now passed on, his written works will retain their importance well into the future. In one small paragraph he gave a different dimension to everything I already thought I knew, putting such concepts as the connections between women, water, the tides and Grandmother Moon in a much larger context. He was writing about the problems many indigenous people have with western psychology and its focus on healing people as individuals: "A traditional native sense-of-self may find a relentless focus on self as alien, disquieting, undesirable or unnecessary. Rather, a general Aboriginal self is one of an 'embedded, enfolded socio-centric self' ... Native mind is therefore a mind-in-relational activity, a mind-in-community."[2]

THE PHRASE "embedded, enfolded socio-centric self" was what really hit me. Dr. Couture had taken it from a 1993 book titled *Multicultural Assessment Perspectives for Professional Psychology*, written by R.H. Dana, because it struck him as an essential phrase if people wanted to understand the aboriginal sense of self. When he gave me that phrase, my long-favoured notion of "seeing relationally" started to evolve into something much more complex: the notion of "*being* relationally." Until that moment, I had imagined myself looking at Creation through a relational lens. That meant I was still separate from all of Creation. If I dropped that lens and saw myself instead as embedded and enfolded *within* all of Creation, I was different. I was no longer an observer, seeing from a distance. I was a partner, instead, a co-participant.

Having finally encountered an expression of that difference, I seemed to run across the same perspective everywhere I turned (as often happens). For instance, here is how it is expressed by Marlene Brant Castellano, a noted Mohawk Elder, writer and professor emeritus at Trent University: "The notion is not that human beings are at the centre of the universe, but that our lives are nested in complex relationships."[3]

Embedded, enfolded and nested. When I thought back to the school gym and those disconnected girls and boys showing such delight at hearing about the connections they shared and had a duty to respect, I realized that I had only understood the word *connected* from within my own thing-centred, human-dominated way of seeing the universe. I had not thought of women as being embedded in relations that were ongoing, every moment of every day, between all those things. If you are embedded in those relations, you become a part of each of them in ways that are far more elemental than simply being connected to them. A Nuu-chah-nulth principle from the west coast of Vancouver Island puts it simply: *Hishuk ish tsawalk*—"Everything is one; we are all connected."

When I went back to the plant-in-the-meadow event, the same Teaching was there, but I had missed it. When I was told that a full understanding of the plant required learning its integral role in the meadow, how it interacts with all the other plants, animals, birds and so on, I did not make the leap to seeing it as embedded in the nature of the meadow, to realizing that it participates not just by being connected but by being an integral component of the larger whole. Whatever it does has an impact on the whole of the meadow, just as changes in the meadow have an impact on it. While individual things obviously have a separate physical existence, their significance, their true nature and meaning, can be seen only in the context of their being part of a changing whole, with all parts contributing. When I hear the word *connection* now, I hear it very differently, as meaning "embedded within."

I read about how the wolves in Yellowstone Park had been hunted until they became extinct, and the various consequences that flowed from their absence. To follow only one of those chains, the elk population that the wolves had feasted upon then exploded. As it did, their food supplies were put under heavy pressure. The elk started eating the leaves off bushes along stream beds. Over time, those bushes began to die out. That meant that their root systems died as well, and the soils they once held in place began to wash into the streams. As the water clouded, the fish habitat was altered until certain spawns stopped happening and some fish species were themselves threatened with extinction. Without the wolves, the park became a fundamentally different—and poorer—place. Once wolves were reintroduced, however, everything began to re-establish and reassert their roles, and with surprising speed. The elk population was reduced by wolf predation, the bushes grew, the soil was retained, the water regained its clarity and the fish spawn was restored. The wolves, once thought to be a threat to the health of the environment, had been truly embedded in that ecosystem, and it changed dramatically when they were taken out of it.

Alex Skead knew that. It is why he saw his values of respect and sharing and caring when he looked out the windows at the water, trees, rocks and animals.

I have no idea what other chains were affected when wolves were taken out of the equation, but I can imagine all sorts of them. The rabbit population, for instance, might also have exploded with no wolves eating them, and certain grasses and leaves would be consumed to dangerous levels, causing the rain runoff to escalate clouding of the stream water, further affecting the fish spawning. Looked at from this perspective, every component of the Yellowstone system was embedded in that system and was essential to its overall health. As Alex Skead would have said, every part was sacred, and that sacredness came from its vital role in the health of the whole.

Two other aboriginal people have been helpful for me in understanding this notion of embeddedness. James Dumont, an Anishinaabe Elder who holds a fourth (or highest) degree in the sacred Medewiwin Society of the Anishinaabe people, was a professor of native studies at the University of Sudbury. His writing partner, Carol Hopkins, is a Delaware woman who holds a master's degree in social work; she was the co-chair of the First Nations Addictions Advisory Panel when I met her. In a lengthy paper, she and Elder Dumont articulate this bedrock view as follows: "All things work together in an interdependent fashion, forming an interconnected web of integrated wholeness. Though each part is a recognizable unit, it only has meaning when in relationship to the whole."[4]

How much do we understand that "whole" and the roles played by all the recognizably separate units that make it up? In my travels, I had heard that many aboriginal cultures refer to Creation by a longer phrase, often interpreted as "the Great Mystery." While I liked the humility of that thought, I originally found it a little overdramatic: even if we didn't yet have the entire universe studied, dissected, chronicled, mapped and named, I could imagine getting to that point someday, especially with computerization. At least, that's what I thought when I saw the universe primarily as a collection of things. Then I was given the plant-in-the-meadow

Teaching and, over time, began to contemplate the meadow not as a collection of things but as ever-modifying relationships. At that point my expectation of ultimate knowability began to break down. While the meadow might have a thousand things in it, it therefore had one thousand times one thousand relationships, all of which were in constant flux over days, weeks, seasons and years. In what sense could that dimension of the universe be known by us? Could it ever be known well enough to grant us accurate prediction? Or predictable intervention? Or would we always find there were relational dimensions we had never contemplated, such as the impact on fish spawns caused by taking wolves out of the balance? Everything has meaning only insofar as it acts within relationship to everything else.

In a similar vein, who could have predicted that an increase of just a couple of degrees in the winter temperature of British Columbia would mean that the population of pine beetles would explode and lay waste to thousands of hectares of pine trees, right over the mountains and into Alberta? That little beetle was (truly!) an embedded part of the forest. I found it so sad—and somewhat terrifying—to drive for hundreds of kilometres down valleys filled with red and dying trees, all because of a little beetle unleashed by such a minimal change in weather. As I looked at those dying trees, I thought about our obligation as nested or embedded participants in the natural world to act toward every other entity with care, humility and accommodation. I thought about our duty to never alter the balances that sustain everything within Creation, including ourselves.

And that takes me to something I never expected: the thought that our need for caution is founded not just on personal interest, but also on the ethical obligations we owe to every one of our relations within Creation.

ETHICAL RESPONSIBILITIES
TOWARD ALL OF CREATION

As I have learned, this notion of an embedded and nested self goes much deeper than mere appreciation of the connections between things. What has given me a much greater challenge is the notion that our responsibility to accommodate the natural world has a deeper foundation than the self-preservation of human beings on this planet. The indigenous understanding is that we carry an *ethical* responsibility toward rocks, trees, water and all life—an ethical responsibility identical to the one we recognize when we deal with other human beings.

In the Dumont-Hopkins paper cited above, they put the concept of ethical responsibility this way:

> Within Indigenous culture … all things are regarded as "persons" and as "relatives." Personhood not only applies to human persons; plants, trees, animals, rocks and both the visible and the unseen forces of nature are also considered as "persons." Because they are persons, they have the range and qualities of personhood that are commonly attributed in western ideology exclusively to human persons. Once this is accepted, other-than-human beings are elevated to a higher quality of being, and the nature of the relationship moves to an all-inclusive, ethical level. We are all related to one another as persons, and are responsible for maintaining good and harmonious relationships within the "extended family" of persons.[5]

Once I read that, I seemed to see the same perspective everywhere I turned. Betty Bastien comes out of Blackfoot culture, and in her book *Blackfoot Ways of Knowing: The Worldview of the Siksikaitsitapi,* she expresses it this way: "The fundamental premise of Niitsitapi ways of knowing is that all forms of creation possess consciousness. The non-separation of nature and humans is one of the demarcations between Eurocentered and Indigenous philosophy. This demarcation creates completely distinct paradigms of reality, truth and knowing."[6]

James (Sákéj) Youngblood Henderson, a member of the Chickasaw Nation and Cheyenne Tribe in Oklahoma, now research director at the Native Law Centre at the University of Saskatchewan, asserts a similar contrast between European and aboriginal perspectives: "While Eurocentric laws separate humanity from the natural world, there is no such separation in First Nation laws. Rather, a deep spiritual connection exists between humanity and the natural world."[7]

Vine Deloria Jr., a noted Sioux author and professor from South Dakota, describes that same perspective this way: "The world, and all its possible experiences, constituted a social reality, a fabric of life in which everything had the possibility of intimate, knowing relationships because, ultimately, everything was related."[8]

For the moment, let me just say that if my travels within the indigenous world have convinced me of anything, it is this: indigenous people are determined to re-articulate that whole vision and build it into daily life once again. Every indigenous author I have read, and every speaker I have heard, carries the same message: they will restore their belief in the traditional sanctity and equality of all life forms to a central position.

So where does that concept come from, the concept that all things in nature should be regarded as persons who are the ethical equivalent of humans? Let me begin by offering the words of Elder James Dumont, whom I mentioned earlier. They come from his 2006 Inaugural Newbury Lecture at the University of Sudbury, and they describe the traditional Anishinaabe Creation story, a story from which he asserts all other Teachings flow:

> Just as the spirit is at the centre of each of us, so the spirit is also at the centre of everything else within this creation. The spirit is always at the centre. When we live our life with other spirit-centred beings in this creation, our relationship to the Creator is from spirit to spirit. Our relationship to one another is also, first of all, from spirit to spirit. Our role as human beings is to preserve that relationship, to maintain the spiritual order and structure of the world.... Indigenous psychology and Indigenous culture can only be fully and properly understood from within this belief: that spirit is the central and primary energy, cause, and motivator of life.[9]

Within the Anishinaabe Creation story, he says, there was a time when there was nothing at all, not even consciousness. There was just darkness and silence. It was a time he describes as "not yet." Then sound began. In the darkness, Creator began to think and consciousness emerged. By becoming able to see his thoughts, Creator knew he existed. That established one aboriginal truth: that we can know ourselves only when we are in relation to something other than ourselves. Alone, we cannot be certain that we even exist. As Elder Dumont puts it, "It is only in relation to someone else that you come to know yourself. That is the way it is in our reality."

Elder Dumont goes deeper still into the Anishinaabe Creation story. Creator wanted to see his thoughts reflected back to him, so he sent them radiating out into the darkness, where each "left an imprint as a star." A voice then told him that "if the mind who seeks to create wishes to make something real from his thoughts, it must be guided by 'her' from whom all life flows: the heart." Creator knew what to do when he listened to the heart: "On the pulse of the heartbeat at the very centre of the darkness, as it moved out in ever-increasing circles—on each wave of that pulse—the star-thoughts gathered and formed the universe." That set up a second aboriginal truth: that the heart embraces everything into itself, gives the universe its circular shape, and thus creates what Dumont calls "forever peace, forever unity and forever stability." Mind or spirit is always the originator, the motivator behind all activity, but it is always heart that guides that creativity and gives shape to the things in the universe.

Elder Dumont then speaks about how Mother Earth was created as the most beautiful place Creator could imagine. It was there that Creator could see the evidence of his own thoughts, "the most beautiful thoughts," reflected back to him. Dumont insists that earth is not a place "where we are sent to learn the lessons of life, or to be tested, or to suffer"; instead, our essential duty is to experience the beauty that sprang from Creator's thoughts, and to reflect that beauty back to him. Dumont expresses it this way: "The human being was designed in order that the spirit would be able to experience this life in all of its depth, in all of its beauty, with all of its joy."

He speaks of aboriginal languages being structured to help people see Creation "as animate, recognizing the spiritual aspect of earth, plants, animals and other living species." As such, those languages indicate that "it is spirit that establishes the relationship between all elements of Creation." That is why Elder Dumont draws the following conclusion: "Indigenous psychology and Indigenous culture can only be fully and properly understood from within this belief: that spirit is the central and primary energy, cause and motivator of life."

He also speaks of the importance of the circle, the shape of Creation guided by the heart. Each component of Creation, though recognizable as a separate unit, "only has meaning when in relationship to the whole." Even though humankind is "a special creation event," the fact that we were "created from the land and ... placed on the land means that we are personally related to the environment, the landscape and the forces all around." He argues that "western man, carrying an exclusive and disconnected view, has lost his sense of relatedness, or gives little credence to it."

I want to suggest that this vision of the beginnings of Creation deserves as much respect as other visions. In fact, it seems much more akin to the evolutionary view of western science, given that it traces every single creature alive today back to the atoms, molecules and chemicals found in Mother Earth. To me, this version is far more likely than the one expressed by the millions of Creationists in North America, who insist that man emerged full-blown between six thousand and ten thousand years ago, at the same time that the whole world began. Many members of the American Senate and House of Representatives subscribe to that belief, as well as one former member of the federal Cabinet in Canada, but I don't see anyone holding that belief system against them. In my view, the aboriginal vision is also as well founded as many aspects of traditional Christianity, whether the virgin birth, the parting of the Red Sea, or a few loaves and fishes feeding the multitudes. Aboriginal creation stories are, however, routinely written off as primitive myths—that is, when they are given any thought at all.

I have provided only the smallest fragment of Elder Dumont's long and complex recital, but I hope to have given a sense of the world view out of which he speaks. As he makes clear, the human focus must be on relationships, on the heart guiding the creative force of the mind, on spirit being within everything as the essence of everything, and on the conviction that the primary role of humans is to reflect the joys and wonders of all life back to Creator.

I want to underline how surprised I was to discover so many well-educated aboriginal people speaking in similar—if not identical—

terms. Whenever I had heard those kinds of perspectives before, I had always given the speaker a sort of poetic licence to articulate the world in rather fanciful terms. As I started to delve into aboriginal writings, however, my view began to change. I was impressed by the fact that so many people, all of them highly educated in the western tradition, were nevertheless promoting identical visions. And their numbers are increasing: thousands of aboriginal people are now enrolled in Canadian universities and colleges, and they are learning about their history and about traditional thought. It began to dawn on me that perhaps I should look more closely at what they all appeared to be studying and saying.

What really struck me, however, was something said by Dr. Laurence Kirmayer, a non-aboriginal psychiatrist who is director of social and transcultural psychiatry at McGill University and editor-in-chief of the scholarly journal *Transcultural Psychiatry*. In one of his pieces, he wrote about how widespread this vision of an embedded self was in the world *as a whole*:

> The notion of a self that is defined in relational terms is well articulated in many cultural concepts of the person, throughout Africa, Asia, and, indeed, most parts of the world ... such alternative metaphors situate the value of the self in its social embeddedness and connection to others rather than in its detachment and inviolability.[10]

There was that word *embedded* again. Suddenly, the aboriginal insistence on the validity of their vision took on a whole new meaning. If there were people in many other places on the planet who held similar views, then there was a chorus of societies articulating similar visions—and taken together, they demanded respectful study. That was important for me to hear, because I confess that, as I said, I had wondered if these beliefs were just romantic expressions of an idealized but unreal past. Reading about Dr. Kirmayer's findings gave me confidence that I was hearing ancient understandings being brought to life in the twenty-first century.

Ultimately, however, it was discussions about indigenous languages that really convinced me that such a vision of spirit-centred interconnectedness truly prevailed in traditional times— and is now being promoted to help struggling communities regain their health and find useful roles in the modern world. Even a quick look at several of those languages will illustrate what I mean.

LANGUAGES BUILT ON SPIRITUAL CONNECTIONS

I am now convinced by the structure of indigenous languages that people did indeed live in a spiritualized and embedding universe, speaking about the world in reverential, connecting terms, positioning everything with and within everything else, and colouring daily life with a rich spirituality that almost defies western understanding.

One of my teachers over the last several decades has been Leroy Little Bear, of the Blood Tribe of the Blackfoot Confederacy in southern Alberta. He was a professor of Native American studies at the University of Lethbridge before becoming director of the Native American Program at Harvard University. He writes the following about his Blackfoot language:

Our elders repeatedly tell us that our language is a spiritual language. For example, "miskisik" means an eye. In this word, "mis" refers to a body part, and the root word, "kisik," means the heavens; it reminds us that our ability to see is a spiritual gift, that we are related to the Creator, and every relationship carries responsibilities.... Our languages guide us in our relationships.... English words simply cannot convey words contextualized in relationships with the sacred.[11]

In her book *Blackfoot Ways of Knowing*, Betty Bastien describes other formations of words in the Blackfoot language:

> An example of the organic nature of Siksikaitsitapi language is the root "aato" which can be found in a number of concepts that form an intricate and complex set of relationships. This group of letters or sounds is found in the words for sun, sacred, prayer and power. The sun is referred to as Naatosi, meaning "sacred power." Naatosi is found as a particle in such words as Aawaa-toyinnaiyi [to sing powerful sacred songs] and Aato'si [to have (healing) powers] ... people who have great influence are described as Aato'si, as having sacred power.... The Blackfoot language and the good heart are one and the same. If Niitsitapi lose their language, then the way of life, the good heart and prayer, the connections to the cosmic world of alliances, and, subsequently, the good path will be altered.[12]

Angayuqaq Oscar Kawagley, professor emeritus of education in the College of Liberal Arts at the University of Alaska Fairbanks, writes about the Yupiaq language in similar terms, noting where certain root portions reflecting aspects of spirituality are grafted onto other syllables to describe daily things. *Ella* is a root for weather, awareness, world, God or creative force, universe and sky:

- *Qaill' ella auqa:* "How's the weather?"
- *Quaill' ellan auqa:* "How are you feeling?"
- *Ellam nunii:* "The world's land"
- *Ellaqpiim yua:* "Spirit of the Universe"

- *Ellapak:* "Universe"
- *Ella amigligtuq:* "The sky is cloudy."[13]

Leona Makokis, a Cree woman who is president of the Blue Quills First Nations College in St. Paul, Alberta, explains, "The ability to speak an indigenous language is an indispensable part of our indigenous identity, as these languages convey a sense of identity, a sense of responsibility, and a sense of *spiritual* relationship to the universe: plants, animals, Mother Earth, rocks, and people."[14]

When I began to see how many indigenous authors saw their distinct languages as expressing a similar focus on the spiritual dimension, insisting that all things existed within a spiritual framework and participated in a spiritual interconnectivity, I began to understand what Joe Couture meant when he said, "It seems to me that the Indian spiritual mind, or spiritualized mentality, perceives or experiences the Creative Mind in all, everywhere."[15]

I was shocked at how readily European settlers assumed that those complex, spiritualized languages were merely crude attempts at basic communication. Children in residential schools were expressly forbidden from using them, and punished if they did. Here is how one aboriginal man described to researcher Jo-Anne Fiske what happened when he spoke his own language in residential school:

We were up at a hillside on a Saturday and we were on like a walk. We were walking around in a big group, and again I forgot about my language. I'm not supposed to speak it, and the next thing I knew the supervisor, he got really angry with me and hit me around the head a few times there, and then grabbed the back of my head there, walked right over and then, he was looking around there, and then he found some cactus. And he stuck some cactus in my mouth. "You cannot speak ... you cannot speak your language. Do you understand? You hear me?" And he forced my mouth open and he stuck that in my mouth, and ... he had his hand underneath my jaw and his hand on top of my head, and then he pushed my jaw closed on the cactus. And it hurt. It hurts pretty bad, that day. I couldn't eat anything there for three or four days ... my mouth was swelled up there from those cactus. And they were just torturing me.[16]

It is difficult to imagine the confusion indigenous children must have felt at being punished for speaking about their spiritualized world, and at having to learn to express themselves in the impersonal form of the English language instead. Most non-indigenous North Americans have no idea how indigenous people experienced the prohibitions against speaking original languages, or the punishments that followed their breach. How would it have felt as an aboriginal child if, by force, you learned to abandon a comforting, connecting and context-laden world for one that had only unfeeling rigidity? As I reported in *Returning to the Teachings*, I clearly recall one Anishinaabe woman describing in a justice discussion in northwestern Ontario her own determination to maintain her language:

Boarding school was supposed to be a place where you forgot everything about being Anishinaabe. And our language too. But I said "I am going to talk to myself"—and that's what I did, under my covers—talked to myself in Anishinaabe. If we were caught, the nuns would make us stand in a corner and repeat over and over "I won't speak my language."[17]

When she told us that story, the entire room broke into applause.

As an English speaker, it's almost impossible for me to conceive of speaking in ways that connect and spiritualize everything surrounding me. I cannot imagine actually speaking about the connections between things like weather, awareness, world, God, universe and sky every time I refer to one or another. While I can philosophically see myself as "embedded" in the universe, I can't see myself speaking out of that embeddedness every time I open my mouth. I can, however, understand why indigenous people insist on resurrecting their languages, simply because that means resurrecting their distinct sense of the world and their place within it.

As it happens, I visited the Hollow Water First Nation in late 2013 and was told that they now have Ojibway immersion up to grade three in their community school. They are excited by the program and have plans to expand it into higher grades. I was also told that their school officials had just returned from visiting a Mohawk community in Quebec that now has Mohawk immersion for all students up to grade five. About a month later, I was invited to make a presentation at the Tyendinaga First Nation in southern Ontario, and was overjoyed to see that the day's events were opened by a formal five-minute greeting by a dozen children, all of whom were speaking Mohawk. The parents and grandparents in the room were absolutely beaming with pride, especially given that they had never learned Mohawk themselves. They told me they could actually feel the restoration of their culture beginning with those children learning their own language once again.

In my view, children who grow up in their traditional languages are growing up in a different world than the one my language has given me, a much richer, more interdependent and spirit-filled world than I will ever know. It won't be long before they are also university graduates with their feet solidly planted in *both* worlds, ready and eager to bring their rich ways of thinking to the rest of us, whether in the fields of justice, philosophy, spirituality, community governance or science—or, what they might think of as exploring the foundational patterns within Creation. The more I have explored indigenous thinking, the more I have seen how different those foundational concepts are. I will now do my best to outline a few of them.

PLACE, SPACE AND THE MEDICINE WHEEL

As we have seen, indigenous languages spoke of the world in ways that emphasized the spiritualized, ethical embeddedness of everything. When I began to look at how those languages described the world, I ran across something written by Leroy Little Bear, which I initially found puzzling:

> Aboriginal paradigms include ideas of constant flux, all existence consisting of energy waves/spirit, all things being animate, all existence being interrelated, creation/existence having to be renewed, space/place as an important referent, and language, songs, stories, and ceremonies as repositories for the knowledge that arise out of these paradigms.[18]

While I understood much of what he said, I was intrigued by his indication that "space" and "place" were important referents in traditional times. In follow-up conversations, Leroy argued that while European languages spoke of the world with time as their central organizing theme, indigenous languages did not. Instead, they relied on place or space as their central organizing force.

At the time, I recalled encounters with aboriginal witnesses who consistently appeared unable to give their evidence in chronological order. Instead, they would flit from event to event, with no attempt to put them in the order in which they had happened. I acknowledge often wondering what the impediment was, and I admit that there were times when I suspected the witnesses were too mentally disorganized to be able to give a chronologically accurate account. When I ran across Leroy's assertion, a new line of inquiry opened up. What did it mean that for aboriginal people space and place might stand for our chronological time in talking about events? The more I looked at the issue, the more I found other indigenous voices making similar statements.

Marie Battiste, a Mi'kmaq woman from Nova Scotia who is a professor in the College of Education and director of the Aboriginal Education Research Centre at the University of Saskatchewan, describes this concept in a paper written with James (Sákéj) Youngblood Henderson: "Indigenous knowledge is ... inherently tied to land, not to land in general but to particular landscapes, landforms, and biomes where ceremonies are properly held, stories properly recited, medicines properly gathered, and transfers of knowledge properly authenticated."[19]

Naomi Adelson, associate professor and chair of the anthropology department at York University in Toronto, speaks to this issue when she writes that "the history of the people and the history of the land do not simply correspond to each other—they are one and the same."[20]

When I really looked at it, I could see how place would become an essential referent for people who thought of themselves as embedded in the universe that they knew. For instance, they would create names for the months of the year based on various land-and-season-dependent elements in their particular environments. Here are the names of the full moons originally given by the Algonquian people of Ontario:

January	Wolf Moon	Hungry wolf packs howl at night.
February	Snow Moon	Heaviest snow falls in the middle of winter.
March	Worm Moon	Spring begins, as earthworms and robins that eat them begin to appear.

April	Pink Moon	An early spring flower called moss pink starts to bloom.
May	Flower Moon	Many types of flowers bloom in May.
June	Strawberry Moon	Strawberries are ready to be picked and eaten.
July	Buck Moon	New antlers of buck deer coated with velvety fur begin to form.
August	Sturgeon Moon	Sturgeon, a large fish, are easily caught at this time of year.
September	Harvest Moon	Farmers can continue harvesting until after sunset by the light of the harvest moon.
October	Hunter's Moon	Hunters track and kill prey by moonlight, stockpiling food for the coming winter.
November	Beaver Moon	Time to set beaver traps before the swamps freeze to ensure a supply of warm winter furs.
December	Cold Moon	The cold of winter sets in.

People who occupied different landscapes would name the months according to their own landscape and seasonal variations. Here, for instance, are the names for the full moons originally given by the Nuu-chah-nulth people of Vancouver Island:

January	Moon of the Most Snow
February	Beginning of Spawn (fish)
March	Herring Spawn
April	Geese Moon
May	First Seal Hunting
June	Salmon Berry (ready for picking and eating)

July	Bee Moon
August	Spring Salmon Run (fishing)
September	Dog Salmon
October	Fish Cutting
November	Getting Ready for Elder Sibling (time for feasting)
December	Younger Sibling (time for Potlatch)

From this, it's easy to understand why people's language, their ways of referencing many things in their lives, would refer to local geography and the seasonal experiences within it. In that sense, it's obvious why certain places became central referents within language and thought.

Within each group's habitual territory, particular locations would take on special significance over time, and ceremonies would develop to consecrate those locations. Certain landforms would develop spiritual significance for people and would come to contribute substantially to the community's spiritual life. As such, they needed to be protected from ordinary use, for people's spiritual lives would be affected if they were not.

People also were given personal names that reflected their interaction with the birds, plants and animals of their region, taking them from the characteristics that had been observed and recorded over centuries. The clan names and structures showed those embedded origins, as well. People of the Crane Clan of the Anishinaabe, for instance, were born to assume the highest leadership responsibilities because of three traits: all bird clans were known as leadership clans because they had voices; the crane's voice caused the other birds to stop singing and listen; and the crane spoke less often than other birds, preferring to listen instead, just as a good leader should speak as little as possible but command the greatest attention when he does.

If the clan into which you were born and your personal name were taken from what happened in the natural order that surrounded you, it would be impossible not to see yourself as embedded in that natural order. And if that natural order involved plants, animals, birds, locations and environmental factors specific to your region, then place would indeed be an important referent in your life. Herman Michell, a Cree-speaking associate professor and vice-president of academics at First Nations University of Canada, suggests that the role of place comes out of the cross-familiarity between humans and nonhuman creatures:

> Place is a spiritual relationship with the tangible world that connects other aspects of life.... Place is multidimensional. It entails both physical and emotional characteristics and refers to more than just a geographic space.... In other words, Place is the interaction between location and resident.[21]

Gregory Cajete, a famous Tewa author and educator from Santa Clara Pueblo, New Mexico, describes how widespread this emphasis on place and space really is to the indigenous peoples of North America:

> This relationship is predicated on the fact that all Indigenous tribes—their philosophies, cultural ways of life, customs, language, all aspects of their cultural being in one way or another—are ultimately tied to the relationships that they have established and applied during their history with regard to certain places and to the earth as a whole.... Native people interacted with the places in which they lived for such a long time that their landscapes became reflections of their very souls.[22]

By happenstance, I ran across an article titled "The Unexpected Canyon" in the January 2006 edition of *National Geographic* in which a Hopi man articulated his relationship with the Grand Canyon:

> All this canyon land is covered with our footprints. It's where we had our genesis; where some of our clans farmed and lived until we were called to the mesas. It is where we make our sacred salt trek. It is where our spirits go when we die. It is where we learned the Hopi way of life, and the lessons that guide us. And the key lesson is the lesson of humility.[23]

As I began to understand it, if aboriginal people's languages spoke out of a sense of embeddedness in their particular geography and environment, then descriptions of all things would necessarily engage a spiritualized component as well. In other words, so many observations, descriptions and ceremonies would involve the natural surroundings that it would be impossible to talk about them or perform them without referencing the landscape. If people saw themselves as essential, integrated and performing parts of the world around them, and spoke in ways that signified that integration, then references to specific places would necessarily be a part of describing all of life.

I noted earlier that Leroy Little Bear mentioned both space and place as important referents. I've talked about the importance of specific locations—of place—in people's self-definitions, but what about space? How does nonspecific space become an important referent? What squeezes time into second place as an organizing principle? Surely you can live firmly embedded in nature and still see the chronological passage of time as a central organizing dimension of existence?

I may be well off the mark here, but I suspect that part of the answer lies in something else that was central to many aboriginal cultures in North America: the medicine wheel.

I won't try to teach the medicine wheel, because it is not mine to teach and it is too complex, containing as it does every lesson you can imagine for individual and social human development. What I will do is provide a basic description of its structure to make my point: if you see your life as existing on the medicine wheel, if you strive for the balances it urges and defines, then you come to see yourself positionally rather than as occupying a specific moment in linear time. As a result, space may replace time in your self-definition.

The medicine wheel is a teaching tool. It is an imaginary circle upon which almost everything can be plotted. That circle is fundamentally broken into four quadrants, known as the four directions of east, south, west and north. Everything revolves around that wheel, beginning in the east and then rotating clockwise into south, west and north, before returning to the east.

A single day, for instance, involves the sun rising in the east, hitting its highest point in the south, setting in the west and then moving into darkness and rest in the northern quadrant before returning to sunrise in the east. You can plot a year on the same circle, with spring in the east, summer in the south, fall in the west and winter in the north before the return to spring. You can also plot a lifetime on the wheel, with birth in the east, youth in the south, adulthood in the west and old age in the north. Oddly enough, when you plot all three time-related events of a day, year and lifetime on the same circle, and your emphasis is upon what is similar at the various stages of each, the importance of time is replaced by the importance of position. The central question becomes *where* you are instead of *when* you are.

While westerners might think that finding parallels between sunrise, springtime and human birth is interesting as a metaphorical exercise, such parallels take on much deeper significance for aboriginal people. Each day, year and lifetime are seen as being essentially the same—and time is almost irrelevant. What does become important is where you are located on the medicine wheel. If you are a child, you share the passion of each new day and the magnificent flowering of springtime. If you are an old man, you share the stillness of night and the preparation for both deep winter and your final sleep. In other words, you occupy a space on the medicine wheel far more than you sit within a passing second, minute, hour, year or lifetime. When you think of yourself, and speak of yourself, you do so out of a spatial context on the medicine wheel, not a temporal one. If you are truly embedded in the relational world, you understand your participation to be in ever-repeating cycles, not finite and linear time spans. The spirit that binds everything together as relatives does not expire; it merely transforms and reasserts itself as the circle repeats.

When I first encountered the medicine wheel, I was fascinated to discover how much thought had gone into finding all the parallels within the various quadrants. As I mentioned, the start of a new life is equated with the start of a new day and the start of a new year. As each day, year and life move into the southern quadrant, they develop similarly: the south, for instance, is the time of full light from the sun of each day, full seasonal flowering in the natural realm and the full energy that comes with youth. As all three time spans move toward the western doorway, they become associated with late-afternoon calm, with a slowing of physical growth as plants and animals achieve physical maturity and with the development of mature skill sets and systems among adult people. When all three move into the northern quadrant, each day grows into the silence and stillness of night, each season turns into winter's rest and each human shifts more deeply into reflection and contemplation. Elders, with their white hair, reaching the winter quadrant of their life, are understood to have gained their greatest wisdom.

I remember hearing one man speak about how residential schools had fundamentally damaged the medicine wheel. He spoke about how, traditionally, youth were placed in the southern quadrant and Elders directly opposite them in the northern quadrant, straight across from them over the centre of the circle, often the place where the sacred fire glowed, giving life to everything that surrounded it. When winter came and activity was restricted by snow, cold and shortened days, that was the Elders' time to teach youth the things they would need to know to grow into healthy adults. With the youth being taken to residential schools for (at least) the Teaching period of winter, there was no one facing the Elders across the sacred fire. For the first time in centuries, the Elders had no one to teach during those long winter nights. Left without a role to play, they suffered terribly.

At the same time, the youth never got to hear the words of the Elders, never got to understand their language, their history, the lessons learned or the sacredness of life. The connections between generations suddenly ceased, leaving everyone gasping for spiritual breath and confidence in the future. Everyone, and everything, was suddenly disconnected—and much poorer. Now the white hair of old people meant only that they were useless or, worse still, a burden on the adults who had to care for them. Elders often descended into despair, and youth grew up with no connections. The medicine wheel had been broken.

In *Reclaiming Connections: Understanding Residential School Trauma Among Aboriginal People*, Deborah Chansonneuve, a consultant on aboriginal culture and gender equality, expresses that breaking this way:

Communities and Elders [were] denied their role in raising children through teaching and reaffirming language and customs and became, over time, fragmented and conflictual.

Loss of language to communicate between the generations and loss of cultural pride created a breach between the generations that is still felt today.[24]

I thought of that quotation when I listened to the children at Tyendinaga give their formal greeting in Mohawk, and when I heard parents talk of never being given the chance to learn their language. While this may seem to non-aboriginal people to be a relatively insignificant impact of residential schools, nothing could be further from the truth. The very structure of aboriginal languages reflects their embedded and spiritualized universe, and denying those languages meant that the universe they describe cannot be passed from generation to generation in any of its original fullness.

What kinds of Teachings would the Elders have shared from the medicine wheel? I'll mention one small one that has played a role in my own family. In traditional Teachings, various animals were associated with each of the four directions. Two creatures associated with the east (or what is often called the eastern doorway) were Fieldmouse and Eagle. Eagle soared highest of all, closest to Creator, and saw Creation from a unique vantage point. High up in the sky, he could see the migrations of animals, the greening of trees and bushes up the slopes as spring emerged and the browning going down the slopes as fall came along. He could see the balance between all the populations, like the deer and wolves. He could see how rain swelled the creeks and then the rivers and then the lakes and oceans. Truly unique within the animal world, his eye saw the large patterns that were always missed by those animals that could not attain his height. By the same token, he was terrible at particular activities, such as building himself a nest: it was always a slap-dash affair, with sticks and roots jammed together every which way, looking ready to fall from the tree at any moment. Fieldmouse, by contrast, was able to focus on his many small tasks, whether digging a burrow or husking tiny seeds for storage. His capacity for giving all his attention to discrete tasks was unmatched. Such powers of concentration were dangerous, however, often keeping him from observing bigger problems, such as Owl swooping down from above to take him as a tasty meal. The Teaching was that human beings needed to pay attention to both skills sets—that of large-pattern recognition and that of small-scale accomplishment—going back and forth between the two rather than focusing too much on one or the other and becoming out of balance.

When I told that story to my family, it was an instant hit: most of the time my children would say something like, "That's enough Eagle, Dad. Time for some Fieldmouse from you!" I learned that I too often got lost in my thoughts, ignoring the daily details of life that were of primary concern to them.

This is just one small illustration of the medicine wheel Teachings that sat at the centre of traditional life, organizing priorities and reminding people of their responsibilities to all other aspects of Creation. Needless to say, those Teachings formed no part of growing up within residential schools. Instead, they were replaced by punishment-based rules that imposed a very different vision of human relations.

The notion of balance was also central within medicine wheel Teachings; people who were unhealthy were described as being *out* of balance. The medicine wheel named the four quadrants to represent the four dimensions of human beings: the mental, physical, emotional and spiritual, and people thought of themselves as positioned somewhere between all four. I recall a pre-sentence report prepared by one community healing team that suggested that a particular accused, a well-respected businessman in the community who had nevertheless abused his children, had succeeded in developing his physical and mental dimensions, but was deficient in the emotional quadrant and almost completely empty in his spiritual dimension. The community saw his abusive behaviour as a sign of imbalance, not as proof that he was a bad person who should be shut away in jail. They saw their task as helping to bring him back into balance by working with him to develop his emotional and spiritual dimensions. Once those quadrants were developed, they believed he would be aware of the damage that his violence caused others, and he would develop the love and sense of connection that would make him want to bring happiness to others instead. In that way, the abuse would end and balance would be restored to the family. Everything was a question of balance.

As I mentioned in *Returning to the Teachings*, Kathy Louis, a Cree member of the National Parole Board, gave me a book back in 1991 called *The Sacred Tree*. Put together by Phil Lane Jr., Michael Bopp, Judie Bopp and Lee Brown, it gave voice to more than thirty aboriginal Elders, teachers and spiritual leaders from many native communities across North America. The Teachings contained in the medicine wheel were found to be central to many of those societies. For instance, here is how those aboriginal leaders described their understanding of the eastern doorway, where each day, year and lifetime began:

It is the place of innocence, guilelessness, spontaneity, joy and the capacity to believe in the unseen. When we travel to the East we will be tested with lessons that will teach us many things. There we will learn of warmth of spirit, purity, trust, hope and the uncritical acceptance of others. We will learn to love as a child loves; a love that does not question others and does not know itself. Here courage is born and truthfulness begins. The East is a place of all beginnings. The human being must return many times to the East in the course of a life's journey. Each time, there will be new things to learn on a new level of understanding. Not only is the East the direction of birth and rebirth, it is also the direction of illumination. It is the direction from which light comes into the world. Hence it is the direction of guidance and leadership. Here the gifts of beautiful and clear speech that help others to understand is acquired.[25]

Such Teachings are only the smallest part of the medicine wheel. It insists that everyone search for balance and harmony within their own lives as well as in the lives of each family and community. Each of the four doorways is understood to offer different visions for self-awareness and self-development, all of them intended to help people carry their responsibilities to all their relations. When you work within aboriginal healing processes, you see that the medicine wheel is often the primary tool, the device that helps people locate themselves and gain a clearer picture of where they are strongest and where they are most in need. By examining their position on the medicine wheel, they can readily see how they can move themselves into greater balance. In the hands of healers, the medicine wheel is a teaching tool that is premised on never-ending birth, life, death and rebirth, where time is of little consequence and your placement within its detailed collection of values and the directions you must pursue to change your position are the critical components. As I said before, wholesale reliance on the medicine wheel leads you to ask yourself *where* you are. The issue of *when* is largely immaterial.

In a healing program studied by James Waldram, a medical anthropologist and a psychology professor at the University of Saskatchewan, one participant summed up his thoughts about the utility of the medicine wheel this way:

I see the use of the Medicine Wheel ... as the basis of [the] healing process for the Native people of Western Canada. Canada in general, actually, wherever the residential schools were that attempted to replace the traditional Four Directions way with a European way. And I am not saying that those European teachers were altogether evil in what they did, but they were wrongly directed in their false assumptions that the Four Directions way was unable to help people live in the modern world. They were wrong! Taking that away from the Indian people of this country was the biggest mistake that was made. Other mistakes were made as well, but taking away the belief system, the foundation, connectedness with human life and the world around a person, was the most harmful thing that the people could experience ... because it completely demoralized them and disoriented them.... The future is to return [to] the Medicine Wheel, the Four Directions way of looking at yourself and the world.[26]

The more I have learned about traditional Teachings, the more I agree with such statements. There is absolutely nothing primitive about those Teachings. Instead, I find great sophistication in them. In my view, they reflect deep thought about the human condition, whether aboriginal or non-aboriginal, as well as great creativity in how its dimensions and dynamics are expressed. I also admire the fact that all traditional Teachings are simply open to people to accept or reject on their own, without any notion of compulsion. I have taken many of those Teachings into my own family life, sharing them as best I can, and trying to honour them as I go along.

THE CENTRALITY OF THE CIRCLE AND CEREMONY

It seems to me that seeing the world "the four directions way" means that everything is understood to be engaged in a never-ending, always re-emerging circle. And that takes us to another

fundamental organizing principle of traditional societies: reliance
upon the circle in almost everything. Black Elk, a noted Lakota
Shaman, describes the significance of the circle:

> You have noticed that everything an Indian does is in a circle,
> and that is because the Power of the World always works in
> circles, and everything tries to be round ... Everything the
> power of the world does is done in a circle. The sky is round,
> and I have heard that the earth is round like a ball, and so
> are all the stars. The wind, in its greatest power, whirls. Birds
> make their nests in circles, for theirs is the same religion as
> ours. The sun comes forth and goes down again in a circle.
> The moon does the same, and both are round. Even the
> seasons form a great circle in their changing, and always come
> back again to where they were. The life of a man is a circle
> from childhood to childhood, and so it is in everything where
> power moves.[27]

Clearly, life as positioned on the medicine wheel is lived in a
circle, from birth to youth to adulthood to status as Elder, then
death and rebirth. The centrality of the circle extends into virtually
every facet of aboriginal life, and every circular aspect strengthens
the circular whole.

In the introduction to this book, I spoke of the Cree Elder
Maria Linklater and her words to aboriginal youth about what it
means to live a good life. She was originally scheduled to make
her presentation in a room at the RCMP academy in Regina, but
when I went there at the appointed hour, a small sign on the door
indicated that she had moved it outside. When I found the group,
she was explaining her decision to come outside as an important
one, pointing out that rooms have corners that are difficult to reach
into, and outside we could sit in a circle and include everyone.

Virtually all group discussions among aboriginal people are held in circles. Everyone sits as an equal to everyone else, and a talking stick, feather or rock is passed from one person to the next. Each person who holds it can speak as little or as much as she likes, and all others must listen. In this way, the conversation goes around the circle carefully, excluding no one.

I recall one talking circle put together by a group of non-indigenous academics who thought they knew what they were doing. At one point, the speaker said something that another person sitting across the circle disagreed with. That second person jumped right in, out of turn, with his objections, and everyone else sat mute while those two had it out. I looked at the few aboriginal people who were present, and they were slowly shaking their heads at how the circle had been broken by the second speaker. Because of that interruption, the two combatants completely missed one of the advantages of circle speaking: it avoids open or hostile disagreement, simply because of the buffering that happens as a number of people speak on the issue before the talking stick comes to the person who may be most hostile to the matter. In that way, what others say gives him a chance to reflect on his own views and to incorporate those of the others who responded before he did. The process is certainly preferable to outbursts that hijack the entire discussion and result in one-on-one hostility before anyone else has a chance to offer more moderate views.

The circle is everywhere in aboriginal communities. In pipe ceremonies, the pipe is offered in a circle, touching each of the four directions, then the heavens and then Mother Earth. The sweat lodge itself is circular, and people sit in circles within it. Group discussions take place in circles. Healing activities that involve more than a couple of people are called healing circles. Every gathering uses the centrality of the circle, which mirrors the cycles within the natural order. Participating in circles is participating in the cycle of life, being embedded in the structure of the natural order.

Deborah Chansonneuve discusses what happens when people lose their conviction of embeddedness within the many circles of life:

> Within this worldview, the circle connects the spirits of all beings and things in a great, sacred whole. When connectedness to any part of the whole is lost or interrupted, the sense of sacredness is lost. As the sacred is the most fundamental of all connections, when it is lost, people will destroy others, the environment or themselves.[28]

As I said earlier, when that happens with individuals, it is understood that they have become out of balance. As long as they stay out of balance, they will continue to bring about disharmony within the group, simply because they are embedded in the group, just as the plant is embedded in the meadow. The very notion of casting people out of the group is seen as silly, because there is no existence outside the circle. Everyone is a part of it, whether they are contributing well or poorly.

When you look at all life as participating in an endless, repeating circle, and when you celebrate life within that circle in ceremonies, you are given a conviction of belonging that brings immense comfort and a feeling of deep thankfulness. You somehow know that nothing is missing, or the circle would have collapsed long ago. That, in turn, leads traditional aboriginal thinkers to contemplate the universe as giving humans all that we truly need. In short, it leads to the notion of the benevolence of Creation, and of the need for humans working within it to constantly express—and feel—their gratitude.

THE FUNDAMENTAL POSTURE
OF THANKFULNESS

When I first read that the universe was seen as manifesting goodness, kindness, compassion and the like, I didn't know what that meant. Traditional creation stories give this account, always speaking about the need for humans to achieve a state of reverential thankfulness in everything they do. I didn't understand our dependencies the way I now do, and I failed to see the power behind assertions that Creation has supplied everything we need for wonderful lives. Everything suggests that we should live our lives in an attitude of gratefulness for what Creation bestows on us, and of reverence for the uncountable contributions that every individual makes to the whole.

Why had I not clued in to this much earlier? I remember having many talks with Charlie Fisher. He often spoke about the old days, about trapping with his dog team between Kenora and Red Lake, and he always emphasized that everything he did had to be done with reverence. In his final years, Charlie committed some of his thoughts to paper, and here's how he described the Anishinaabe approach to trapping:

Trapping in the Anishinabe way is first and foremost a spiritual activity. At its most basic level, it means giving respect for the land and animals ... so that life on the land will be renewed, and giving respect for those people who had the sacred knowledge of how to trap in a sustainable way.... In our sacred way of respect in trapping, we followed the practices that are necessary to renew life on the land.... When we trapped a beaver, we put as many as seven parts of it back in the water. When we trapped a muskrat, we put three parts back in the water. This was the way of respect that we followed for all animals.[29]

Charlie never explained the significance of putting certain numbers of body parts back into the water. I suspect that, since the act was ceremonial, the numbers had significance, as did the body parts chosen. What was clear to me, however, was that his participation in the natural order was surrounded by reverence and the ceremonial posture of thanksgiving. He did indeed see himself as embedded in everything around him, as owing his life to complex sets of intertwining circumstances that he had a duty to study and accommodate, as best he could.

Charlie's service to others stands as a testament to his sense of obligation as an embedded partner in Creation. While he often used tough love in his role as a Justice of the Peace, the operative word was *love*. Just before he passed on, I asked him how he looked back on his life. He immediately spoke about thirteen men and women whom he had helped to overcome their alcohol addictions and get off the street. They not only managed to survive, but they returned to their community to have families and to make them healthy, as well. He saw himself as embedded in his community and charged with the responsibility to help that community however he could.

In many aboriginal cultures, each day begins with a short sunrise ceremony at daybreak to thank the sun for returning with its warmth. When the saplings are cut to build sweat lodges, tobacco is placed where each was cut as a way of giving thanks to Mother Earth for giving up the saplings for humans' use. Pipe ceremonies begin with thanksgiving, with pointing the pipe in all directions to honour the gifts that come from each. When a youth kills his first deer, moose or caribou, he gives it to the community and eats none of it himself. When youth receive their names, the ceremony begins with an expression of thanksgiving, and the names themselves carry the obligations that their community believes are best suited to those individuals' unique and developing gifts. Thankfulness is paired with responsibility at every turn.

And, as everyone familiar with aboriginal people can attest, no meeting can begin or end without a prayer of gratitude. We are asked to think of all our blessings, from the sun that rose that morning to the food that nourished us at the start of the day. It is only after that fundamental gratitude has been expressed that there is any notion of a request in aboriginal prayers, whether it is for safe travel home or for the good health of our relatives. In most sweat lodges, the expression of thanksgiving is central, whether for the old people who went before or the young ones just being born. The only request is for the strength, knowledge and love to serve both groups well.

THE NOTION THAT HUMANS ARE FUNDAMENTALLY GOOD

The aboriginal vision suggests that it is not only the universe that is fundamentally good, but also all the people who share its wonders. When missionaries began to insist on the opposite through their teachings about the doctrine of original sin and the need for constant confession to avoid damnation, that message was, of course, at odds with how indigenous people saw themselves. The noted Anishinaabe scholar Basil Johnston expresses the traditional view this way:

> The men and women who were created as the last and most dependent of all beings took a name in its collective form, "Anishinaubeg," for themselves. Such a designation represented their understanding of the fundamental goodness of human nature derived from the supposition that men and women generally meant well in all their undertakings and aspirations.... The belief in the innate goodness of human nature remained, and conferred on men and women a sense of worth, equality and pride.[30]

Recall what Elder Dumont said about how Mother Earth was created as the most beautiful place Creator could imagine, a place where Creator could see the evidence of his own thoughts, "the most beautiful thoughts," reflected back to him. Recall, as well, his insistence that Mother Earth is not a place where we are to be tested, or to suffer, but a place where we are given the opportunity to experience the beauty that sprang from Creator's thoughts and to reflect that beauty back to him. What a wonderful task to set yourself at the start of every day!

I also remember what Carol Hopkins described to me as a turning point in her work with youngsters in a treatment program for gas sniffers. She said that she had always watched each new group coming in the door with a critical eye, wondering which ones would cause the most problems for her. One day when a new group was arriving, she thought back to the strength-based Teachings that she had seen in her studies of traditional thought, and she changed her silent question. No longer asking what problems were arriving, she asked herself, "What gifts are walking in the door today?" From that moment on, as she focused on bringing each youth's unique gifts into fuller bloom, the problems began to melt away and were replaced by an awakening of potential in each of them.

And that brought me back to something else Charlie Fisher told me. He said that every child presents four gifts to the community. One is physical, another mental, a third emotional and the fourth spiritual. These gifts might appear to be not very significant—the ability to run fast, or to listen carefully, or to use fingers in weaving, or to speak soothingly to the old people. It doesn't matter what they are; it is the duty of all adults to watch carefully for whatever gifts each child presents, and to help the child develop, use and expand those gifts. The basic premise, though, is clear: all children come with four ways of contributing to their families and communities, and each gift has to be honoured and all children valued for what they bring.

Two American aboriginal writers, Iris HeavyRunner and Joann Sebastian Morris, speak of it like this:

> Cultural resilience is a relatively new term, but it is a concept that predates the so called "discovery" of our people. The elders teach us that our children are gifts from the Creator and it is the family, community, school and tribe's responsibility to nurture, protect, and guide them. We have long recognized how important it is for children to have people in their lives who nurture their spirit, stand by them, encourage and support them. This traditional process is what contemporary researchers, educators, and social service providers are now calling fostering resilience. Thus, resilience is not new to our people; it is a concept that has been taught for centuries. The word is new; the meaning is old.... One [training] participant said, "Now I have a word for what I have always known and struggled to explain to the children and adults I work with."[31]

I should point out that the notion of fostering resilience by stressing the positives in each person's makeup is now gaining hold within western psychology. Condemning and punishing negative behaviour is increasingly seen as counterproductive, given that it further alienates people who already feel significantly estranged from others. The goal, instead, is to send signals of welcome and to stress how *able* people are to earn and enjoy that welcome. Prison reform, especially in the United States, is now moving in this direction, emphasizing the teaching of new skills and the building of self-confidence as the best way to reduce recidivism, a distinct change from the angry denigration and belittlement that has been so common. I recall a discussion with Rod McCormick, a Mohawk who is an associate professor of counselling psychology at the University of British Columbia, when he stressed the traditional belief that "pulling forward" into goodness is far more productive than guarding against "slipping backwards" into sin.

I'll have more to say later about this insistence on emphasizing the positives, because it seems to establish an important difference between the processes that have dominated western therapies and those that prevail within indigenous healing. For the moment, it is enough to observe that it is especially difficult to establish good relations with people whom you intentionally condemn and marginalize. In my view, it is to the immense credit of indigenous people that so few have responded with anger or violence to the intense and pervasive denigration they have suffered for centuries at our hands. Their insistence on maintaining an open, welcoming posture despite that history is proof, to me, of their allegiance to the principle that the best way to achieve healthy relations involves resting on the positives rather than descending into the negatives. I frankly doubt whether I could maintain that emphasis after so many years of insult and injury, and I admire their capacity intensely.

RIGHT RELATIONS AND TRUE KNOWLEDGE

For years, I have looked for the right words to convey my overall sense of what life was all about in traditional times. The best I've been able to come up with is this: traditional life centred on striving at all times to create "right relations," not only with people but also with everything else that surrounded you, not only in the present but also in the past and future, and not only within the physical realm but within the spiritual realm as well.

Because the focus was on relations, it was understood that they had to be experienced and felt, not just thought about. Relations centre on emotional connections, not cerebral ones, and everyone's duty is to focus on helping all relatives bring the best they can into each and every relationship, whether with trees, rocks, bugs or other people. It is not a religious activity, not something separated from your every moment; rather, every moment is an opportunity to deepen engagement in right relationships.

As an example, here is how a Cree Elder, Mary Lee, describes what could be seen as a mundane activity, constructing a tipi: "Before making a tipi, I offer tobacco. I don't just stand there and let that tobacco fall; I sit on the ground with humbleness, because I am offering something for something I will use from Mother Earth. Because it's not ours; everything we take is borrowed."[32]

When that "everything" is seen as spiritually equivalent to human beings, obligations of respect are owed to everything. A child born in traditional times was born into a world that was, in its essence, deeply spiritual and centred on striving to maintain a balance between the emotional, physical, mental and spiritual dimensions inherent in everyone. Children were expected to join the adult world in honouring the spirit of all things, and in giving thanks for the blessedness of being embedded in the life of all things. Betty Bastien, the Blackfoot author, phrases it this way:

> There is no separation between the sacred and secular as in the Christian or Eurocentered sense.... As human beings, we Siksikaitsitapi see ourselves as cosmic, because we are interconnected, related to all of time and all that there is.... Following Niitsitapi logic means experiencing the whole, the interconnectedness of an indivisible universe.[33]

A. Oscar Kawagley, the Yupiaq professor from Alaska, sees it this way:

Wherever the Native person is, that place serves as a kind of cathedral, deserving of respectful behaviour. In concert with the above is the giving of thanks to Ellam Yua, the Spirit of the Universe. This was and is done through rituals, ceremonies, singing, and dancing, which reinforce the belief that all nature is alive and everything has its own being.... Rituals and ceremonies were created to show honour and reverence for the Ellam Yua, and to center oneself to maintain or regain balance, ordering one's life.[34]

When Anishinaabe people went out on the land for four days in their vision quest, they were expected to sit on Mother Earth in the midst of their animal and plant relations, as well as sky and weather, to relearn humility and to open themselves to whatever instructions might come from visions or dreams. Those dreams and visions were treasured in traditional life, and regularly sought through a wide variety of ceremonies and cultural practices. They were understood to be a gateway into the spiritual plane of existence, a world as real as the physical one that the five senses delivered. They were understood to be the source of what is often called "true knowledge." Leroy Little Bear discusses the place of such knowledge in Blackfoot society:

Knowledge is about relationships.... Knowing is represented in the Aboriginal context as multiple and diverse processes and includes other ways of knowing, i.e. dreams, visions, insights and teachings that validate one's sensory experience ... spirituality, relationships, language, songs, stories, ceremonies, and teachings learned through dreams form the axiology of Aboriginal knowledge.[35]

Joe Couture makes similar observations about the kinds of knowledge that are essential if you wish to gain an understanding of yourself and to nurture your capacities to be of service to others:

> To come to "know" as an Indian knows, to "see" as an Indian sees, that is the key objective. It is a process objective, requiring conscious sidelining of discursive reason, or intellectual mind, to let intuition, or intuitive mind, play.... The primal "experience" embraces the inner and outer worlds. In Native cognition, these are together and equally real and functional. The sense world, as well as the spiritual world, each have something to reveal that only each can express. The spiritual and the physical are both acknowledged as inseparable and recognized as belonging centrally to the sphere of Native, human knowing.[36]

Couture's words about the need to "sideline" discursive reason and the intellectual mind before the intuitive mind could come into play struck a chord with me. I am one of those westerners caught up in the intellectual sphere. Only rarely do I remember my dreams, and I have no experience with interpreting them. I have had almost no personal engagement with this parallel spiritual universe, with learning through dreams, visions or the appearance of otherworldly figures.

That being said, I do know that gaining access to the spiritual world was, and often remains, a central preoccupation for indigenous people. Shake-tent ceremonies to gain spoken contact with deceased people are not uncommon in Ojibway and Cree communities today, and I have heard (with some awe!) many trusted non-aboriginal people speak about the variety of voices they have heard come from within the tent that only one person entered. I have also heard of people seeing fireballs cascading around ceremonial rooms, leaving everyone present in rather stunned silence.

One particular event convinced me that there can be interplay between the spiritual and the physical plane. A man I know reluctantly attended an Anishinaabe cross-cultural program that included a sweat lodge. As he told me himself, he was skeptical of most aboriginal Teachings at the time but was required by his employer to attend. Although he had no interest in the sweat lodge, he liked steam baths and, seeing no big difference between the two, agreed to be a part of it. During the sweat lodge, however, something happened that changed his life. At one point, as he sat in total darkness, the "sky" inside the lodge turned a beautiful blue. Spiralling out of it and coming toward him was a brilliant red speck that, as it got closer, turned into a large eagle-like bird. It came right to him, face to face, and knocked him onto his back. He lay there for what felt like a long time, wondering what had just happened to him. He said nothing to anyone that night, but he left feeling strangely refreshed. Still mystified the next day, he approached the keeper of the sweat lodge and described what had happened to him the night before. The keeper listened closely and then smiled, telling him not to worry. The red bird meant that he had aboriginal blood, and the bird had appeared as his protector. The keeper then carried on with his regular duties of the day, as though nothing unusual had happened. My friend fully believed that the keeper was wrong and decided to dig back into his family history to prove it. A genealogical search that cost several thousand dollars revealed, however, that the keeper was correct: there was aboriginal blood in his family history that he had never known about.

He has no explanation for what happened, and neither do I. He and the keeper were almost strangers to each other, having met only a couple of times before. No one participated in the sweat lodge to prove any point. Most significantly, the keeper made his startling (and correct!) interpretation almost offhandedly, as though it was just an everyday sort of occurrence.

The people who told me such stories did so very quietly, fearing that I would reject their accounts as far too fanciful. Their rational minds had told them that their experiences had no logical explanation, and they doubted they would be believed. I do believe them, however, despite having no explanation for what they described. In a way, I'm a little jealous of what they have been through. At the same time, I suspect that I am afraid of putting my rational faculties to one side and surrendering myself to forces that are not within my conscious control. Perhaps that will change as I close in on the last years of my life.

Regardless, it must be recognized that the traditional world was primarily a *felt* world, a world to be *experienced*. Each of the thousands of relationships that surrounded every person was primarily a felt relationship, centred on values like thanksgiving, respect and humility. As such, it was a rich and comforting world, a welcoming and appreciative world that honoured the striving good spirit in all things. It was a world in which children thrived, surrounded as they were by love, respect, caring, sharing, a conviction of their own worth and a vision of interconnectivity on the physical, mental, emotional and spiritual planes.

Then the white man arrived, and he didn't see things the same way at all.

Because the white man did not see writing, he assumed an absence of sophisticated thought. He had no idea about the medicine wheel and its elaborate understandings of human development. Nor did he have any sense of the complex metaphysics of embeddedness developed over thousands of years of living successfully—and lightly—in North America.

Because he did not see churches, he assumed spiritual poverty and rushed to fill that gap. He failed to understand the healthy spirituality that touched (and was grateful for) everything, and he outlawed the multitude of ceremonies that offered aboriginal experiences of the spiritual plane.

Because he did not see European-style buildings, he assumed a primitive physical existence. He had no idea that within the tiny, round sweat lodges people routinely re-dedicated themselves to helping the Elders, the children, the planet and all people's search for balance and harmony in their lives.

Because he did not see institutions of judgment and punishment, he assumed social disorder. He did not see the elaborate counselling regimes that brought people back into harmony with themselves and their communities.

Because he chose to speak only with men, he missed the wisdom, power and influence of the women.

Because he saw children running about with little parental supervision and almost no punishment, he assumed parental failure. He did not understand the many Teachings and tests those children faced, nor did he value the adults' determination to let the children develop their own sense of responsibility over time.

Because he saw people living in the bush, he assumed they had nowhere fixed to live and could be moved to make way for dams or roads. He had no idea about the spiritual, linguistic and cultural ties to particular segments of the landscape.

Because he seldom learned aboriginal languages, he assumed primitive articulation skills. He had no idea that indigenous life and ceremony were woven into complex spoken metaphysical constructs like traditional Creation stories.

In short, the European settlers who came to North America were almost completely ignorant of the ways of indigenous people and the lives they had constructed for themselves over centuries. When this lack of knowledge was coupled with a sense of superiority over all other peoples, the newcomers caused wholesale upheaval in virtually every aspect of indigenous life. In the centuries since, this upheaval has deepened significantly in far too many places, and only recently has recovery begun.

PART TWO

COLONIZATION

CHAPTER 4

THE MANY SOURCES
OF HARM

In 1651, more than a hundred years after Jacques Cartier explored the St. Lawrence River, Thomas Hobbes wrote that where man has "no arts; no letters; no society; and ... continual fear and danger of violent death," then his life is "solitary, poor, nasty, brutish, and short." Sadly, it is probably not an exaggeration to suggest that the Canadian government, the churches and most settlers of that time saw the aboriginal people in exactly that light. We have, for instance, the words of Prime Minister Sir John A. Macdonald in Parliament in 1883 as he proposed the closure of day schools in aboriginal settlements and the opening of residential schools at distant locations:

> When the school is on the reserve, the child lives with his parents who are savages; he is surrounded by savages, and though he may learn to read and write, his habits and training and mode of thought are Indian. He is simply a savage who can read and write.[1]

Before that, we see similar attitudes from the church. Cynthia Wesley-Esquimaux and Magdalena Smolewski describe four ways in which Jesuit Father Paul LeJeune planned to "civilize" the Montagnais-Naskapi of the St. Lawrence Valley in the mid-sixteenth century.[2] He supported taking aboriginal children far from their homes and placing them in Jesuit-run institutions, writing that "the Savages prevent their [children's] instruction; they will not tolerate the chastisement of their children, whatever they may do, they permit only a simple reprimand." He went much further, however. He advocated the practice of punishment, arguing, "How could they understand tyranny and respect it unless they wielded it upon each other and experienced it at each other's hands?" In that connection, he expressed his distress that the "Savages," as he termed them, thought physical abuse a terrible crime. He also wanted to establish permanent settlements governed by official authority, saying, "If someone could stop the wanderings of the Savages, and give authority to one of them to rule the others, we would see them converted and civilized in a short time." Finally, he aimed to "introduce a new social structure in which Aboriginal people would adhere to the rules of patriarchal institutions of male dominance and female submission."

It must be understood that colonization refers to much more than these four components. Colonization, in the aboriginal scheme of things, also includes the diseases that came from Europe; the relocation of aboriginal people from traditional lands; the discriminatory legislation passed to control them and their movements; the Sixties Scoop, where aboriginal children were taken from their families under child welfare laws; and the heavy use of incarceration today. I'll speak briefly about each of these issues in this chapter.

It is the impact of residential schools, however, that has really captured my interest, especially the psychological connections between those schools and the desperate situation of too many aboriginal communities today. It is my view that addressing that psychological damage is the first step in indigenous recovery. Until this step is taken, few others, such as creating jobs or building better housing, will make much difference. I've watched many employment programs fail to have a lasting impact: people went into them and did well for a while, but eventually fell back into various addictions, family breakdown and depression. Until all four human dimensions—the physical, mental, emotional and spiritual—are moved into healthy balance, many families and communities will continue their long histories of addictions, violence, loss and sorrow.

DISEASES

I remember being in Anchorage, Alaska, and having lunch with a group of aboriginal women. They indicated that their history did not include the same heavy emphasis on residential schools that existed in Canada, but their communities showed a very similar breakdown. In their view, the primary colonization force had been the diseases that Europeans brought to North America. They talked about entire villages being wiped out, about lost souls wandering out of the wilderness as the only survivors of once-thriving small settlements. They talked about how traditional medicines fell into disrepute because they were powerless against the diseases that left the white man virtually untouched. They talked about the almost complete loss of culture when so many older people died, taking the songs, stories, history and ceremonies with them to the grave. With no written records, with so few learned people remaining to speak of them, and with the sudden loss of faith in traditional medicines and ceremonies to save lives, it was no wonder that aboriginal people began to forsake traditional ways.

To be honest, I had never learned much about those early days just after contact, and I started looking into the history. What I found shocked me. Instead of North America being an almost empty land, scholars now estimate that perhaps seven million aboriginal people lived here. They also estimate that 90 percent of them died during the many outbreaks of infectious disease that spread across the continent. That's a staggering loss.

Leigh Syms, a former archaeologist for the Manitoba Museum, went into the records of the Hudson's Bay Company and discovered that "there was one year where so many people died at a Hudson's Bay post near the Saskatchewan border that the natives left the bodies under the snow on the ground. They didn't have the energy to bury them."

In fact, scholars are now unearthing records showing that some *deliberate* attempts were made to spread lethal diseases among aboriginal populations. Cynthia Wesley-Esquimaux and Magdalena Smolewski report that Lord Jeffrey Amherst, as the Governor General of British North America, openly advocated biological attack. In letters to his subordinate officers in 1763, Amherst suggested that they "inoculate the Indians by means of [smallpox-infested] blankets, as well as to try every other method that can serve to extirpate this execrable race."[3] The authors report that several officers followed his suggestion, which resulted in smallpox epidemics in several aboriginal communities. This was not the attitude of benevolence toward aboriginal people that non-aboriginal Canadians like to believe in.

Intentional or not, deaths on that scale must have wreaked havoc with traditional culture. European societies suffered similar plagues, but the total loss of life never approached 90 percent of the population. Just as important, much of European history and culture had been captured in writing, painting, sculpture and architecture, and as such it could be brought back to life with relative ease. Aboriginal culture was, however, an oral one, residing in the minds, hearts and words of the people. When so many of them died, a great deal of their culture died with them, and what remained was only the barest skeleton of its traditional sophistication. The disconnection from traditional culture had begun.

THE DENIGRATION OF WOMEN AND THEIR ROLES

As I mentioned when discussing the goals of Jesuit Father LeJeune, removing women from positions of power and authority was an important step in colonization. Here is how Cynthia Wesley-Esquimaux and Magdalena Smolewski describe the damage done by displacing women from their traditional roles within aboriginal life:

> Many contemporary Aboriginal thinkers are convinced that, historically, the destruction of the social sphere began with a rearrangement of gender roles in Aboriginal societies and the devaluation of women. Christian missionaries, like their secular counterparts, could not tolerate peoples who allowed women to occupy prominent positions and decision-making capacity at every level of society.... The colonizers saw (and rightly) that as long as women held unquestioned power ... attempts at total conquest of the continents were bound to fail. In the centuries since the first attempts at colonization in the early 1500's, the invaders have exerted every effort to remove Indian women from every position of authority.[4]

Janice Acoose, who was an associate professor in the English department at First Nations University in Regina when I first ran across her work, is a Nehiowè-Métis Nahkawé woman whose roots stem from the Sakimay (Saulteaux) First Nation and her mother's Ninankawe Marival Métis community. In her 1995 book *Iskwewak:*

Neither Indian Princesses Nor Easy Squaws, she describes the colonial policy with regard to women:

> Of specific importance ... is the removal of women from all significant social, political, economic and spiritual processes. Where women once participated and contributed in meaningful ways as part of clan, tribal and council consensus governments, under the colonial regime ... they were generally excluded.[5]

For my own part, I have seen the near reverence with which most aboriginal people greet their *Kokums* (or Grandmothers) today. They have certainly been at the forefront of my own learning! I think of Mary Anne Anderson of Big Trout Lake asking why my western justice system takes their money and their people out to jail and leaves them with the problem. I think of Murdena Marshal of Eskasoni setting me in the right direction to understand healing. I think of the Cree Grandmother who led me to consider how abusive people learned to behave that way simply because they had only experienced relationships based on fear and anger. I think of the Cree Grandmother who spoke about needing to restore her granddaughter's trust in the church, the schools and adults in general. I think of Burma Bushie, who brought me into the healing circles at Hollow Water, insisting that I had to participate and feel, not just observe. I think of the many Grandmothers who told me about the reverse hierarchy within Creation. All of them—and so many more I have not yet named—have continued to speak out, and they do so without anger, even to people like me, a white Crown attorney.

I cannot imagine how much healthier their communities might have been today had those strong women been welcomed by non-aboriginal governments instead of shunted aside. One male aboriginal leader explained, only half-jokingly, why it was that women played such an essential role in family and community life. "It is because," he said, "they're the only ones who can see past their own egos!" Unfortunately, the prominence of women in traditional societies fell prey to a European insistence on dealing only with men. While aboriginal men initially insisted on continued consultation with the women, over time that habit began to break down, especially with the imposition of residential schools and the complete separation of boys and girls during their formative years. Those schools left most aboriginal communities unconnected to their past social structures and dependent, instead, on replicating the male-dominated structure of non-aboriginal societies. It is only recently that many indigenous communities have begun to reassert their matrilineal social structure and restore women to honoured positions within both families and community governance.

LEGAL DISCRIMINATION

We should not be surprised to find legal attacks against aboriginal self-determination, but few Canadians understand the degree of subservience that was demanded. Aboriginal people were not equal under the law with everyone else. Here are just some of the legal restrictions imposed by Canadian governments over the decades:

- "pass laws" where aboriginal people were not permitted to leave their home reserve unless specifically permitted by the Indian agent;
- laws that denied them the right to vote as long as they remained on their reserves as "status Indians," a situation that prevailed until well after World War II;
- laws that forbade them from selling farm produce to anyone outside the borders of their home reserve;

- laws that made it illegal for them to take governments to court to enforce any treaty or other rights, a situation that existed from 1927 to 1951;
- laws that made it illegal to even consult with a lawyer about appealing to the courts;
- laws that made it illegal to "receive, obtain, solicit or request" any money to assist any Indian band in any such claim against government; and, perhaps most important,
- laws that imposed jail terms if people participated in traditional ceremonies like sweat lodges, the potlatch in British Columbia or the sun dance on the prairies.

On that last point, I recall an Elder from Lake of the Woods telling me that when he was a boy, he and some friends snuck through the woods one night to a tiny clearing where some of the old people were conducting traditional ceremonies around a fire. When the old people discovered them, they were told never to do that again or to conduct such ceremonies themselves, because all of them could go to jail if the white man caught them. To this day, that memory remains a vivid reminder for the Elder of the degree to which, as he grew up, everyone he knew lived in fear of being punished by the white man for doing things they had always done with—and for—each other.

I haven't even mentioned the legal subordination contained in the Indian Act, passed at various stages without indigenous input. Entire books have been written on that subject, and I'll leave it to them to tell the story.

RELOCATION OF FAMILIES AND COMMUNITIES

Canadian governments not only restricted rights of movement, voting, association and legal appeal. They also took it upon themselves to simply create entire communities where none had existed before, primarily so they could flood aboriginal lands and build hydro dams. I saw evidence of that movement first-hand in northwestern Ontario, an area the size of France. There are now roughly sixty First Nations communities there, ranging in size from perhaps two hundred people to over three thousand. We made those communities, moving seasonally nomadic families into them. I'm not sure we understood the impact of what we were doing.

While such new communities made it easier to provide schooling and medical services, I suspect that we had little sense of the challenges posed by that sudden switch to community living. We ignored the difficulties the people faced as they had to learn about new locations for good traplines, safe routes across winter ice, places where the best sloughs to harvest wild rice were, the most likely sites for berry picking, the locations of major spawning grounds for fish populations, the paths taken by deer and moose during rutting season, areas where the geese landed in spring and fall, places where medicinal and sacred plants could be found and harvested. Every pattern of living deep in the bush had to be rebuilt when people were moved out of their traditional, semi-nomadic landscapes and into new communities, often far away.

Then there was the issue of once-separate families having to create new sharing arrangements over their new communal geography, dividing up increasingly scarce resources. Community governance, traditionally involving only single families or related groups, now included many strangers as well. Voter-based democracy was then imposed under the Indian Act, contrary to other forms of choosing leaders that had existed for centuries. And leaders were given powers over others that they had never had before.

Perhaps most disruptive, however, was the flooding of vast areas for the development of hydroelectric power systems. When that happened, the flooded lands simply disappeared from people's lives. It seems to me that we regularly fail to recognize what that loss of traditional land meant to the people who were displaced. Joseph Gone, a member of the Gros Ventre Tribe of Montana and an associate professor of psychology at the University of Michigan, gives us one young man's reflections on what was lost when his traditional lands were flooded in Manitoba:

> But then, as the water was rising, I think there was sort of a grief and loss because a lot of times I heard my father complaining about what Hydro was doing to the land and their trapping grounds…. And I guess they sort of started to depend on the welfare system…. I'd seen some things happening that, I don't know, I didn't understand back then. And I'd seen some abuse going on. There were adults arguing and fighting and I heard guns going off at night, and there was drinking going on…. It was getting kind of depressing for me to be out there. It wasn't the same any more, once you saw the trees in the water, and there's no more places that were nice. You couldn't walk around the shore no more…. I guess the adults were grieving. Sometimes I saw the adults cry when they were drinking when the spring flooded, and I guess that was when one of my older brothers was telling me, "It's time to go back to school and get some education, because the environment is getting ruined. You can't move along or live off the land no more like in the old days."[6]

I suspect that the young man was not aware of the spiritual loss, the loss of self-definition, that his parents and grandparents suffered. After all, the ceremonies that expressed those spiritual connections had first been made unlawful, then were ridiculed and ignored during residential school days, and finally were made virtually senseless by the destruction of the unique geography that had nurtured them. Although he might not have known in any detailed way about all the sources of spiritual strength that now lay submerged, he certainly sensed the enormity of those losses to his people.

Most non-aboriginal Canadians have no concept of the disconnection such relocation causes. To us, the bush is just the bush, and it doesn't really matter where you are within it, because it's all pretty much the same. We wonder at the opposition we now encounter when we plan to simply relocate indigenous populations in the bush, just as we wonder about all the compensation claims now being made over relocations that happened decades ago. What we have difficulty understanding is that those specific landscapes had, over centuries, informed and shaped the ceremonies that sustained spiritual life. Conducted in a new environment, significant portions of those ceremonies no longer made sense, because they had no roots in that particular location.

When the importance of place is understood from an indigenous standpoint, the dislocation caused by moving people becomes clear: we were uprooting them from their long-familiar spiritual context, built as it was around specific locations. When you are suddenly taken from the source of your belief in mutual interdependency, how can you not feel displaced or without roots in your new reality?

In the Far North, the dislocation suffered by Inuit people when they were forced to adapt to community life is perhaps even more pronounced. They, too, lived an essentially nomadic life, defining their home as the entire expanse of ice, snow and water through which they moved, according to the seasons, in purposeful and repeating activities. They never had communities like those they live in today, nor did they ever wish for them or struggle to create them. In some cases, governments simply flew entire family groups hundreds of kilometres away and dropped them into entirely new surroundings. Their plight is only now being recognized. Kristiann Allen, who has a master's degree in medical anthropology from McGill University, describes it as follows:

> The problem is that many (Inuit) hamlet dwellers do not consider their community to be home and understandably so.... The communities seem like artificial constructs.... They know that their true home stretches across a quarter of the Canadian Arctic itself.... Consequently, no one actually feels ownership over a hamlet. They have never planned it, never fought for it, and most certainly did not build it. A settlement of people only becomes a true community when sufficient numbers of people come to call it home and are willing to work for it.[7]

In short, indigenous people were forced to live where they were told, in circumstances that were foreign and confused, while being deprived of the physical environment on which they had built a sustaining social structure, economy and spiritual home over thousands of years. That is a big part of what colonization means to indigenous people in Canada. I find my thoughts returning to the day in Regina when Maria Linklater took the aboriginal youngsters outside to sit under a tree on Mother Earth and talk of serious things. Her people had been sitting on that same soil for thousands of years, but in five hundred years or so, almost everything had changed.

Perhaps the biggest source of change, however, involves the deliberate destruction of aboriginal families over many generations—along with the cultural structures that had supported them for thousands of years—by the imposition of the residential school system on aboriginal children.

CHAPTER 5

THE RESIDENTIAL SCHOOL SYSTEM

I once thought the whole issue of residential schools ended when most of them closed forty years ago. I thought it was silly to keep blaming them after all this time, a belief that is echoed by many Canadians. I have since learned how wrong I was, and I want to explain why I now feel so differently.

We have already seen what Prime Minister Sir John A. Macdonald said about aboriginal parents, calling them "savages." Researcher John H. Hylton, in *Aboriginal Sexual Offending in Canada*, describes the general feeling of the day:

> The prevailing view was that every aspect of the traditional Aboriginal way of life was inferior to the ways of the dominant culture.... Youth were considered to be especially suitable objects for the state's assimilation efforts, since the government and the missionaries could "guide them from a state of impurity, incompetence and ignorance, to a state in which they would function as adults acceptable to white society."[1]

And that's what Deputy Superintendent of Indian Affairs Duncan Campbell Scott meant when he testified about residential schools in 1920 before a special committee to the House of Commons: "Our object is to continue until there is not a single Indian in Canada that has not been absorbed into the body politic and there is no Indian question, and no Indian Department, that is the whole object of this Bill."[2]

Yet the "Indian question" is now greater than it ever was, and perhaps growing, thanks to the emergence of the Idle No More movement in late 2012. For one thing, the number of aboriginal communities showing signs of social breakdown is large and, in my view, growing larger. Their demands are increasing, not disappearing. For another, many present-day aboriginal leaders are pushing for the re-establishment of aboriginal education systems that include a strong focus on traditional Teachings. And we haven't really begun to see the full scale of aboriginal resistance to environmentally disruptive activities like Alberta's oil sands and the pipelines being proposed to carry oil to distant markets. The "Indian question" has clearly not gone away.

For the remainder of my discussion about colonization, I want to focus on what really happened to children, over generations, when they were forced to leave their families and attend residential schools. My questions have slowly boiled down to four:

- What happens to children's personal development when their youth is spent in circumstances of helpless captivity where their race and culture are insistently denigrated?
- Are there emotional capacities that remain undeveloped or underdeveloped?
- What kinds of adults do those children become? What kinds of parents?
- How are their children and grandchildren affected?

Before getting into these questions, a few issues need to be clarified, because most Canadians have never been given a clear picture of the residential school system.

First, it is important to recognize that not all aboriginal children went to residential schools. Those schools were able to accommodate only about half the population of aboriginal children at any time, with the result that many children never went at all. I know of one Elder who grew up with her grandparents, both of whom were traditional people, keeping her language and gaining their insights into right relations. She went on to Harvard University and earned her master's degree in education. She, along with many others across Canada, has remained vibrantly attached to traditional visions of those right relations. She has dedicated her life to passing traditional Teachings—and her language—on to the children of her people. However, most of the children in her community were not so lucky.

Nor did all of those who went to residential school stay for the full ten years. Many attended for only a couple of years, sometimes because their parents hid them after learning of the treatment their children suffered within those schools.

Because most of the schools existed between the 1880s and the 1960s, with approximately 140 being built over that time, their nature and attitudes could not help but change over the decades. The calibre and sensitivities of their staff also varied from school to school, and from year to year. Many students recall good experiences with some of the staff, but many describe sexual and physical violence at the hands of others. There were teachers who learned to speak aboriginal languages and schools that supported learning about traditional values, but in many other institutions, indigenous language and culture were constantly criticized, often ferociously.

As I have begun to understand, there is no single story created by these institutions, and no standard template into which all communities fall. Individuals, families and communities have shown tremendous differences in their responses to to the forces of colonization. For instance, a recent study demonstrated that while the rate of aboriginal suicide in British Columbia was much higher than the national average, most suicides were clustered in a few aboriginal communities, and many showed no recorded suicides at all. Some remote First Nations in northern Ontario are thriving and primarily Christian, while some other Christian communities are in deep social trouble. Other healthy communities maintain strong ties to traditional culture, while struggling ones assert similar grounding in name only. There are also communities that are thoroughly modern in their business dealings, but hide serious degrees of sexual abuse and family violence just beneath the surface. To repeat myself, there is no single story among aboriginal communities, just as there is no single story to be told about the families that live within them.

I am drawn to the conclusion that the primary cause of differences among communities lies in the distinct experiences of their populations within residential schools. The degree of trauma they then took home, and the capacity of their communities to absorb that trauma in healthy ways over subsequent generations, seems to vary dramatically.

Two psychologists from the University of Toronto, Rosemary Barnes and Nina Josefowitz, describe that variety of experience in their paper "First Nations Residential School Experience: Factors Related to Stress and Resilience," presented to the Canadian Psychological Association.[3] In it, they set out the many factors that children might have faced, and how different they were. For instance, if parents wanted their children to attend the white man's school, the children would leave home with a very different mindset than those who were forcibly taken from their protesting parents' arms. If parents set out good reasons for going, such as learning the white man's language and customs, the children would have a goal to achieve, and the foreignness of the experience would be an expected component. If the schools were close enough that family visits could be frequent, the sense of dislocation was lessened. Similarly, if the children went to school with siblings or friends with whom they could feel a continued connection to home, they would also feel less isolated. If children were older when they first attended, or stayed for fewer than the expected ten years, they would have absorbed more of the sustaining aspects of their own culture, language, traditions and sense of belonging, and so could more successfully return to their home community. Some children went home every summer, maintaining connections with family and culture. Others, staying much longer, went home alone and were virtually unrecognizable to their family, friends and community. If the families and communities they returned to were peaceful, self-sufficient and steeped in traditional Teachings, the children were more likely to psychologically resist the racist denigration of their residential school years. If, however, their home communities were violent and disorganized, they stood little chance of surviving in healthy ways.

What aboriginal children found at school also varied widely. When staff were kind, open and nurturing, fear and isolation were reduced. If staff did not put down everything aboriginal, the children could better sustain pride in themselves, their families and their culture. If, however, staff constantly denigrated their heritage, or, much worse, assaulted them physically or sexually, the negative impact would be large, deep and lasting. Similarly, in those schools where there was substantial student-on-student violence, the fear, helplessness and anger would only multiply.

Here, to illustrate just one person's experience, is part of the story told by an aboriginal woman from Vancouver Island in *Residential Schools: The Stolen Years*, a book in which Phil Fontaine, former Grand Chief of the Assembly of First Nations, wrote about his own sexual abuse. Three of her brothers were sent to the Port Alberni Residential School on Vancouver Island, but at age five she was sent by train with an older sister to a residential school in Edmonton, over a thousand kilometres away:

> At first I found this exciting. We ran around and ate in the diner. But as the train took us farther and farther away, I began to feel afraid. At each stop, more and more Native children were put on the train. Soon we were packed in like sardines. All around there were other children like us, looking and feeling afraid....
>
> Finally, we stopped in Edmonton, a place far away from home, a place I had never heard of.... We were crowded into buses, which took us into the country. The trip was quiet. We all sat and stared out at everything. We stopped in front of a huge red brick building full of windows....
>
> As soon as we entered, some women took away our clothes, and gave us clothes with numbers on them. We never saw our clothes again until the end of the year.[4]

In these few paragraphs, it's easy to see a five-year-old's sense of dislocation from her family, her fear of the unknown, and the loss of traditional things such as clothing. She, like so many others, also had her name replaced with a number. On that issue, here is the story given to researcher James Waldram by another former resident:

> I didn't even know my name, had no idea who I was or anything. All I had was a number. And I still know my number, it was number 59. And I used that ... all through that time, until I was nearly ten. Until I got out from wherever I was for a doctor's appointment or dental appointment, or anything like

that, I'd be there, number 59, that's all they knew who I was, by that number. I guess they told us [at] about ten or eleven, that I started to know who I was and ...find out later that I had siblings in the Rez with me and in school. And it was just like a shock to me, I didn't know that I had any because ... I didn't know what happened, if they died or whatever, eh? I didn't know what happened to them, I had no clue.[5]

The little girl from Vancouver Island was fortunate in having some support, including parents who agreed that she should attend the school and an older sibling to stand beside her. As it turned out, she went to residential school only for grades one, four, five and six, spending the other grades in normal day schools close to home, and then made her way to university. But many others had no such support, and many spent a full ten years in residential school. Their traumatization would have been substantially greater.

I cannot explain why some people, families and communities have absorbed so much colonization trauma that they are now almost wholly dysfunctional, while others are not. I doubt that anyone can penetrate all the layers going back several generations.

I am, however, certain of one thing: it is wrong to assume that because one aboriginal person reports having a good experience at residential school, every other student's stories of abuse are either lies or exaggerations. These are just people telling honestly what happened to them, and the stories of abuse, some of them horrendous, are just as real and valid as those of being treated well. If you look at the proportion of those stories speaking of abuse, you realize that abusive behaviour was far from rare and needs to be looked at closely. You cannot spend time with the Truth and Reconciliation Commission hearing about the terrible situations children faced without recognizing that those things happened, and that they are still heavily influencing those people today.

This is one of the goals of this book: to point out what I see as the major negative forces that were at play in the lives of those students who did face abuse—forces that continued to plague the children they raised when they went home. I'll first identify each of the forces that I think were most threatening to good health, whether mental, physical, emotional or spiritual. I don't claim a specialist's knowledge about them, but I think it's important that we at least start to explore them. I will also address the growing research that is starting to define how those forces change personality over time, leading us to so much of the violence and dysfunction we see today.

THE CHILDREN WERE PRISONERS,
NOT JUST STUDENTS

To understand the impact of residential schools it is critical to acknowledge that the children in those schools were not simply students. They were prisoners, and their captive status began as early as age five. They were helpless, dependent and lost. That is why, as adults, they now call themselves "survivors," not "former students." They are offended that non-aboriginals would think of them as students in the same way that they think of their own children going to school. They survived forced imprisonment by western culture and governments, and they want the world to understand that.

Fred Kelly, Anishinaabe from Lake of the Woods and the spiritual adviser to Phil Fontaine when he was Grand Chief of the Assembly of First Nations, paints his own picture of what he encountered at residential school in the Kenora area:

> Immediately upon entry into the school, the staff began to beat the devil out of us. Such was my experience. We were humiliated out of our culture and spirituality. We were

told that these ways were of the devil. We were punished
for speaking the only language we ever knew. Fear stalked
the dark halls of the school as priests and nuns going about
their rounds in black robes passed like floating shadows in
the night. Crying from fear was punished by beatings that
brought on more crying and then more punishment. Braids
were immediately shorn. Traditional clothing was confiscated
and replaced by standard issue uniforms. Our traditional
names were anglicized and often replaced by numbers. Those
who ran away were held in dark closets and fed a bread-and-
water diet when they were brought back. Any sense of dignity
and self-esteem turned to self-worthlessness and hopelessness.
We came to believe that "Indian" was a dirty word, oftentimes
calling each other by that term pejoratively.[6]

Even more tragic, some died while trying to escape for home.
The authorities in the Kenora area are currently considering a new
inquest into the death of a young boy who, many years ago, fled his
Kenora residential school in mid-winter and was found frozen to
death beside the railway tracks, heading home. When children were
captured after they tried to escape, they were punished. Another
man told Joseph Gone about what happened when he was caught:

We used to run away too. I was trying to run away from that
pain, and we were trying to run away from the way we were
treated. But when we run [sic] away, and we were caught, they
used to shave our head…. And they used to have a movie
at that school. We used to sit there. [They] displayed us….
And this priest and nuns thought it was funny putting us in
front of the screen while they're watching the movies, and
they would not allow us to watch the movies because that's
our punishment.[7]

It has recently been revealed that students in some residential schools were used in projects generally called "nutritional experiments," where groups of children were fed different diets to see how their bodies responded. One of those schools was in the Kenora area, and many people here are feeling intense anger at such treatment.

In other words, when we think of residential schools, we must not think of them as schools at all. They were much more like prison camps. And the prisoners were not adults. They were children. And there were generations of them.

THEY SUFFERED A DEEP SENSE OF ABANDONMENT

It is hard for many to imagine what these children must have felt. Maggie Hodgson is a member of the Carrier Nation in Alberta. She has managed an aboriginal health promotions institute for eighteen years; has written four books on aboriginal issues; and has presented on community healing in Canada, the United States, Australia, New Zealand, France, Germany and Norway. She writes about the loneliness children felt:

> Water spirit is the gift we use when we cry. In residential school, many people learned not to cry. When children cried in residential school and there was no response except "I'll give you something to cry for!" they learned to shut down sadness. Over time, they built such a wall around sadness that when they cry now, they say "I broke down." When children cried themselves to sleep because they missed their parents so much, they eventually learned that they could cry all they wanted but they were still not going home.... The sense of abandonment was experienced by many children. They wondered why

their parents did not come to visit them. After one hundred years, there was not much water spirit left; in its place was hopelessness, a deep sense of abandonment, and anger.[8]

The sense of abandonment was complete: it was not only the children who felt it, but also their parents and their entire communities. Janice Acoose speaks about the rule that boys and girls be completely separated, even though they were in the same school: "My oldest brother, Fred, became only a passing face behind a wire fence. During all those years in residential school I remember seeing him only through that fence."[9] Peter Ernerk reports the same experience for Inuit people in the Far North:

I had no brothers or sisters at Chesterfield Inlet but a lot of the people had sisters right upstairs which was the third floor from the ground. I remember the other boys were not allowed to see their own sisters upstairs. Bonding with relatives was an important part of Inuit culture that we were denied.[10]

Researchers Madeleine Dion Stout and Gregory Kipling confirm this isolation from family:

Moreover, not only do former students remember not having anyone to turn to when they were sick or in need of comfort but, in many cases, family estrangement was reinforced by the fact that children were forbidden from interacting with siblings, particularly those of the opposite sex.[11]

This estrangement was widespread across regions and traditions. Another man described its impact to Lee Brown, a member of the Cherokee Nation and director of the UBC Institute of Aboriginal Health when we first met:

Grief, fear, abandonment, alienation, those were the big ones for me. Alienation was the big one ... alienation from self. Alienated from family, alienated from culture. Getting back to it was like I had finally come home. Like I had been lost all these years and I had finally got home.[12]

We have all felt alone at times, but few of us have felt as alone as those children taken to residential school. I repeat what Maggie Hodgson said about the repercussions of that loneliness over many generations: "After one hundred years, there was not much water spirit left; in its place was hopelessness, a deep sense of abandonment, and anger." Is it any wonder that such abandonment would lead to anger later in life?

THEY LIVED WITH POVERTY, DISEASE AND SOMETIMES DEATH

Here is something else that many do not know about the residential school system: it was so poorly funded that it was common for the children to spend half of each day working, not studying at all. The boys worked at farm chores, raising crops and tending animals. The girls worked in kitchens, did laundry and sewed clothing. Complaints were made by many people, including students, their parents and school investigators, about how little education the children really received, spending so much of their time just keeping the schools running, but they fell on deaf ears.

Diseases took an extraordinary toll in the schools, and medical attention was often nonexistent. As Deborah Chansonneuve explains, it has been known for over a century that a high proportion of the children died from illness:

In 1907, both *The Montreal Star* and *Saturday Night* reported on a medical inspection of the schools that found aboriginal children were dying in astonishing numbers. The magazine called the 24% national death rate of aboriginal children in the schools (42% counting the children who died at home shortly after being returned because they were critically ill), "a situation disgraceful to the country."[13]

Imagine what would happen if nearly half the children in a local public school died or were sent home to die instead. Even more incredibly, the parents of many children were never notified about the death of their children, much less given an explanation. The children simply disappeared, and the schools went on. Figures released by the Aboriginal Healing Foundation suggest that at least three thousand children died over the history of residential schools, yet many of them were never named in any report.[14]

The residential school experience was far from that of an English boarding school. These were children held in entirely foreign captivity, on threat of punishment, and many of them suffered extremes of deprivation and abuse that affected their entire lives.

EVERYTHING ABOUT THEM WAS DENIGRATED

I have already talked about the incessant denigration, beginning with Sir John A. Macdonald's view of aboriginal people as savages. That attitude was pervasive across Canada. John Amagoalik, former chief commissioner of the Nunavut Implementation Commission, was born in a hunting camp near Inukjuak in northern Quebec and grew up in the High Arctic. This is what he says about the Inuit experience of residential school:

Non-Aboriginal Canadians cannot fully understand the crushing effect of colonialism on a people. They do not appreciate the negative self-image that people can have about themselves when another culture projects itself as being "superior" and acts to impose its laws, language, values, and culture upon the other. Canadians must understand that their leaders had assimilation policies designed to kill Aboriginal cultures and traditions. In reference to Inuit, the *Report of the Royal Commission on Aboriginal Peoples* quoted an unnamed federal administrator as writing in a 1952 report, "Their civilization, because it is without hope of advancement, should be ruthlessly discouraged."[15]

Imagine being told, in every way possible, that your civilization should be "ruthlessly discouraged" because it is "without hope of advancement." Imagine, as a parent, that your child was being told such things, day in and day out. Here is how one woman described the after-effects to researcher James Waldram:

I guess my self-esteem ... was broken.... I had no sense of identity, I had no sense of belonging.... I didn't even know what I [was] supposed to do or what was expected of me because, you know, being constantly told that ... I don't have no Mom or nothing and ... that the only good Indian was a dead Indian and all this sort of stuff. So I started ... to believe that stuff because if [they] start constantly pounding, pounding it into you, you know, you just [believe it].[16]

Cynthia Wesley-Esquimaux and Magdalena Smolewski have studied the long-term impact of the constant denigration of culture and race, which they describe in these terms:

When people's expert knowledge about the world around them is discredited, they are incapable of understanding the outside forces that forcibly shape their lives.... Without cultural remembering, there is no cultural knowledge, nothing to pass on to next generations, nothing to teach young people and nothing to use as social resources in times of crisis. Without shared cultural knowledge, there are no societies, just groups of culturally orphaned individuals unable to create their shared future.[17]

In fact, Erica-Irene Daes, chair of the United Nations Working Group on Indigenous Populations, has seen exactly the same result among colonized people around the world: "Isolation is an important tool, and a devastating result, of colonization ... one of the most destructive of the shared personal experiences of colonized peoples ... is intellectual and spiritual loneliness."[18]

When experienced by children, constant denigration leads to lifelong shame. This shame remains a destructive force in aboriginal communities today, and it is a topic I will return to in a later chapter.

THEIR RELATIONSHIP WITH STAFF WAS OFTEN ABUSIVE

Abusive relationships between students and staff at residential schools have drawn the most attention thus far in Canada. Clearly, many schools were the source of physical and sexual abuse, but many more were not. That deplorable behaviour was widespread enough, however, that it had a serious, long-term and pervasive impact.

Madeleine Dion Stout and Gregory Kipling provide an overview:

If the physical setting seemed foreign, the treatment students received at the hands of school staff only served to exacerbate their feelings of dislocation. Rather than playing the role of surrogate parents, staff behaved, all too frequently, like prison guards by acting coldly and without sympathy toward the children, while forcing them to adhere to a highly regimented schedule.[19]

There need not have been actual sexual abuse to cause psychological damage to children, given the rigidity of church doctrine forbidding sexual activity of any kind.

In many instances, our role models were the same priests and nuns who were our sexual predators and perpetrators. To be absolutely certain, not all the religious staff committed such sexual atrocities. To their credit, many appeared pure and conscientious in their duties. But having taken their vows of lifelong chastity and celibacy, and even giving them the benefit of any doubt, they were understandably hard-pressed to talk about the act of procreation, personal parenting, and other normal facts of life in a Church that taught us that sex was a taboo subject in school. In fact, there was no such thing as a healthy sex education. Sex was dirty, and even thoughts about sex were sins—matters, indeed, for the confessional. Touching a girl in any way would lead ultimately to "one dirty act," said the nuns invariably. Once planted in the mind during the formative years of an adolescent boy, this notion was insidiously inescapable…. The psychological damage was done. Many fathers to this day are unable to express their love to their children, especially their daughters. Personally, I was not able to hug or kiss my mother until she was seventy-three, the final year of her life.[20]

Punishment at the hands of staff was often a routine part of the residential school day. One Inuit survivor told David King about the physical abuse the children suffered:

I've seen students being pulled by two grey nuns by the ears, taking them upstairs.... They would hit us, they would slap us, they would pull us by the ear which was completely contrary to Inuit teachings. We were always told to never hurt people by the areas that broke easily such as the eyes, the nose, the ears and so forth. So when they gave their punishments they did their job very well.[21]

Janice Acoose has a similar story:

My older sisters, Iris and Vicky, were whisked away to the "big girls" dormitory. They soon discovered one Sister's private chambers were used to punish girls who did not follow the rules. It was equipped with a wooden horse which allowed the Sister to lay the girls across it while she whipped their bare backsides until they screamed out or cried.[22]

The abuse goes far beyond simple punishment. Beatings that involved sexual abuse were not uncommon. Researcher Gwen Reimer reports that an eighteen-month investigation uncovered more than 230 possible instances of physical and sexual abuse in one school in what was then the Northwest Territories.[23]

After leaving the schools, these children had to live with the impact of what they had suffered. Jo-Anne Fiske reports what one man told her about his childhood sexual abuse by a priest, and how it connected to his later life:

You know, they teach you there that sex is dirty, sex is a sin and it's evil and everything else, and the priest sexually abused me, so I didn't know what's going on. If sex is a sin then why is he hurting me there? So when I went home there I was totally confused.... Sometimes I have a girlfriend or sometimes a woman that gets in my way there, and I don't know what happened, and I'd be hitting them or pushing them or something ... saying get out of my way, don't touch me.[24]

While it is true that not all children were abused in such a way, just being a witness to abuse can be powerfully destructive, especially to children, and especially when there is nothing you can do to escape it. A Grandmother once told me about a time when she and an older female student were taken to the superintendent's office to be punished for trying to run away. She stood frozen as he ordered the older girl to bare her upper body and stand there while he strapped her. She remembers the superintendent turning purple in the face, then quickly leaving the room, an erection visible in his trousers. Both girls stayed there, frozen, wondering what was next, unable to move without permission, until someone else came along to shoo them away. As she told that story, I could sense the helplessness she felt then, and the fear that she might be next. That event occurred more than forty years ago, and it remains as vivid to her now as when it first happened.

How did children respond to such abuse? Madeleine Dion Stout and Gregory Kipling report one of the ways they chose to live with it, and I find it as obvious as it is disturbing:

Some students felt their best chance of survival was to reach an accommodation with those in positions of power ... to co-operate with the nuns.... "I learned to use sexuality to my advantage, as did many other students. Sexual favours brought me protection, sweets (a rarity in the school), and even money to buy booze."[25]

Clearly, that perversion of right relations between children and supervising adults turned everything upside down. Abused children were forced to become compliant partners in continuing abuse, with all normal boundaries for healthy sexual encounters abandoned. I'll have much more to say later about the lasting impact of sexual abuse. For now, it is important to note that it happened, it happened to children, and those children had no one to go to. They simply had to find ways to bear what was imposed upon them.

While physical and sexual abuse by adult staff has been proven in a number of criminal prosecutions across Canada, we still have no idea about its full extent. The Truth and Reconciliation Commission is in the process of filling that information gap, and I have no doubt that its findings will shock Canadians. I have heard many of the stories, and they are truly frightening—particularly because they speak of the abuse of children.

Those children faced another source of harm, but it's one that has largely remained secret until recently: violence, including sexual abuse, between the students themselves.

THEIR RELATIONSHIPS WITH OTHER STUDENTS WERE OFTEN ABUSIVE

It should not be surprising that students abused other students, simply because residential schools were themselves institutions centred on power, position and force. The children who came into them were without defences, living completely at the mercy of their surroundings. Many aboriginal people have confided to me, and now to the TRC, that they were never abused by nuns, priests or teachers—but they were abused regularly by older students. They told me that gangs flourished, bullying was common and the only protection was membership in parallel gangs. Joseph Gone was told by a survivor about one of the reasons for the formation of antagonistic groups:

> Most of them didn't speak English. They spoke their own Native language, and I couldn't communicate with them because they speak Ojibwa, and they speak Dene.... And there was some Cree.... And it was confusing.... Fear was in with me. All these people, and I didn't understand a word they're saying. So we went into little groups. There's a Cree group, there's a Dene group, there's Ojibwa groups. Separated.... It was crazy sometimes among us, among our own Aboriginal people. A Dene didn't like a Cree. The Ojibwa didn't like a Cree. The Crees were in the middle of most fights. Nobody liked us. We used to fight amongst each other as Aboriginal people. "Oh, go fight that Dene."[26]

When abuse happened between students, they had no one to complain to. As survivors have described it to me, you just shut up and took it—or plotted revenge of your own. Many who were first abused as younger students became abusers themselves as they grew older. Many have kept this secret for forty years or more, even from their own families, because they knew no one wanted to acknowledge it. Much of that abuse was likely witnessed by other students, but they too remain silent today.

I have had women tell me in confidence about being raped by older students. One of them confided that she had been raped by three boys, all of whom were now men, living locally and seen as respected people in their own communities. She runs into them in stores, and she freezes. She didn't want charges laid, just meetings at which they could be honest and admit what they had done. For many reasons, no such meetings ever took place. All her life she has struggled with those memories, and fallen back on alcohol to numb her pain. She is far from alone.

THIS CHAPTER HAS ONLY BRIEFLY depicted the kinds of abuse that many generations of aboriginal children suffered. As I said before, these things did not happen in every school, nor did all children fall prey to all of these examples of harm. But what is true is that a startling proportion of children suffered some or all of them, and they are still suffering today.

The next chapter speaks to how aboriginal children dealt with whatever kinds of abuse they suffered or witnessed. Once again, not all responded in the same ways, not only because there were different kinds and degrees of abuse, but also because the children drew on different sources of strength. In psychological terms, some were far more resilient than others. What follows is my best attempt to outline the various responses we can see from the people who, as children, found themselves alone and suffering in residential school.

EXPLORING THE PSYCHOLOGICAL DAMAGE

THE PHENOMENON OF SILENCE

One of the things that most surprised me about the abuse suffered in residential school was that no one ever talked about it. It is only in the last ten years or so that the topic has begun to emerge, and it didn't come fully into the spotlight until many survivors decided to take government and the churches to court. How could that silence have lasted for forty years or more, especially when the abuse was so widespread?

The silence of children at the time of their abuse is easily understandable. They were helpless, far from family and without allies. One survivor told Joseph Gone why she never talked about anything:

Reporting such violations to other staff members would be met with wanton disregard. I would try and tell the Sister. She says, "Oh you can't say that (about) this priest, he's a man of the cloth. You'll go to the chapel and say your ten Hail Mary's to be forgiven." It wasn't me that [should have] asked for forgiveness, it was that priest who did something to me that later on in my adult life would affect me.[1]

After learning in this way that reporting the abuse would do no good, it is understandable that the children would grow up and never discuss what had happened to them. Another survivor explained to Joseph Gone:

Back then, I could not disclose myself to anyone because I figured that it was only happening to us.... [Now] sometimes I have trouble with authority figures.... I can see myself like I'm a little kid again and that I'm still seeing that teacher, he scared me, and that's how I feel sometimes. And [I] want to talk back and I can't seem to say what I say because I get a bit upset and I start shaking, and words don't come out right.[2]

It is clear from this statement that the children couldn't talk to anyone about the abuse, not even one another. Under those circumstances, it is easy to imagine that they would have thought it was only happening to them, and that they might even be at fault. That guilt would add to their silence. I recall talking to a man who had been sexually assaulted in his dormitory room by a priest after everyone else had fallen asleep. To this day, he freezes when he hears the sound of footsteps on a wooden floor, because that was what announced the priest's arrival those many horrible nights. He, too, likely thought it was only happening to him.

After the years away, and the abuse suffered, all those students went home. Many people might think that being home meant the children were free from the pressure to maintain silence, that the stories should have started to come out at that point. That is not the case with most survivors. During visits home, children were afraid to tell members of their family or community about what was happening to them. Distressingly, the children received direct warnings at the residential schools against speaking to others about their experiences.[3]

Even when children did tell family members about the abuse, however, most found no response at all. These children were devastated by something they never expected: parental failure to accept the allegations as true. Janice Acoose speaks of her own experience:

> As a child, I tried to tell anyone who would listen about those night visits to our dorm, the cruel punishments and the deadly threats, but my voice was silenced by my family's fears, the community's pressure and the church's power. As a result, I grew up believing that what I felt, heard and saw was not real! Looking back at my parents, aunts, uncles, grandparents and great-grandparents, I understand how they were also silenced.[4]

One man I spoke with told me about a priest in his home village, not in a residential school, who sexually assaulted him as a child. He told his parents when it happened, but they did not believe him, and it was that nonbelief that hurt him the most. Later, when his family moved to Winnipeg so the children could get a better education, the priest was often invited to stay with them when he came into town. He was given an upper bunk in the boy's room, and he slipped down into the boy's lower bunk at night to sexually abuse him. The boy knew that he could not tell anyone. He just accepted it—that is, until many years later, when he pleaded guilty in my court to beating his wife. At sentencing, the judge asked him where he thought all of his anger came from. I remember him sitting before the judge in that northern courtroom, head down between his knees, for several minutes. His silence was so long, we knew he was debating disclosing something serious. When he finally answered that he'd been abused by a priest as a child, we knew what priest he was talking about, because we had convicted him of many such offences, especially in that community. We adjourned the man's case, and I was given permission for a long interview. As he told me his story, it became clear: it was the failure of his parents to believe him and protect him that had hurt him the most and made him the angriest. As he spoke about that dynamic, I shuddered at the thought of thousands of aboriginal children facing the same situation, year in, year out, in residential schools. I could not imagine the depths of loneliness that would cause.

That failure to understand or believe is far more common than most Canadians assume. Garnet Angeconeb, an aboriginal leader in northwestern Ontario and a member of the Order of Canada, tells of his father's long refusal to believe his stories of abuse, and what it meant to him when his father finally became convinced:

When the police investigation of my case started, my father said that maybe I should drop it and move on with my life. It wasn't until after my father realized that two of his other sons (this meant three of his six children) were also abused by the same man that he started to change his views and became more supportive. Father also began to recognize and understand the patterns of behaviour of his sons—the anger, drinking, short tempers, and so on—that we'd been using to cope with our abuse, as well as with the shame and secrecy that had surrounded it. The sign that my father was really supportive was when he went to court on the day that [the offender] was being sentenced.... He realized that day that there were sixteen other men who had been abused in addition to my brothers and me. When my father showed up that day, it was one of the greatest gifts I ever received. It was a victory in the sense that I started feeling that my father was listening and that the denial had been overcome.[5]

Though the Truth and Reconciliation Commission will make every effort to create an accurate record of sexual abuse within the schools, their task may be compromised by a further psychological dynamic that is unique to children who are harmed within environments of captivity. Two American specialists in child psychology, Rachel Goldsmith and Jennifer Freyd, speaking about abusive American homes, describe it this way:

> Since their home environments are for the most part uncontrollable and inescapable, children living with abusive caregivers must find ways to either understand or disregard the treatment they receive … attributing abuse as stemming from one's own inherent badness inhibits the scarier prospect that a caregiver cannot be trusted, and may help create an illusion of control.[6]

I wonder if that dynamic helps explain why so many aboriginal victims of abuse have been reluctant to tell their stories thus far. Can the childhood self-blaming become so entrenched that disclosure feels more like confessing one's own sins than accusing others of theirs? When we consider that in the residential school context this particular self-shaming comes on top of the shame imposed by systemic racial belittling, its power seems dramatically magnified. A prison psychologist once told me of inmates who honestly believed that when Creator took the lives of family or friends through addictions, suicide, accidental deaths or homicides, he was simply punishing the offenders for their inherent badness.

The intense psychological damage led to silence and made it easier for entire communities to ignore what was happening to their children. If a situation cannot be changed, then perhaps it's better to just ignore it. And that leads to the next damaging force created by residential schools.

LEARNED HELPLESSNESS

I recall speaking one day with a man who had served a number of years in jail. He was talking about how hard it was to move from a society in which everything was done for him into one where he had to do everything himself. He talked about the day of his release, when he picked up his civilian clothes and a few personal articles at the front desk, then walked to the front door ... and just stood there, waiting for someone to open it for him.

Residential schools had a similar impact. Children were to do as they were told, nothing more and nothing less. They were not given opportunities to make their own decisions. They were not given opportunities to indulge their curiosity. Individual assertions of personality were not welcome, and neither was creativity in response to challenges. There was no room for individual, self-chosen activities: everyone was expected to simply do as they were told. Survivor Bev Sellars describes her own experience with this disempowerment in residential school:

Normal children learn by being allowed to experience life and to explore their curiosity, and to make mistakes without being ridiculed. We were not normal children at these schools. We were more like robots, always taking orders and never being involved in decision-making of any kind. We were never asked what we thought or even encouraged to think for ourselves. We learned very soon after arriving at the schools not to express ourselves. We got into trouble when we spoke our minds, expressed feelings, or dared to question anything.

On top of all that is the constant message that because you are Native you are part of a weak, defective race, unworthy of a distinguished place in society. That is the reason you have to be looked after.[7]

Researchers Raymond Corrado and Irwin Cohen are direct in how they describe the psychological challenge:

One of the more general consequences of the residential school experience was that it instilled an institutional dependency mentality in the students so completely that many of them found it difficult to leave behind as adults. In addition, this dependency mindset perpetuates a discomfort with the responsibilities of everyday life and a lack of self-confidence and initiative when dealing with non-Aboriginal people.[8]

About five years ago, I was talking to the former Chief of a large, progressive First Nation about how few people showed any initiative in tackling community problems, and I wondered out loud about the learned helplessness that was unconsciously taught at residential schools. He immediately picked up on the idea, and told me about going to visit his brother-in-law and finding no handle on the front door. His brother-in-law explained that it had fallen off. "Why," he asked his brother-in-law, "don't you fix it?" The brother-in-law had no answer; he just looked at him, rather perplexed. The Chief then spoke to me about how many of his people have no experience of doing things for themselves, no experience of trying to figure something out or experimenting with different approaches to solve challenges. His conclusion was that too many people don't believe they can do things, simply because, as children, they were never given the chance to try.

I thought back to my own childhood, and all the chances I had to work on things in my own way. Curiosity was rewarded and so was initiative. I learned about trying and failing, then trying again, until I got it right. I was being raised as an independent thinker and as someone who could make choices on my own and see where they led me. Stan McKay, a member of the Fisher River Cree Nation in Manitoba and former moderator of the United Church of Canada, looks back on how residential school affected the development of his capacity for initiative:

> The residential school experience was for me an incarceration that limited my development as an independent and interdependent person. While in the residence, I was told what to wear, what to eat, and how to stand. I was given an identification number. In the classroom I was taught English and French. I was expected to memorize dates from British history texts. Leaving the residential school was traumatic because after years of being instructed I had very little confidence in my ability to make decisions. I had been made compliant and, in many ways, I was dependent like a young child. Back on the reserves, welfare was creating dependent communities without options. Students were leaving residential schools with low self-esteem and few prospects for successful reintegration into our communities, and the communities themselves were disintegrating because of poverty and loss of dignity.[9]

Western psychology describes an empowering environment as one in which people are given "sufficient opportunity for autonomous behaviour" so that they can begin "believing in their capacity to effect change in the environment in pursuit of goals."[10] What opportunities did children have for autonomous behaviour in residential schools? What experiences were they given that would cause them to believe they could ever change their environment in pursuit of goals, when every facet of their lives was so strictly controlled? The constant assertion that nothing of value could be created out of aboriginal traditions led to great disempowerment that went far beyond the individual. In essence, everyone was told that, as "Indians," they would be followers, not doers.

Over time, as more and more people came out of residential schools lacking both curiosity and confidence, and as the trapping economy slowly gave way to welfare, that learned helplessness became much more common. William Mussell of the Skwah First Nation in British Columbia, a psychologist and past chair of the Native Mental Health Association of Canada, gives his perspective on how it all unfolded over time:

> No wonder we have few people in our communities who have voice and vision, who question, wonder out loud, or express a point of view on matters of personal and social importance. No wonder many family members show evidence of attachment difficulties and distrust, and so many, especially males, have difficulty asking for help, reaching out, and exploring the world.[11]

When that lack of experience in autonomous behaviour is piled on top of the silence, loneliness and trauma of residential school, is it any wonder that people are so passive? Never having experienced the joy of accomplishing things on their own, why would they be expected to even try? Cynthia Wesley-Esquimaux and Magdalena Smolewski articulate the resulting learned helplessness well:

> Faced with inescapable situations ... individuals and groups often exhibit what social psychologists label "learned helplessness" ... this kind of behaviour occurs when an

individual (or a group) perceives that his or her behaviour cannot control events and that no action on his or her part will control outcomes in the future. Moreover, if the traumatic experience should endure across time ... then failure in the present should create generalized expectations for failure in the future.... In consequence, even if a person finds herself or himself in a situation where she or he could act and react to outside pressures, she or he fails to make any attempt to do so. A person or a group becomes passive, inactive and hostile.[12]

If that doesn't describe the troubled First Nations in my region of northern Ontario, I don't know what does. To be sure, not all communities show such passivity, just as not all families or individuals do. Before retirement, I worked as a criminal prosecutor in the troubled communities for twenty-six years, and very few showed any signs of improving their circumstances. In fact, some of those with the most severe problems now seem to be facing a future filled with even greater social chaos.

There are, however, other negative forces at work in those communities, forces that are more serious than anything I've mentioned so far. Discussing them requires a much deeper plunge into psychology, and I rely heavily on the expertise of those working in that field. Over the last several years, I have sought out a number of psychologists (and I'm pleased that many are now friends), hoping they could help me understand what happens to children who are cut off from family members, left with virtually no one to turn to or confide in, and then subjected to constant denigration of everything they knew about themselves. I needed to understand what happens if they are physically or sexually abused in those circumstances, either by fellow students or by the only adults in their narrow world. I want to thank all the people who have responded so thoroughly to my questions, because I have been able to make connections between the residential school era and today's troubled dynamics that had eluded me in the past.

Oddly enough, my introduction to all these concerns came about in a way that was totally unexpected, and from a woman who had never been engaged in aboriginal issues before.

COMPLEX POST-TRAUMATIC STRESS DISORDER

In 2005, I was invited to attend a conference for Crown attorneys in Toronto on the psychological impact of spousal violence on women, with special reference to their difficulties in coming to court and giving convincing testimony. One of the presenters was Dr. Lori Haskell, a clinical psychologist in private practice and an assistant professor of psychiatry at the University of Toronto. Her area of concentration involved the psychological state of battered women with lengthy exposure to family violence. I was interested, given the frequency of domestic assault in the more troubled aboriginal communities, but I didn't expect to learn much that might be applicable. How wrong I was.

In her presentation, she introduced the theory of complex post-traumatic stress disorder, a diagnosis I had never heard of. This disorder was first described by American psychologist Dr. Judith Herman, in her 1992 book, *Trauma and Recovery: The Aftermath of Violence—from Domestic Abuse to Political Terror*. As Dr. Haskell explained it, what made spousal violence different from "normal" PTSD was that it involved repeated acts of violence, and the victim was substantially helpless throughout. When I later got hold of Dr. Herman's book, I saw that she explained the differences this way:

The diagnosis of "post-traumatic stress disorder," as it is presently defined, does not fit accurately enough. The existing diagnostic criteria for this disorder ... are based on prototypes of combat, disaster, and rape. In survivors of prolonged, repeated trauma, the symptom picture is far more complex. Survivors of prolonged abuse develop characteristic personality changes, including deformations of relatedness and identity. Survivors of childhood abuse develop similar problems with relationship and identity; in addition, they are particularly vulnerable to repeated harm, both self-inflicted and at the hands of others.[13]

As Dr. Haskell began to list the symptoms of complex PTSD, I noticed that almost every one matched what I routinely saw in the most troubled aboriginal communities. The more I listened, the clearer it became that I was seeing those symptoms not only in the women but also in the men and children. Dr. Haskell described the following major symptoms of complex PTSD:

- substance abuse in a vain attempt to regulate emotional states;
- significantly greater suicidality, self-harm, insomnia and sexual dysfunction;
- chronic, low-grade depression, which the victims considered a "normal" way to feel;
- disruptions in consciousness, memory, sense of self, attachment to others and the establishment of sound and durable boundaries within relationships;
- reduced ability to trust one's own judgment, assert needs or cope with others;
- uncontrolled vacillation between pronounced dissociation and extreme fear;
- a sense of emotional numbness and a retreat into silence; and
- a smouldering anger.

I want to look, very briefly, at each of these symptoms and their appearance in the most troubled First Nations communities in my region.

At the top of the list was substance abuse, and that is almost a given in any case I have ever prosecuted. In fact, substance abuse in some communities has taken over almost every aspect of their lives. One Chief estimated that 80 percent of her community was addicted to prescription painkillers like Percocet and OxyContin, not to mention the use of alcohol, drugs and vapour sniffing.

Regarding the next point, on suicide and self-harm, aboriginal suicide in Canada is five times the national rate. Among Inuit youth, it is ten times as frequent. I recall coming into one aboriginal community with great social problems to get ready for court, and finding that the police had failed to put the witnesses I needed under subpoena. I approached the female constable responsible for those subpoenas and asked her why they had not been served. As she stood in front of me, tears formed in her eyes and fell down her cheeks. I tried to be comforting (we'd been friends for some time) and asked her what was wrong. She told me that in the past two weeks she and her fellow officers had "cut down" five children who had hanged themselves. Only one had survived, and he was in hospital in Winnipeg. I knew that there had been 118 suicides in the last eighteen years in that community, out of a population of fewer than 2500 people. Now those kids were no longer just statistics: I knew three of them by name, because they had all appeared in my court, either as victims or accused—or both. Suddenly, my subpoenas meant nothing, just as the cases they were supposed to serve meant nothing. There was nothing a court could do that would change the dynamics leading children to take their own lives in such numbers.

This relates to Dr. Haskell's next point on chronic, low-grade depression as a normal way of feeling. I have often thought that in the more traumatized communities, too many people—especially children—have no light in their eyes. They walk around at a slow and aimless pace, engaging in almost no conversation, looking forward to nothing. That state of depression stands out so much because I remember seeing the opposite one night at a powwow in Kenora when the Whitefish Bay First Nation Dancers were performing onstage. I noticed a little aboriginal girl, perhaps five or six years old, standing beside me, moving to the music, a big smile on her face, her eyes lit up with fascination and energy. I remember thinking at that moment of all the communities where there was no such light or energy in anyone's eyes, and I felt so glad to see it in hers. One of the dancers noticed that little girl down on the arena floor, called her to the stage, lifted her up and encouraged her to join them in the dance. I found tears streaming down my face then—and as I write about this now. There were many other signs of that "chronic low-grade depression" in the North, but I won't go into them now.

Dr. Haskell also listed "uncontrolled vacillation between pronounced dissociation and extreme fear," and I found that described far too many of the men, women and children I dealt with. When faced with various kinds of pressure, including the pressure to come into a courtroom to give evidence against someone, many people retreated into complete, and what appeared to be stubborn, silence. One day, three women who had been victimized were brought to me by the police to go over their evidence on the day before court; one after the other, they simply sat silently in front of me. They didn't even say hello, just stared at the wall. I tried everything I could think of to get them to talk with me, but nothing worked. Knowing that many victims were afraid of making their abusive spouses even more angry by giving evidence and causing them to be incarcerated, I promised that I would not ask the court to send their assailants to jail, but that didn't get their attention either. They wouldn't even acknowledge their own names, much less mine. It was not just that they were silent. Instead, each was simply not there in the room with me, or with the female victim–witness coordinator who was also present. Wholly confirming Dr. Haskell's observation that battered spouses are reluctant to trust their own judgment or assert their own needs, they removed themselves from the court process completely by simply not coming to court the next day, and their assailants were freed. While three in one day was the most extreme example, I've had far too many people do exactly the same thing.

Numbing and silence were also symptoms that Dr. Haskell noted, and they too struck a chord with me. In fact, they led me to remember one of the most dispiriting moments I've ever had as a prosecutor. The case involved two men charged with killing a Grandmother during a twenty-four-hour alcohol binge involving many people. Our only substantial evidence against them was that the Grandmother's blood was found on their clothing. We knew that perhaps a dozen other men had come and gone from the party house that night, but we didn't have their clothes. At the preliminary hearing, we therefore called the wives of those other men to the witness stand and asked them what clothes their husbands had worn that night, and where the items were now. All of them told the court they didn't know the answer to either question. In cross-examination, defence counsel asked them if, once they learned that the Grandmother had died in that house, they had ever talked to their husbands about what went on that night. All of them denied ever talking to their husbands about it. With some exasperation, they were asked, "Weren't you at all curious about what happened that caused that Grandmother's death?" Very carefully, each one answered that they were not curious. Something about the slow and quiet way they said it led all of us to believe them completely, and we could only arrive at one explanation: their lives were so full of unmanageable grief and tragedy that they simply could not consider searching out more. Their only survival choice was just what Dr. Haskell suggested: numbing and silence.

The symptom of complex PTSD that most resonated with me, however, was "smouldering anger." I have had many cases where extreme violence seemed to erupt out of nowhere, all on its own, causing everyone to ask: Where did that come from? To illustrate how potent (and deeply hidden) that smouldering anger really is, I'll mention just one of the cases I've prosecuted.

It involved two teenage boys who hosted a party where homebrew and hairspray were consumed when their parents were out of the community. When a third older boy started bragging about how tough he was and made advances toward the girlfriend of one of the two boys, they attacked him. For approximately an hour, with other young people coming and going, those two teenagers inflicted forty slash wounds and nineteen stab wounds on their victim, cutting his carotid artery and killing him. While he lay helpless on the floor, one of the boys stomped on his forehead, leaving three distinct running-shoe impressions on the skin. They then dragged him outside and covered him with boards, before going back inside to try to clean up the blood. One of them spent the rest of the night having sex with his girlfriend in the same house. Only one of the two accused had a criminal record, and it was minor. Everyone asked the same questions: Where did that anger come from? How could the extreme violence of their assault be in any way connected to the minor misconduct of the older boy? None of us had any answers.

When Dr. Haskell listed the *causes* of complex PTSD, however, I began to wonder if I was on the verge of finding an answer, because every single one of them gave an accurate description of life within many residential schools and many of today's communities:

- growing up in an environment of neglect and deprivation;
- having a sense of powerlessness and helplessness;

- experiencing social, psychological and legal subordination;
- being a target of sexism and racism;
- living with homelessness and/or extreme poverty; and
- having a sense of repeated interpersonal victimization, including childhood abuse and other physical violence.

Clearly, each of these circumstances was present in the residential school experiences of the parents and grandparents of those two teenagers. Without doubt, those schools were environments of neglect and deprivation, openly premised on racial denigration. They demanded complete psychological and legal subordination, where the language, clothes, food, spirituality, ceremonies, instruction and structure of every day were both enforced and entirely foreign. Corporal punishment was routinely threatened and employed. Physical and sexual abuse was not uncommon. Food was often inadequate, and diseases were sometimes fatal. It would not be at all surprising to find that the parents and grandparents of those boys returned from residential school to their village with the same kind of "smouldering anger" that we saw from the teenagers many years later. I began to ask myself if there was a connection between the two.

The answer, I have since learned, lies in what is called the *intergenerational transfer of trauma*. That is a topic I'll return to in more detail later. For now, it is enough to say that when the parents and grandparents brought their residential school trauma home and had children of their own, they could not model strong, healthy behaviour. When they retreated into alcohol, refused to discuss or honour feelings, let their smouldering anger explode into violence, and built relations based on fear, mistrust and force, their children took those behaviours as "just the way people live" and began to live the same way. Growing up within that chain of dysfunctional, often violent behaviour, they could not help but perpetuate it. The more I learned about that intergenerational transfer of trauma, the better I understood the claim of aboriginal people that residential schools started it all. I was coming closer to a reason behind the sudden violence that erupted from those two boys.

Going back to life within residential schools, I was especially interested in the fact that repeated interpersonal victimization was only one of the factors contributing to complex PTSD. I found myself asking whether all the other causes of complex PTSD, working together, could have created that condition *in the absence of* real physical or sexual abuse. Would the fear of such abuse be enough, especially if it lasted over several years? And did it make a difference that it was children who found themselves trapped in those circumstances? What if their fear was accompanied by constant racial denigration? What if their sense of helplessness was absolute? I knew that I needed to look more deeply into the whole area.

As fate would have it, shortly after I returned to Kenora, a counsellor there gave me a copy of the book Dr. Haskell had referred us to, Judith Herman's *Trauma and Recovery*. He told me that it was the most important book he'd read in his work with aboriginal people. When I read it, I had to agree—at least as far as her description of the symptoms and causes of complex PTSD was concerned. The route back to "good health," I have since learned, depends on how you define that good health, and it has slowly become clear to me that the aboriginal vision is not at all the same as ours.

In her book, Dr. Herman described the kind of psychological environment all children need if they are to grow into healthy adults:

A secure sense of connection with caring people is the foundation of personality development.... The developing child's positive sense of self depends upon a caretaker's benign use of power. When a parent, who is so much more powerful than a child, nevertheless shows some regard for that child's individuality and dignity, the child feels valued and respected, she develops self-esteem.[14]

A secure sense of connection with caring people? How many aboriginal children have ever described finding anything like that in residential school? One person told Joseph Gone how upset people were to even visit the site of a shut-down residential school today:

> And in a lot of cases, we have people that won't even want to go there. We have cases of people that are resistant about going there for whatever reason. And we have a lot of people yet that can't open up. Whatever happened over there, they just as soon leave it over there.... And yeah, we've had people break down. I've had people that are so overcome by emotion that they go into convulsion. We've had people like that. And that's how powerful this experience about residential school is.[15]

I have attended Truth and Reconciliation gatherings and watched as survivors came to tell their stories. They approached that storytelling in much the same way that they approach the former schools, with fear, anger, confusion and often an almost childlike sense of vulnerability and hopelessness. These are people recounting events from forty years ago, and they still appear overwhelmed.

Dr. Herman also wrote that where the violence is long-lasting and touches not just individuals but entire segments of a community, whole populations can fall prey to complex PTSD, "trapped in alternating cycles of numbing and intrusion, silence and re-enactment."[16]

There was a moment in reading Dr. Herman's book when I suddenly realized why so much of it felt familiar to me: she had built her argument about battered women by drawing parallels with people being abused while trapped in situations of real captivity, such as concentration camps, prisoner-of-war camps, satanic cults, the sexual slavery of criminal brothels and, most significantly for me, the industrial schools of Ireland. When she looked at those institutions, she saw so many correlations with the situation faced by women trapped within long-term domestic violence that she had to compare them. I didn't need to have parallels drawn, simply because Canada's residential schools were so similar to those other institutions of captivity.

Here, for instance, is how she describes the tactics used by the perpetrators of domestic violence. They clearly have much in common with the abusive psychological atmosphere intentionally created within institutions like residential schools:

> In addition to inducing fear, the perpetrator seeks to destroy the victim's sense of autonomy. This is achieved by scrutiny and control of the victim's body and bodily functions. The perpetrator supervises what the victim eats, when she sleeps, when she goes to the toilet, what she wears.... The methods of establishing control over another person are based upon the systemic, repetitive infliction of psychological trauma. They are the organized techniques of disempowerment and disconnection.[17]

And there they were, the magic words: *disempowerment* and *disconnection*. Sir John A. Macdonald wanted to create an almost total disconnection from family, community and culture when he promoted residential schools to Parliament, and the means he chose promised the almost complete disempowerment of aboriginal parents, as well as their children. Madeleine Dion Stout and Gregory Kipling put it this way:

> The physical separation of students and their families was merely the first step in a more generalized attempt to sever any connection children had with their culture and history. As Isabelle Knockwood puts it in her description of life at the Shubenacadie Indian Residential School in Nova Scotia: "We were being forcibly disconnected from everything our parents and elders had taught us."[18]

Dr. Herman also describes how battered women are seen by the outside world. As I read her words, I began to recognize something from my own past responses to them—and to other victims of violence—that I am not proud of:

> Most people have no knowledge or understanding of the psychological changes of captivity. Social judgment of chronically traumatized people therefore tends to be extremely harsh. The chronically abused person's apparent helplessness and passivity, her entrapment in her past, her intractable depression and somatic complaints, and her smoldering anger, often frustrate the people closest to her.[19]

On reading that, I had to acknowledge that I had begun to blame many aboriginal adults for not being conscientious parents who cared about their children, and for failing to do anything to change things for the better. Knowing so little about residential schools and the kinds of damage they inflicted, I confess to having made harsh judgments of many victims, especially for their pronounced passivity in failing to confront their abuser in court—or to at least get themselves out of their dangerous situations. The more I thought about residential schools, the more I became convinced that the traumatization of children in residential school led to traumatized behaviour once they returned, and to the modelling of that behaviour by subsequent generations. Every symptom of complex PTSD shown by survivors would lead their children into similar kinds of behaviour.

I am not the only one looking at the intergenerational impact of complex PTSD on First Nations today. After I heard Dr. Haskell introduce that diagnosis to Crown attorneys, I spoke with her about its application in many aboriginal communities, and I invited her to an aboriginal justice session. After that, her growing interest in the subject led her to join with Melanie Randall of the Faculty of Law at the University of Western Ontario to study the issue further. Ultimately, they wrote a paper titled "Disrupted Attachment: A Social Context Complex Trauma Framework and the Lives of Aboriginal Peoples in Canada," published in the *Journal of Aboriginal Health*. Here is one small excerpt:

> Children exposed to complex trauma often experience lifelong problems that place them at risk for additional trauma exposure and other difficulties, such as psychiatric and addictive disorders, chronic medical illness, and legal, vocational, and family problems. Moreover, chronic abuse in childhood, physical and/or sexual, has been repeatedly demonstrated to increase vulnerability to developing substance abuse problems, a range of mental health difficulties and other physical health problems later in life.[20]

Marlene Brant Castellano, a respected Mohawk Elder and former professor at Trent University, sees things in much the same way:

> Indigenous counsellors and researchers in the United States and Canada have proposed a theory of historic trauma to describe

the consequences of multiple stressors experienced by whole communities over generations. Images of traumatic events and adaptive or maladaptive responses become imbedded in shared memories of the community and are passed on to successive generations by storytelling, community interaction and communication, patterns of parenting, emotionally laden memories, and inherited predisposition to PTSD.[21]

Summarizing much of this, Cynthia Wesley-Esquimaux and Magdalena Smolewski offer the following unhappy picture of too many communities:

These experiences have left Indigenous cultural identities reeling with what can be regarded as an endemic and complex form of post-traumatic stress disorder.... There continues to be compelling evidence of a negatively altered and unhealthy psychological atmosphere in Aboriginal culture.[22]

I have come to see the troubled First Nations families and communities of my region in a very different light. I now understand that their passivity and descent into social chaos began with the repeated abuse of children within an environment of captivity, and that the abuse extended over generations. The fact that some communities appear healthy today doesn't alter the fact that others are not; as I said earlier, there is no single story of residential schools. Instead, there are thousands of stories, and sometimes, in some communities, they come together in ways that leave those communities almost wholly chaotic. When that happens, succeeding generations magnify the chaos—until you get to the point where 80 percent of a population is addicted to drugs, or 80 percent of the population has been involved in sexual abuse.

When I began to understand it, I thought that complex PTSD gave me a full explanation for everything I saw. I soon discovered, however, that there were several more forces that began in residential school that I hadn't yet seen, and they were layered on top of the destructive effects of complex PTSD. The next factor, as I discovered, not only contributed to continuing dysfunction, but also stood as perhaps the most important roadblock to community healing.

EMOTIONAL SUPPRESSION

Earlier, I mentioned an aboriginal man who asked the Truth and Reconciliation Commission to explain to him why he couldn't cry. I had always wondered why so many victims and witnesses (not to mention a great many offenders) seemed to tell their stories with a strange absence of emotional connection, as if the things they described had happened to someone else. For many years, I assumed that detachment came from cultural rules against keeping tragic events alive in your heart or burdening others with them. I think that culture was indeed part of it, but I was no longer certain that was the whole explanation. I then learned that the symptoms of complex PTSD include numbing and silence, but that still didn't explain how deep the silence was. Were those people going through the same experience as the man who wondered why he couldn't cry?

I discovered that many aboriginal people had been raising the same issue. Cynthia Wesley-Esquimaux, a member of the Chippewa of Georgina Island First Nation in Ontario and now the vice-provost of Aboriginal Initiatives at Lakehead University in Thunder Bay, Ontario, wrote about the feelings that aboriginal people "had unconsciously learned to deny, suppress and hide within themselves." She argued that those feelings "were not given appropriate acknowledgement and therefore any accurate expression." In her words, they had not been "brought into consciousness where they could be processed and healed."[23] I wondered if she was asking the same questions that were just beginning to occur to me.

Then I came across the writings of Maria Yellow Horse Brave Heart, a leading aboriginal educator in the United States. Now I had no doubt—she was clearly speaking about the same kinds of issues:

> You shut down all feeling because you are trying to avoid the pain. It helps you get through the immediate crisis and the trauma. But if they persist, if they go on for a long time, they become a problem and you don't feel much of anything. You numbed yourself from the pain, but you stunted your feelings, your warmth and your joy."[24]

A number of questions arose for me. How widespread is this suppression of emotion in aboriginal populations today? What role did the residential school system play? What are the consequences of long-term emotional suppression, both individual and social? Could it lead some people to a wholesale disconnection from normal emotional engagement with life? Could it affect entire communities in a similar way? What happens then?

Just as I started to ask those kinds of questions, someone sent me a paper written by two psychologists at the University of British Columbia (UBC). It was called "An Exploratory Study of Emotional Intelligence and Domestic Abuse,"[25] and that title really got my attention. I had never heard of emotional intelligence before, and domestic abuse was startlingly high in the communities I served. Was there a connection?

As I read the article, I was first surprised to find that what they called "emotional intelligence" (or EQ) was not thought of as a fixed, genetic or predetermined capacity. Instead, it involved emotional skill sets that people might have, or might not have, developed. Those skill sets, the authors suggested, normally developed during childhood, in the family context. I wondered about how well they would develop in the captive environment of residential school.

In their study, the psychologists assessed the emotional skill sets of forty-four men, none of them aboriginal, who had been convicted of spousal assault. Those psychological assessments suggested that

- they might not be aware of their emotions;
- because they are *unable to express* their feelings and needs, they resort to intimidation and aggression;
- they lack insight into how their emotions arise, such that all arousal-producing emotions get expressed as anger, which in turn gets translated into aggression; and
- they are unable to modulate thoughts, emotions and behaviours to correspond to changing environment and demands.

I was intrigued, asking myself whether the elevated levels of violence in many First Nations might be connected to people's inability to access, understand, express and modulate their emotional lives. I also wondered what would happen if people hadn't developed those emotional skill sets as children and then carried the "smouldering anger" that complex PTSD theory suggests is a natural result. Could that combination give rise to the mindless explosions of horrific violence—and patterns of daily abuse—that had come to dominate so many communities?

Lee Brown is a member of the Cherokee Nation and the Wolf Clan, and presently director of the Institute of Emotional Health in Vancouver. In researching his doctoral thesis, he studied a training program for aboriginal social service workers that ran from 1980 to 1987 in Kamloops, British Columbia.[26] In particular, he was interested in how frequently the students had chosen to put their course work aside and form talking circles to explore what residential school had done to them. He wanted to find out how they looked back on that experience, and whether it had an enduring impact. As I read their reflections, I found a riveting resonance with the words of Cynthia Wesley-Esquimaux and Maria Yellow Horse Brave Heart. For instance, the students spoke about how their habit of emotional suppression had begun in residential schools:

- "We weren't allowed to cry. Because we were taught that way, it was really, really hard to cry, [or] even laugh."
- "When we look at aboriginal people, because of their history, it is like they don't feel, don't talk about the feelings."
- "I had built this wall around me, all over … ever since I was small. I wouldn't allow anybody into that space of mine. I think it was really hard to take that risk and letting that down and letting people in…. I have always shielded myself from other things that had happened, so … for me, that was one of the biggest things … letting go of that shield. Not a shield, it was an armour, so thick, right?"
- "A lot of times I might be having a feeling and not really know where it came from … something present may have triggered it in my life, but when I look back it was, you know, a mood swirl, a lot deeper. So starting to really look and find … the first time that pain was planted, and (was) buried."

I found it difficult to read what those people said, to imagine feeling so trapped within yourself and so intentionally self-numbed. At the same time, I recognized what they were talking about, because I had seen that numbness so often over the years. This was the first time, however, that I had heard people speak of breaking through it, of the ways in which they had begun to learn how to get in touch with, and express, their feelings:

- "What (the program) really did is it gave the group ... permission to feel ... to feel their emotions and actually express them ... not only people learned how to do that but they were given permission to do that.... I think some people started to learn how to do that."
- "The learning and the teachings and the teachers helped you feel and explore those areas of your life that you wouldn't even touch. Especially if you were hurting in some areas of your life and you never dealt with it."
- "And I think the big thing is opening up and trusting, being able to talk about those feelings and being able to identify those feelings."
- "Being given permission to cry and not have to explain why you were doing it, and people supporting that, just allowing you to do that, was a new experience to me. Because I don't show emotion that well."

The words those people chose said so much to me. I was struck by the notion of needing "permission" to cry, of needing to be "allowed" to do it. In residential school, emotional displays were indeed forbidden, and punishment often followed when the emotions were too strong to be suppressed. What also leapt out at me was that people in the study felt they needed to *learn* how to identify their feelings and express them to others. Those were, to me, just natural ways of living, but they amounted to foreign territory for those survivors. I was not, however, surprised to hear such things, because I had seen the same emotional deadness in so many of the victims and witnesses I had dealt with over the years. It was as if they had become almost wholly separated from their emotional selves. As I've noted earlier, no matter how extreme the violence that had engulfed them, many spoke about it as if it were nothing at all.

Lee Brown then described how the students believed that learning to monitor and manage their feelings also helped reduce the pain they seemed to carry with them:

- "Now, if somebody bothers me I can tell them 'I hear what you say and I don't think you should say that,' whereas before I would just let you say it and forget about it. Not really forget about it, but actually it would build up inside me and then I would just blow off at the next person, but I don't do that anymore."
- "So (the training program) opened doors to be able to see better, to hear better … to communicate more, more lightly or in a civil manner."
- "I think that … it is learning to listen, learning to express my feelings, express my opinion without getting angry, without getting upset."

What struck me was this: these were the words of people who were in a training program, moving up in the world, improving their lot in life. They were not people whose lives had been overwhelmed by addictions, violence or despair. Yet, despite their relative good health, they still spoke about how much the emotional suppression of residential school events had affected their lives. Given that my work often involved people for whom addictions, violence and despair were constant companions, was this an explanation for the fact that their emotional suppression seemed so deep and automatic that they often appeared wholly disconnected from their emotions?

Recall the case I mentioned where the two teenage boys killed an older teenager who was bragging about how tough he was and trying to move in on one of their girlfriends. When the two younger boys were interviewed by police on video, both admitted what they had done to the victim, but in such casual, flat and unemotional tones that you'd think they'd been charged with jaywalking instead of murder. More disturbing still was the nonreaction of all the other youngsters: they not only failed to intervene, but on the witness stand they too spoke about those horrific events as if they were a minor occurrence. Perplexed at such apparent indifference, one of the defence lawyers reminded a young female witness that it was a murder we were asking her about, where a young man had been brutally killed. When he asked her to pay close attention to his questions and do her best to help the court understand what had happened, she answered by sighing, shrugging her shoulders and muttering an exasperated "Whatever!" All of us were stunned. We wondered at first if she was just dismissing the court proceedings as a waste of time, but the fact that she had casually wandered back and forth past the scene of the stabbing and beating without any reaction whatsoever suggested something else. Besides, we were seeing too many similar cases coming out of remote communities, especially involving young people. In some places, parents were quietly telling us they were terrified of their own children. Could the wholesale disconnection of these children from their own emotions be traced back to the residential schools their parents and grandparents grew up in?

One psychologist writes specifically about the conditions necessary for children to begin developing the critical emotional competencies that the men in the UBC study appeared to lack:

The development of emotion regulation ... is thought to arise through social interaction, primarily within the parent–child relationship. For example, socialization practices are posited to teach children how to label and interpret emotions, when emotional expression is appropriate, and how to manage emotional arousal.[27]

It seems clear that residential schools seldom gave children anything that could be described as supportive experiences. Does that mean that many of them have never developed those emotional skill sets? Another American study set out, in my view, exactly the situation faced by children in residential schools, even though the authors had no experience with those schools:

> In maltreating environments, children can learn that it is unacceptable, threatening or dangerous to express emotions, especially negative ones. Since abuse and neglect produce negative emotions, children may adapt to abuse with general deficits in emotional awareness.... Children learn that they must distance themselves from their own needs and feelings to obtain love and care.[28]

Is that not exactly the situation described by Maria Yellow Horse Brave Heart when she said, "You shut down all feeling because you are trying to avoid the pain"? Is it not what Cynthia Wesley-Esquimaux was talking about when she spoke of the feelings that aboriginal people "had unconsciously learned to deny, suppress and hide within themselves"? We also have the words of researcher Deborah Chansonneuve: "[The children] were faced with the developmental task of forming primary attachments to caregivers who were prejudiced at best and dangerous at worst. For many ... traumatic bonding became a way of surviving childhood in an unsafe, unpredictable environment."[29]

Seen from that perspective, it is clear that many "graduating" survivors went home with few capacities to sort and manage their accumulated pain, and little experience of healthy bonding with others. Relying instead on suppression, distancing and disconnection to keep from being overwhelmed, they then became parents who modelled that same impoverishing behaviour to their children and grandchildren. They couldn't model what they didn't know, and they couldn't teach what they had never learned. Instead, they modelled silence, distance, suppression and, often, numbing through drugs and alcohol. As a result, when pressures became too great, they modelled something else: the violence that explodes from anger sitting just below the surface.

It is also clear that residential schools often made survivors ill-equipped to resist the various pressures in their lives. As one psychologist put it:

> The development of emotion-processing skills, such as the ability to identify, verbally express and regulate one's emotional states, may be obstructed in individuals who are chronically abused and neglected as children. As a result of their deficits in emotional awareness and control, these individuals may be especially vulnerable to the effects of traumatic stressors as adults.[30]

I have seen cases where the anger is so deeply buried that people may not even be aware of their actions when that anger finally erupts. When I was a fishing guide (long before becoming a lawyer, much less a prosecutor), I ferried one of the aboriginal guides to his camp on an island one day after work. We chatted as he filleted his fish on a board nailed between two trees. Though he'd been drinking during the day, he was still his normal pleasant self. Suddenly, he looked up, his eyes clouded over and he started swearing. He came angrily toward me, waving the knife in my direction. I began backing away, saying soothing things I don't think he really heard. Just before he got to me, his eyes noticeably cleared and he stopped in his tracks, looking quizzically at the knife held in front of him as if he didn't know how he got there with it. He went back to cleaning fish as if nothing had happened. After ten more minutes of friendly, casual conversation, the same thing happened again. As soon as he "clicked back in" the second time, I got in my boat and left, shaken. I wondered whether I had triggered that explosion, but I didn't have a clue back then. We became good friends years later when I became a Crown attorney and he was the (sober) teacher of traditional ways at the local jail. I never asked him about those events. I was sure that he had no recollection of what he had done that day.

Madeleine Dion Stout and Gregory Kipling describe that psychological response this way:

> In reading the accounts of Survivors of their years spent in residential school, one of the most common strategies used to deal with traumatic situations was to distance oneself from the source of the hurt. In some instances, children did so by suppressing any manifestation of feeling or emotion as a way of shutting out the pain and fear in their lives. For example, a former student at Kamloops Indian Residential School reports being whipped so often that: "eventually you get so tough that you block those things out and you can't feel things, you'd get hit and you can't feel it no more."[31]

I suspect my friend with the knife had developed such a capacity to suppress his feelings that his anger was buried so deeply that he neither controlled it nor even knew when it erupted. I've seen too many cases of aboriginal people suddenly exploding into extreme violence, often without apparent provocation, then just as suddenly reverting to their regular selves, without any knowledge of what they had just done. I once watched another aboriginal guide sitting at the bar one evening, acting normally, when he suddenly leapt over the bar and attacked the bartender. About six of us wrestled him outside and took him to the ground. Just as suddenly, his eyes cleared and he stopped struggling. He asked us, "What's going on? Why are you doing this?" He had absolutely no recollection of the violent outburst that had led us to subdue him.

I see a vicious downward spiral here that is reinforced over generations. People who are already carrying the burden of unresolved trauma have to face new traumatic events without the ability to process them in healthy ways, and their only option is emotional suppression. As that grows, so does the risk that those unresolved events will explode into further violence, thus escalating the need for greater suppression still. When whole communities become mired in that dynamic, the descent into community-wide fear, despair and violence can, in my view, reach epidemic proportions. I can think of entire communities where the fierceness of emotional suppression is almost palpable; people seem absolutely determined not to react with feeling about anything, with the exception of anger.

As I learn about the lack of emotional skill sets, I find myself asking a further question: Does that lack also explain why so many communities seem unable to take up and sustain the healing challenge? Even when people want to turn things around, can they create sustainable healing teams if they are not able to trust one another with their emotional lives? And how can they do that if they are not able to understand or manage their own unresolved emotional burdens? My question, in other words, is whether the development of emotional competencies is a prerequisite for bringing health to families.

In *Returning to the Teachings*, I discussed a wonderful healing program, designed to address sexual abuse, at the Hollow Water First Nation in Manitoba. In that small Ojibway community, despite their estimate that 80 percent of the population had been involved in sexual abuse as either "someone who had caused harm" or "someone who had been harmed"—or both—they had managed to fashion a community response that was working. They had principles that could be articulated, and visions of their past and their future that could be shared with others. In essence, they had developed a years-long process designed to bring everyone touched by the abuse back into balance again, personally and within their relationships, instead of sending them to jail. I wanted to let the communities in my own region hear about the program and about how Hollow Water had built it.

In my enthusiasm, I organized such a sharing in Kenora. I managed to find government funding to bring three people from each of some forty First Nations together for three days to hear about "the Hollow Water experience." I made sure that each community sent a police officer, social worker and band councillor so that they could start their healing conversations together. For three days, Hollow Water people told the story of how they began, the lessons learned, the cautions developed and the relations established with the justice system. Two of our local judges spoke of their support for such community initiative, giving all the encouragement they could. At the end of the three days, as everyone filed out to return to their communities, I felt that a tidal wave of healing was just beginning to form.

But I was wrong. Only one community even tried to form such a healing group, and at the end of nine months they gave up, primarily because the team members reported that they had too many of their own private issues to begin taking responsibility for the lives of others. As time went by, various communities attempted much smaller projects, such as helping kids who were sniffing gas or starting youth suicide prevention programs, but none lasted more than a year or so. I felt immense frustration: there I was, mired in beatings, rapes, homicides and child abuse that I saw as preventable, but no one was doing anything to bring effective prevention into existence.

I found myself falling into what Dr. Herman described as the "harsh judgment" of people trapped in historic trauma, getting angry at the communities themselves. Why were they not even trying? Did they not care? Were they just too lazy? Too frightened? Or was it incompetence? Was the leadership too selfish? I discovered that many communities had over fifteen people, on full-time salaries, supposedly promoting different healing activities. But they wouldn't even talk together, much less form a Hollow Water–type community response. Meanwhile, life in the traumatized communities grew worse. In one community, police arrested a seventy-two-year-old who had brought in a large amount of crack cocaine by airplane. The local suspicion was that it helped him buy sexual favours from young teenagers. As shocking as that case was, it is far from rare: some communities are in such a downward spiral that no one sees any answers at all, and no one seems to care.

Why was no one doing anything? Why did so many people seem so helpless?

It was Lee Brown's Ph.D. thesis on the B.C. training program for social workers that started me on a possible answer. Several of the former students suggested that emotional suppression compromised their ability to fully engage not only in their own training program, but in other aspects of their lives as well. Lee Brown reports their statements about the changes that began in their talking circles:

- "I was able to share, emotionally cry and let my anger go. And those kinds of things, my trust in things, I had a lot of abandonment issues, a lot of anger. A lot of those things were holding me back on my skills and my social life."

- "There was a lot of pain. I wasn't the only one that had all this pain, and yet when we were sitting around laughing and talking, you would think we were okay, but really when you got to know them, there was a lot of hurt there. That was one of the things that I learned.... I had to get past that before we could do anything."
- "I found that ... at the stage I was in ... I couldn't have feelings from my heart. My heart is (now) something that will come out and do and see and hear a lot of things in life that I could not see before."

If the people in that training program were so wrapped up in their own anger, depression, grief and abandonment that they found it hard to engage with "normal" life, what must it be like for people who carry an even heavier load, who are wrapped up in the violence, substance abuse and family breakdown that plague so many communities? If the discharge of grief and the development of emotional competencies were important for those social-workers-in-the-making, would they not be even more important when people are living in, and surrounded by, violence, alcoholism and despair? Is that why so many people did nothing when they learned about things like that seventy-two-year-old bringing crack into their tiny, vulnerable community?

When I started asking those questions, I remembered something from Hollow Water that I think I failed to see properly when I first became involved with them many years ago. At an early stage in their development, the healing team thought they were ready to start taking on cases. As it happened, they were being visited by a psychologist from California. After listening to them for a while, he expressed his concern about their readiness to take on such demanding work. In conversation, it became clear that they had not yet shared with one another the sexual trauma in their own lives.

Until they were comfortable doing that, he suggested, it might not be wise to take on the sexual trauma of others. As a result, they put their program on hold until they learned how to share openly with one another, a process that ultimately took about two years.

When I first heard that, I thought that what they had accomplished in those two years was the building of adequate trust between each of them, but I now suspect that the real struggle involved much more. I think it also entailed each of them first getting deeply into themselves and wrestling with everything they found there, everything that they had suppressed for many years. They then had to find the language to start sharing those feelings with one another, and to get comfortable with "letting it out." This process required much more than learning to trust others to receive their stories respectfully; it also meant first learning how to tell those stories to themselves, and then to others. I raised that issue on a recent visit to Hollow Water, and the team agreed. A leading member of the healing team spoke about how, on her first disclosure of sexual abuse in her own life, all she could do was cry and cry and cry. "I didn't know how to talk about it," she said. "All I could do was cry."

And all I can really say is this: during my twenty-six years of often intimate involvement in the lives of traumatized aboriginal people, families and communities, I have seen everything these various studies of emotional suppression discuss. As I read them, I had one "aha!" moment after another. From my perspective, emotional suppression and disconnection caused by generations of trauma, secrecy and disempowerment are a primary cause of the tragedies we see today. They are also why it's so difficult for communities to do anything to counter those tragedies. Until affected people are given the tools they need to explore, understand and manage their own emotional responses to those accumulated injuries, it's difficult to see how they can begin turning things around for others.

Learned helplessness, complex PTSD, emotional suppression and the habit of silence are not the only forces plaguing aboriginal communities today. There are several others that, though perhaps less powerful, nevertheless contribute substantially to continued dysfunction and paralysis.

SOCIO-CULTURAL SHAME

Earlier, I discussed the shame that many survivors felt upon returning home from residential school, given that most residential schools routinely belittled children not only for their supposed individual shortcomings, but also for their supposed racial, social and cultural deficiencies. That shame was a powerful force, and it has been passed on to subsequent generations.

James Waldram conducted research among survivors of residential school, which he writes about in "Building A Nation: Healing in an Urban Context." He reports being told by one survivor, "As an individual, I was very ashamed of myself. For what, I really don't know. It was just the way I was raised. I was raised to be ashamed of my being an Aboriginal Indian, full-blooded Cree."[32] Another survivor told him, "I was trained that Native people were dirty, were ugly, a disgrace and because of me being the darker one of the family, they always called me squaw or dirty or filthy things, you know."

Everything about the children was consistently denigrated as the work of "savages." As Deborah Chansonneuve phrases it, "Children ... were taught shame and rejection for everything about their heritage, including their ancestors, their families and, especially, their spiritual traditions."[33]

Children as young as five were put in an impossible situation: the only way to escape that shame was to stop being who they were—aboriginal people. As absurd as it sounds now, some tried to do just that: one friend told me that as a child he had tried to scrub himself into becoming a white person. Many people have told me that the nuns also scrubbed them to excess, and for the same reason: "to scrub the Indian off of you." Shame arising from a sense of personal inadequacy at least leaves hope that you can overcome that inadequacy; when the shame is attached to your race, however, it feels complete and hopeless.

American psychiatrist Donald Nathanson has made the study of belittlement and shame his life's work.[34] He believes that the most important psychological result of being belittled is the feeling of shame, and he suggests that there are four primary responses. I have seen extreme variations of all of them in the more traumatized communities:

- the *avoidance* response, where we hide through such things as alcohol, drugs, extreme pleasure-seeking, denial or a fake machismo manner;
- the *withdrawal* response, where we hide, act shy, run away or grow silent, often leading to frightening feelings of isolation or abandonment;
- the *attack self* response, where we demean ourselves and are overly deferential to others, but at least avoid the frightening alternative of isolation; and
- the *attack others* response, where we feel better about ourselves by using put-downs, ridicule, abuse or sadistic violence to reduce the self-worth of others.

I will address drugs and alcohol as a separate topic later, but it is clear that people rely on them to hide from their pain, sorrow and anger. Avoidance through intoxication is almost overwhelming in some places. I haven't had much experience with the withdrawal response—it is by its nature hidden away. But I have no doubt that it is a prevalent issue.

I want to focus here on the attack responses. The attack self response is almost overwhelming. I have already mentioned the high incidence of suicide and the havoc it brings to communities and families. No one should be surprised that aboriginal people who have absorbed so much trauma and shame often hate their lives so much that they want to end them. Such suicides most often occur after gross ingestion of alcohol, drugs and/or pills. Nor should we be surprised at the incredible levels of self-mutilation we see, especially among young aboriginal girls.

But it is the attack others response that I dealt with every day. Violent behaviour is almost the norm in some communities. On one recent court day in a community of five hundred people, fifty-four of them were facing a total of 285 Criminal Code charges. Those charges included

- four robberies
- one robbery with a weapon
- one sexual assault
- three assaults causing bodily harm
- six assaults with a weapon
- seventeen assaults of police/resisting arrest
- one arson
- nineteen simple assaults
- five impaired driving charges
- two driving while disqualified charges
- two charges of dangerous operation of a motor vehicle
- one criminal harassment
- two flight from police charges
- one escape from lawful custody
- eight break and enters
- four simple drug possession charges
- one drug trafficking charge

Imagine living in a community where those kinds of incidents were just a normal part of every day.

Some people's lives are almost defined by the violence that surrounds them. I knew a woman, a residential school survivor and a Grandmother, who was blind from having drunk antifreeze at a party years earlier. On a single court day, she was required to attend for three cases: as the victim of her son, who held a knife to her throat demanding money for alcohol; as the (auditory) witness to the rape of her passed-out niece on a mattress beside her own bed; and as the alleged victim of a thirty-year-old man who she reported raped her after a night of drinking. I say "alleged" because for that third case the laboratory reported that the DNA found in semen from her vaginal swab had two donors, neither of whom was the man she named. When police went to pick her up for court, she was grossly intoxicated, screaming profanities at the officers and refusing to participate. This was the home the son and niece were growing up in. Their community had only four hundred people living in it, and cases like hers were far from uncommon. One night in this same community, about twenty teenagers were found standing in the lake, heavily intoxicated from sniffing gasoline, all of them howling at the moon. I remember asking others, "What on earth is a court supposed to do to respond to that?"

Stories like these are hardly ever mentioned to the outside world. For many years I wondered why the huge court dockets in so many remote communities were not in the news, along with the poor housing, bad water and other impediments to healthy living. It almost seemed as if communities wanted to keep their social chaos a secret. I'm now drawn to the thought that much of the insistence on secrecy comes from the fact that many aboriginal people haven't learned to trace individual behaviour back to what happened to everyone else as colonization took its toll. Being unaware of the cumulative impact on them all, each of them feels the violence and negativity as personal failures. They blame themselves today, just as they did when they were children in residential school. No one wants to confess personal failure, so it stays buried.

Then, when they see that everyone around them is behaving in the same negative way, people begin to wonder if the outsiders weren't right after all. Those outsiders, when they see communities in disarray, have no idea of the chaos that was created by all the forces of colonization. Instead, they believe that it stands as proof that Sir John A. Macdonald and many of his time were right when they called the aboriginal people savages. Many of the negative Twitter and letter-to-the-editor responses to the Idle No More movement come out of that same lack of understanding. The power of social shame magnifies and sinks deeper into the already fragile hearts of far too many aboriginal people. Dr. Lori Haskell and Melanie Randall speak to that issue in their article "Disrupted Attachment": "In a society saturated with negative and racist images of Aboriginal peoples, it is not difficult to see the ways in which the damaged self-perception associated with complex trauma is layered and compounded by the harmful social (mis)representations of the peoples of the First Nations."[35]

What will it take to bridge that knowledge gap? How can the Canadian public be educated to understand that today's turmoil was caused by that original mischaracterization, and by the steps wrongly taken ever since?

The next question seems obvious in light of everything I've said thus far: Who wouldn't turn to alcohol and drugs when their lives are so defined by pain, grief and anger?

THE ATTRACTION OF ALCOHOL AND DRUGS

With so much pent-up anger and shame, the need for release in some fashion becomes almost unmanageable. While alcohol and drugs are used to further suppress those intense feelings, the irony is that they are also the vehicle that releases them—with often devastating outcomes.

In his research on the Pisimweyapiy Counselling Centre in northern Manitoba, Joseph Gone interviewed one survivor who described the consequences of drinking to cope with trauma:

> We're grieving so much on this reserve, and nobody wants to hear how anybody feels. The only time they bring out their grieving and their frustrations is when they are drinking, and that's not right. They shouldn't do that…. And I like to reach out to them and, like, "It's okay, talk about it, we'll help you," instead of bringing it on when they're drunk.[36]

The suffering that leads to this self-abuse is intergenerational, and this is a difficult thing for many to understand. Here is how Cynthia Wesley-Esquimaux and Magdalena Smolewski describe reliance on alcohol from an intergenerational perspective:

> Aboriginal people picked up drinking not to share and reciprocate, but to hide from an oppressive situation and to become invisible to their own tormented selves. Aboriginal people began to drink because they were emotionally numb from what happened to them and wanted to feel something other than pain and despair. Their grandchildren and great grandchildren now drink for exactly the same reasons: to mentally disassociate themselves from cumulative painful memories; to feel something else and not just mental anguish; and to belong to a group with clearly defined boundaries that shares one's meanings, one's understanding, one's world (even if it is a group of alcoholics or drug addicts); and it is a plea for living on one's own terms.[37]

A Dene friend of mine sent me a piece he wrote about the struggles his people have with alcohol. Though it was written as fiction, he quietly told me it was mostly about his own life:

Lately he has been feeling a lot of remorse and guilt after these drunks. So, he has been trying not to drink too much. He does not want to get drunk. He just wants to have a good time. He just wants to be one of the boys. He knew if he drank just enough, fear went away. Shame went away. And there was a time when anger went away. And that's what he wanted to re-capture. He just wanted to feel normal, to laugh and to be comfortable. Why can't he just drink just enough? He had promised himself he would not drink more than two drinks. Two drinks were just right. He felt he could talk to anybody about anything, even if he didn't know anything about the subject. He felt good, handsome, strong, brilliant and boy, could he tell stories. He sang songs. He told jokes. But, lately it seems like he was getting drunk all the time. The last few years he noticed a pattern in his drinking. It was not too bad at first, but lately he cannot remember some of the parties he's been to. He still doesn't know how he got some cuts on his face.... All he knew was: two drinks and everything is normal again. He had many reasons to quit but he was scared to stop. He also noticed a change in his surroundings. Even close friends did not invite him to parties anymore. He started drinking with the heavy drinkers.... He started to drink alone. He even drank stuff he swore never to touch. But he was justified. He was sick. And a shot of hairspray did the trick. He began to depend on booze and whatever would change his view on the world. Alcohol never let him down. It never lied. It never criticized him and it was always there. Comforting him. Loving him. But lately he has been thinking about that. His drinking has gone steadily worse over the past three years.

The extent to which the children of survivors are themselves living alcoholic, disorganized and self-destructive lives cannot be overstated. In some communities, the need to hide through alcohol, drugs and gas sniffing is almost overwhelming. It grieves me to report that the abuse of prescription drugs like OxyContin has added a new dimension. Whole families are using them and becoming addicted. In the more troubled communities, it is reported that half the population is now hooked on prescription drugs. People are going hungry to buy them. In one community two teenage sisters broke into the nursing station to steal them; when they were charged, and their parents tried to enforce a curfew, they burned down their family home. They underwent withdrawal waiting in jail.

It is clear that this all began decades ago, within residential schools. Dr. Lori Haskell and Melanie Randall report the statistics on alcohol abuse among survivors of those schools:

A review of case files for 127 Aboriginal survivors of residential schools ... revealed that 82 percent reported that their substance abuse behaviours began after attending residential schools. Another study on Aboriginal substance abuse treatment centres across Canada revealed that 80 to 95 percent of their clients had been victims of child abuse. Employees of these programs reported that they now saw "alcohol and drug addictions merely as symptoms, with sexual abuse as the underlying cause."[38]

I recall meeting with the executive director of an alcohol treatment centre many years ago. She wanted to discuss one man in her program who had decided to go back to his home community and openly disclose the names of all the women he had sexually abused and then ask for their forgiveness. She was worried about what effect that might have on those victims and the community as a whole. We decided to refer him to the healing team at Hollow Water so they could help him decide on the best course of action, but I shared her worry that he might cause violent outbursts at home if he went ahead with his plan. In the course of our conversation, I asked her how many of the people who attended her facility for alcohol treatment talked about sexual abuse. She stopped, with a perplexed look on her face, and answered as if it was too obvious to state: "All of them," she said. When I asked how many said they had been abused, she shook her head in the same slightly bewildered way, and again responded: "All of them. One hundred percent." I have since learned how naive my questions were, and how common sexual abuse had become.

Here is what another survivor told Joseph Gone about his reasons for attending an alcohol treatment centre in Manitoba:

> That's the reason why I turned to alcohol, to numb the pain, because that's what it does, it numbs the pain. And so today we address social problems, and oftentimes right away we label it, "Well it's an alcohol problem or a drug problem." Personally, I don't see it that way because there's something far beyond that. That person has an alcohol problem for another reason, for something bigger than that, for something greater than that. You have a drug problem, not by choice, but because of something greater than that.[39]

The notion of "something greater than that" lying behind addictions is only recently gaining ground within aboriginal circles. While gross intoxication was involved in almost every case of extreme violence I prosecuted, in every case people told me, "He's not like that when he's sober—it's the alcohol." I disagree. In my view, the alcohol simply released the anger that had been there all along. People who explode in such intoxicated violence have been carrying their anger with them all the time, locked away so deeply that no one could see it, not even themselves. Under the right conditions, alcohol merely served to release that anger. Conveniently, everyone could then blame the alcohol, forgive one another and carry on to the next no-fault explosion.

An article in the *Winnipeg Free Press* headlined "Drugs Dealing Violence, Death" dealt with six homicides that had occurred in six Manitoba First Nations in just the first twenty-two days of 2013. The Grand Chief of those communities was quick to blame the violence on the drugs, not the anger those drugs released: "You need check-stops to ensure drugs don't reach our communities and don't harm our people. There's a lot of drug involvement, influencing a lot of our young people. Crack cocaine is coming in, there's still ecstasy, and oxys (OxyContin)."[40] Only once did the article mention the Grand Chief speaking about what might have led to such drug use: he said that band councils "need far greater resources, including more community police and more mental health services."

Because of my own experiences, I no longer believe that better law enforcement will ever stop the smuggling of drugs or alcohol into First Nations communities. Too many people want—or need—them. When the Grand Chief used the words "mental health," I hope he was speaking about the need to open up all the secrets about abuse, historic and present-day. Until that starts to happen, the reasons behind the addictions remain too powerful for police roadblocks or anti-drug campaigns to have any chance of success on their own. Dr. Lori Haskell and Melanie Randall give their sense of the root causes of such widespread addictions:

In the absence of more functional and effective coping, traumatized people often use drugs or alcohol to avoid feeling intolerable levels of emotional arousal (pain, grief, despair, loneliness, fear, shame).... Unlike a more traditional and limited "disease" model of alcoholism and substance abuse, understanding that a trauma response ... is at the heart of much substance abuse offers a more expansive and less static understanding of this problem in people's lives.[41]

While residential schools taught children to be ashamed of themselves, their families and everything they knew, children growing up in today's violent families are likely to be internalizing exactly the same depressed view of themselves. As I said before, who wouldn't turn to alcohol or drugs when their lives are so defined by pain, grief and anger, and when no one seems to know how to escape those feelings in any other way?

THE DAMAGE DONE TO ABORIGINAL SOCIETY

I find it shocking and odd: I am a well-educated person in the western tradition, I grew up right next to the Tyendinaga First Nation in southern Ontario, I was a fishing guide with lots of aboriginals in northwestern Ontario for eleven years, and I then acted as a criminal prosecutor for twenty-six years in small aboriginal communities—but I had no idea whatsoever about how residential schools had touched every aboriginal person I met. It is only in the last half-dozen years that I have gained even a sense of colonization and the burdens it has imposed on generations of aboriginal people. As a prosecutor, I went north in astounding ignorance, believing that I would serve those communities well simply by prosecuting their criminals and sending them to jail. I had no idea about the people I was encountering, or the psychological burdens they carried, primarily from residential school. Here is how one survivor described those burdens to Joseph Gone:

> That's how [we get] our low self-esteem. Go down [deeper], and it's fear and anger and all that emotional hurt. The mental hurt, too, that goes with it if you think about it and you feel about it. Basically, you want to punch someone. You began to be a violent person because you're so angry [at] all that abuse you went through, emotional abuse, physical abuse, sexual abuse, psychological abuse, even the spiritual abuse.... I never disclosed that I was abused. It was kept inside me and this negativity kept on piling up in you, and [you] may have destructive behaviour or you have criminal behaviour.[42]

Virtually every researcher I have come across ultimately shares the same sense of how it all began, and how the burdens have only increased since the last school closed some forty years ago. Madeleine Dion Stout and Gregory Kipling give us an entirely typical—but painfully resonant—analysis:

> Although respondents identified a wide range of impacts, nonetheless, it is possible to point to numerous commonalities in the findings. For example, many Survivors reported symptoms reminiscent of posttraumatic stress disorder, including nightmares, sleep problems, blackouts, apathy and depression. Moreover, many also indicated that they found it difficult to relate to others as they were less loving, fearful of being touched and more likely to resort to violence or misdirect their anger towards loved ones. Others reported low self-esteem, feeling alienated from their parents and communities, ashamed of their Aboriginal heritage and consumed by anger and guilt.... The impact of residential

school is also seen in the destructive patterns of behaviour adopted by many Survivors. These range from an inability to say "no" and always putting oneself last, to alcoholism, compulsive gambling and substance abuse.... Furthermore, researchers also point to the high incidence of sexual problems among former students of residential schools, including cases of sexual abuse and incest.[43]

One man summed up his residential school experience to Lee Brown in a different way, by suggesting it was worse than the jails he later came to occupy:

When I look back I guess probably the worst thing that happened to me was the residential school system. It actually acclimatized myself for the penal institution. I actually felt that the penal institutions were treating me a lot better than the residential school because they let you make choices and whatever I performed was rewarded and when I was bad ... there was consequences, but in my mind it was fair.[44]

Imagine suggesting that your experience of jail was preferable to your experience, as a child, at school.

CHAPTER 7

GOING HOME

This may be the subject on which there is the greatest ignorance in Canada. To understand the issue more fully, we must first ask what kinds of communities the children returned to after leaving residential schools. We can't forget that those communities began to change the moment their children were taken. Recall the medicine wheel, and the stationing of Elders directly across the sacred fire from the children. It was the job of Elders to teach those children, to bring them into right relations, especially during the long winter nights when everyone collected in their family tents for the telling of stories. When residential schools opened, those children were suddenly gone. The medicine wheel circle was broken, and the Elders were deprived of their central role in the community. Many despaired, and their adult children despaired with them, because the circle of life had been broken.

Madeleine Dion Stout and Gregory Kipling describe the situation faced by the parents of children taken off to residential school:

> Forced to accept their children's removal from the home under threat of legal action, parents were devastated by the separation and all the more so when they knew their children

were likely to experience abusive treatment at the hands of school officials. Further suffering was inflicted because of the lack of subsequent contact with sons or daughters.[1]

As we saw earlier, most returning children kept their abuse a secret, even from their own families. Professors Raymond Corrado and Irwin Cohen speak of that silence:

> After they returned to their communities ... most abused children did not receive the emotional and/or psychological support needed to assist them in coping with their traumatic experiences. In some cases, the community simply could not or did not understand the nature of the children's problems. However, in other cases, parents who had previously attended residential schools themselves did not relate their experiences to anyone. These parents often felt isolated in their grief and assumed that the experiences of others, including their own children, were not as bad.[2]

I suspect that many parents who had themselves experienced abuse at residential school simply didn't want to know if their children had suffered in a similar way. After all, those parents had, albeit unwillingly, agreed to send their children in the first place, despite their own experience. That was the terrible choice put on parents: obeying the law by knowingly sending their children into situations likely to be abusive, or fighting back against the all-powerful white authorities by hiding their children when the police came to get them. Many did the latter, but many more succumbed. That they never wanted to know about the consequences of their choice should surprise no one. After their own residential school experience, self-numbing for self-protection was almost ingrained.

But there are deeper secrets still. One woman in her late forties told me that she hadn't been physically abused in her ten years at residential school, but when she returned home she was sexually abused, first by an uncle and then by an older cousin. She kept that abuse secret for decades. When she first started to acknowledge it, she was engulfed by a desire to do violence in return. But, as her healing journey progressed, she came to see what was done to her differently, to understand that the adults she came back to were, in fact, changed adults, and that the whole centre of their universe had been taken from them the instant the children disappeared. It took her many years to see them for what they were: collateral victims of the residential school system, people who had been forced to endure the ultimate insult of being told that they were incapable of raising children properly. She told me that everyone had been victimized by that system, and that it took her a long time to understand that the people who abused her deserved her sympathy, not her anger.

I still marvel at the sophistication of her analysis and the fact that she put it into practice by going to her abusers in a spirit of forgiveness and reconciliation. I often wish her story had been captured on film and shown in First Nations across the country, because not many harmed people have been able to reach her level of understanding.

Rosemary Barnes and Nina Josefowitz, the psychologists from the University of Toronto who presented a paper on residential school children and stress and resilience to the Canadian Psychological Association, describe what happened when children returned from residential school and began to have children of their own:

> To the extent that children experienced maltreatment, this would increase their risk of engaging in poor parenting and negatively affecting their children. Thus, the harm caused by the schools is passed on to future generations.... We would

expect that children who attended residential school and were exposed to multiple traumatic events would be at greater risk for becoming aggressive adults, which would place their children at risk for the intergenerational transmission of violence.[3]

Even where there was no immediate abuse of returning students, the social picture in too many communities began to change for the worse. Aboriginal psychologist William Mussell sees it this way:

When they returned home from residential schools, many of the young people experienced isolation and loneliness connected with poor social skills, no work skills and inadequate language skills. Positive relatedness to family and community eluded many of them. Together with people who were similarly deprived and searching for relief, they found alcohol and the kind of togetherness that it fosters, including fighting, assault and breaking the law.[4]

I've already mentioned the smouldering anger that could seemingly erupt out of nowhere, and how frequently I witnessed it. I recall one young boy who exploded in violence one day. As he explained later, the thing that drove him crazy as he grew up was that everyone in the community knew how frequently his father beat his mother, but everyone pretended it was not so. His father pretended, his mother, too, and his brothers and sisters— the whole community. His parents had both been to residential school, but they never learned how it damaged their ability to form relationships based on trust, openness, generosity and respect. Instead, everyone put on a brave face and spoke of things like forgiveness while continuing to live within violence. They not only modelled that violence as a way to respond to frustration or disappointment, but they also gave him a reason for his own anger to accumulate: it was the hypocrisy of everyone's silence that fed the rage building up inside him.

Similarly, I remember a husband and wife who had each become trapped by their own parents' ways of relating to each other. The husband had flown into an alcoholic rage, grabbed a hockey stick and beaten his wife severely, while his children screamed, "Stop, Daddy, stop!" Despite that, his wife wanted to do whatever it took to bring the family back together again. At her suggestion, they all attended a five-week residential family-healing program at the Reverend Beardy Memorial We Che He Wayo-Gamic Family Healing Centre in the Muskrat Dam First Nation, located in northwestern Ontario. When they returned to their own community with good reports from Muskrat Dam, I still waited nearly a year before sentencing to see if the changes were lasting. Two of the wife's friends told me the changes were so positive that they had asked her if she and her husband could share what they had learned, because they too had problems in their relationships. I met with her to ask what she had learned at the healing centre.

She was very clear in her explanation of why the program had worked. She and her husband had both grown up with abuse between their parents, but they had never talked about it with each other or with anyone else. In counselling, they learned that they were still seeing things through the lens of their parents' abuse. When one would get angry about something, the other would receive that anger within his or her own experience of growing up with abuse between parents and respond in a disproportionately resentful, fearful and hostile way. This, in turn, would cause the other one to come back with a similarly disproportionate response, escalating the hostility until both were swept up in exactly what they feared: a level of violence that often became physical. It was as if the patterns were so deeply ingrained that they took over even the slightest disagreement, leading both of them where neither wished to go.

Once they understood the origins of their reactions they could begin to disengage from them. She told me that the two of them learned how to talk to each other, instead of talking as if they were their parents. And they learned how to hear each other, instead of hearing their parents. They were learning how to escape the patterns they grew up with.

Both husband and wife felt it was essential that their children join with them in exploring the past and learning new skills of listening and interpreting. They were surprised to learn that their children felt responsible for being unable to stop the violence, or for starting it in the first place, and the couple were grateful that they had a chance to convince their children otherwise. Their story helped me glimpse the validity of the aboriginal perspective that it is not people who must be changed, but the ways in which they relate to each other. It was out of that perspective that their miracle emerged.

It is important to understand how rare that healing experience is. Muskrat Dam can take only five families at a time in their five-week program. The vast majority of troubled families just carry on in helpless bouts of alcoholic rages, assaults and injury. Madeleine Dion Stout and Gregory Kipling describe the family dynamics that often prevail in survivors' homes and give rise to so many problems:

> Raised in an institutional setting characterized by rigidity, authoritarianism and lack of emotional support, Survivors report problems such as difficulty showing affection to their children or use of harsh discipline methods ... participants whose fathers had gone to a residential school were considerably more likely to report physical violence perpetrated by their father against their mother. At a more general level, failure

of Survivors to be taught positive strategies for dealing with inter-personal conflict has, in many cases, led to high rates of family breakdown and divorce.[5]

A grotesque irony is at work here: taking the children into residential schools to protect them from imagined disadvantage and harm ultimately has created exactly the situation the authorities said they feared. Sexual abuse has become almost normalized in some communities. I recall a case where the father was charged with sexually abusing his youngest daughter. When the daughter finally disclosed everything to police and charges were laid, all her sisters turned on her, saying, "What makes you think you're so special? We put up with it." This normalization of sexual abuse stands as perhaps the darkest secret and requires specialized processes for both truth and reconciliation.

There is something else that is not well known to the non-aboriginal world: the leadership of some communities will do almost anything to protect well-connected abusers. I remember sitting in a circle of aboriginal women from across Canada one day and mentioning a case where we had charged an Elder with sexually abusing his adopted daughter for five years, between the ages of nine and fourteen, subjecting her to both anal and vaginal intercourse. Instead of the shocked denunciation I expected from that circle for accusing an Elder of such a thing, I was swamped with stories of similar abuse in other communities. When I told them that the young girl had first disclosed her abuse to the Chief of her community, and that he had responded by calling the accused Elder and telling him to come take her home, I heard a chorus of stories about similar cover-ups right across the country. And when I mentioned that the Chief and band council, upon conviction of the Elder after a hard-fought trial, asked the court for a healing sentence, despite the fact that he had never admitted his crime and the girl had been banished from the community by the same Chief and council, I got the same response: the power structures in many communities routinely supported the abusers and banished the victims. The Chief and council also attended the abuser's parole hearings to offer their support and held a substantial community feast to honour him when he finally returned from prison. By that time, the girl had vanished into the streets of neighbouring non-aboriginal communities, and I have no idea what happened to her. She may well be one of the over six hundred murdered or missing aboriginal women we hear about so frequently today. The normalization of such abuse in some communities is nothing less than shocking.

Two other cases took me right inside the intergenerational transfer of trauma and the continuation of the smouldering anger that began in residential school.

The first involved a young boy and his even younger sister. Both parents were damaged survivors of residential schools, and their marital relationship was marred by violence and deep addiction to the numbing effects of alcohol. On welfare days, they hosted drunken binges that frequently descended into beatings. On those occasions, the boy regularly took his little sister to hide in a closet. As they crouched in the darkness, he held her against his chest and put his hands over her ears so she couldn't hear the thuds, cries and grunts from the other rooms. That meant he couldn't put his hands over his own ears, so he learned to close his mind and heart instead. In that way, the sounds were just sounds, with no people or pain attached. When it finally got quiet, he and his sister would emerge and scavenge for food among the passed-out bodies. On many occasions, they saw men sexually assaulting unconscious women. To them, these events were all part of the normal circumstances of their survival.

That boy grew into a young man who had no sense of personal

boundaries and no capacity for empathy. He began to sexually assault others, and by the time he came to police attention, there were over twenty victims, most of whom had never come forward, because such abuse was just the reality of their lives, too. We did what we could, placing him for lengthy periods in the most intensive residential rehabilitative programs we could find. Unfortunately, we couldn't give back what had been stolen from him, and he reoffended. He will likely offend against more victims, and he may well spend the rest of his life in jail. I don't know what happened to his little sister.

The second case also involved parents severely injured by their residential school experiences, and their behaviour showed a more direct method of intergenerational transfer of violence. A father and mother were both charged with assaulting their fourteen-year-old daughter, and here is part of her statement to police (with her spelling and grammar):

> It was last night at my house. My Mom and Dad were drinking hairspray … in the living room. I was in my bedroom. They asked me to come in the living room. They didn't say anything to me. They started to fight me. They pushed me around. My Dad threw the chair at me and it hit me in the side of the head. My Mom pulled my hair and punch me in the face and my nose started to bleed. She punch me once in the face. My Dad was pushing me and punch me in the shoulder. It was back and forth. I couldn't defend myself. I ran out of the house. I stand outside.

She was taken into care outside of the community, but was later returned to her parents at the insistence of the community leadership. The child-protection agency didn't argue too vehemently, because one of the last children they had removed from that community had committed suicide while in their care, and they were afraid that could happen again.

As I said at the beginning of this book, it is critical that we understand how many aboriginal people fail to understand the connection between the schools that survivors were trapped in and their often pronounced failures as parents.

Jo-Anne Fiske, dean of graduate studies and professor of women's studies at the University of Lethbridge, researched an aboriginal healing program in British Columbia for a paper she wrote for the Aboriginal Healing Foundation. In it, she relates the struggle of one woman to understand her mother, a residential school survivor:

> I need help to deal with stuff from my childhood that kept coming back and coming back. And even with all the stuff at the treatment centre it still wasn't helping me to deal with all the things that I had gone through when I was a kid. And trying to understand my mom and the way she treated us when we were children, and trying to get her to talk about what she went through as a kid, and I find out she was in the residential school, and so was my grandmother before that, and … and then I started talking to other people trying to understand my mom, because of the way she was. And you know, just trying to get a handle on why we were treated the way we were when we were kids.[6]

This woman, like so many other aboriginal people, grew up unaware of the connection between the residential school experiences of her mother and the circumstances of her own childhood. As much as she had to struggle into awareness, seeing those links is just the first step. Jo-Anne Fiske relates what another woman told her:

I am twenty-eight years old right now, and I have to suffer the consequences of my mother, of my father, without protecting me. I got abused in my home. There was incest in my family from my oldest brother ... my sisters moved out at a very young age, some of them, and it was crazy living like that. And to this day people think it's okay at home to abuse. They've been through the residential school, and these people haunt them to this day ... how are we supposed to stop it? Sometimes I wonder, is it too late to stop it? [long pause] I'm really angry because thanks to the residential school my husband got molested there, and my brothers ... lots of people I know have been.... I feel punished sexually by [name of priest convicted of abuse]. And it's sad that I have to live with the consequences. I pay for who hurt them.... I feel like I've been punished because ... with my brother, he reacted in sexually abusing me and my sisters, and my husband ... he was a very early child abuse victim. He didn't know where to turn his anger to.[7]

That woman was starting to understand where it all began, but it is clear from her frustration that she doesn't know how to change things for the better. And she is not alone. Another woman told Jo-Anne Fiske her story:

I was very lost with myself, since I've been brought up jumping from foster home to foster home. My mother being an alcoholic did her best to raise me, and my dad was hardly ever around 'cause he ran away all the time ... he was in the school, and he ran away from there.... I felt really lost within myself, about my culture ... about who I am. 'Cause alcoholism and that all started in my home a long time ago.[8]

Another case demonstrates the extent of the sudden violence that often erupts from people growing up in such homes, violence that not only shocks everyone but also changes many lives. It involved two young men who got into a drunken argument with an older man at that man's home. The argument escalated until they beat him nearly to death, caving in his skull with wrenches and tire irons. They then tied him up with electrical cords, drove him down a bush road and dragged him into the woods. Because he was still gurgling, they rammed a metre-long stick down his throat and "stirred" it, breaking his teeth and lacerating his tongue. He drowned in his own blood. A twenty-centimetre-long portion of the stick was recovered at autopsy, deeply embedded in the man's throat. There was no prior relationship or reason for animosity. What could possibly have driven those young men to such astounding violence? It was not as if they were bad people; despite being nearly thirty years old, only one of them had a criminal record, and it was for a minor offence. Yet they committed this incredibly violent act, on a man who was almost a stranger, in his own home.

The intergenerational transfer of the anger, violence and silence begun by residential school is now being more widely recognized within aboriginal circles. Maria Yellow Horse Brave Heart, associate professor of social work at Columbia University, explains it through her theory of historic trauma response, and in an eloquent passage summarizes so much of what I have seen and heard about the impact of racism and residential schools down the generations on men, on women and on their children:

Historical Trauma Response theorizes that this sense of loss has been transmitted down through the generations, affecting many generations of Indian men with a deep sense of pain, anger and powerlessness. These destructive feelings manifest themselves as violence toward their loved ones, substance abuse, suicide, and an inability to communicate feelings and experiences. Many Native men adopted the oppressor's ways of operating: power through control, intimidation, manipulation, lack of respect for equality and nurturance of women, abandonment of family and responsibility, and a lack of honesty. For Native women, the traditional role of educator, healer, nurturer, head of the home, and sustainers of the family and Nation was gone. Faced with being victims of abuse and abandonment, women turned to substance abuse, suicide and hopelessness.[9]

So far, I have provided examples of how children felt growing up within abusive families. We have not, however, heard much from the parents in these situations. They too are victims. Here is survivor Elsie Chartrand's explanation of what she passed on to her children:

I did a terrible job as a parent. Our first child was born a year after our marriage, then a baby followed every two years. My children were growing up with my abusive behaviour of slapping, whipping and screaming at them for everything that they did. I loved them in a very sick way. Hit them, then kiss them. It was worse when my husband and I drank. I started drinking in bars when I was twenty-four years old. By then I had five children. My oldest child was mother and father to the rest of the children. I became more violent to everyone around me. I was that ugly person I had been told I was since a child. My anger and rage were killing me and killing my children's spirit. Many times I tried to commit suicide in an attempt to stop all the pain and hurt in my life. I didn't teach my children any values, beliefs, culture or language. I didn't have anything to give except my rage.[10]

Rage. I saw it far too many times in my prosecutions, and I used to wonder how people could be filled with so much anger that they could suddenly, without any cause we could see, turn to the most inexplicable violence. I now think people are right when they look back to residential schools and the trauma that began inside their walls. Cynthia Wesley-Esquimaux and Magdalena Smolewski speak eloquently about how that trauma plays out over the generations:

> The combined effect of numerous incidents of emotional abuse may lead to similar symptoms of repressed emotions, numbness and the irrational thinking that comes with unresolved issues and loss of inherent identity. People will not respond to the world outside. They will perceive the world as hostile and beyond their control. They will feel alienated, detached, alone and lonely. They will pass their loneliness and alienation onto their children who will also become lonely and despairing. Their bodies will be the only things over which they will have control and, even then, the sense of control will be tenuous because of their own lifetime experiences. They will start abusing their bodies; they will drink themselves into oblivion, they will sniff glue and gasoline, they will cut their arms and they will kill themselves. They will not be able to love…. Their helplessness will make them angry and they will beat and rape their wives and children. Their children will not have the sense or the knowledge that they are reliving the past of their parents, grandparents and great grandparents. For them, the terror will be happening here and now. Abandoned and neglected, they will not see the future as anticipated opportunity. They will not see any future at all.[11]

It is now clear to me that while the initially traumatizing experiences may have been long ago, and may have directly touched only the parents, grandparents or great-grandparents of the people today, their psychological distress is magnified through the intergenerational transfer of that trauma, and is still poisonously alive for far too many people in aboriginal Canada.

It is because of this intergenerational transfer of trauma that the Truth and Reconciliation Commission must find ways to articulate the impact of residential schools, not only on the children captured within them, but also on the children the survivors later raised. If aboriginal people could be helped to distinguish cause from effect, then perhaps they would be more inclined to seek reconciliation with those who caused them such harm.

Residential school was not, however, the only force of colonization, and other colonial practices are still affecting aboriginal people today, decades after the last school was closed.

CHAPTER 8

CONTINUING DISCONNECTION

THE SIXTIES SCOOP

I have already mentioned that the trauma inflicted by residential schools did not end when the last school closed. Not only was that trauma carried home and passed on to subsequent generations, but new forms of harm were introduced as well.

In the 1960s, aboriginal children were removed from their homes and placed with foster families at an alarming rate. While some of these apprehensions were based on parental abuse, many others were based on allegations of what was called "parental neglect." That accusation of neglect usually came out of a failure to understand aboriginal methods of raising children, methods that often granted children far more freedom to experiment and learn on their own than is the case in western society. Nor were the impacts of extreme poverty and inadequate housing taken into account as factors that few could avoid, and that had nothing at all to do with valuing the children living within those impoverished households. Dr. Kirmayer, together with Gregory Brass, Tara Holton, Ken Paul, Cori Simpson and Caroline Tait, looked at those issues in *Suicide Among Aboriginal People in Canada* and drew the following picture:

By the late 1970s, about one in four status Indian children could expect to be removed from their homes for most of their childhood.... Aboriginal children were removed from their homes and placed in "care" for a variety of reasons. Like the residential school system ... the need for welfare (child and economic) was often a result of perceived parental moral shortcomings. The Department of Indian Affairs expressed concerns about the ability of Aboriginal parents to provide proper "care" for returning residential school students following the closure of many schools. It was argued that because of such factors as alcoholism, lack of supervision, and parental immaturity, returning students required continued departmental supervision. This supervision came in many forms; one practice adopted by the department was to place responsibility for returning students into the hands of child care agencies. It was believed that finding foster homes for former students would be a cost-effective way to address the "void" left by the closure of residential schools.[1]

In light of everything discussed so far, it is easy to see the removal of children from the home as a further instrument of colonization. In the autumn of 1991, the Manitoba Justice Inquiry criticized the scoop for exactly that reason:

Between 1971 and 1981, over 3,400 Aboriginal children were shipped away to adoptive parents in other societies. Aboriginal children have been taken from their families, communities and societies, first by the residential school system and later by the child welfare system.... The Sixties Scoop was not coincidental; it was a consequence of ... the child welfare system emerging as the new method of colonization.

John Coates, a professor at St. Thomas University in Fredericton, New Brunswick, studied indigenous approaches to healing in social work in an article co-authored with Mel Gray and Tiani Hetherington. They drew the following conclusions about the Sixties Scoop:

> In the main, social work has acted as an agent of colonization, especially in transferring inappropriate mainstream theory and practice models to work with indigenous groups. Perhaps nowhere else has this been so vividly demonstrated as in child welfare where mainstream criteria, values, standards and interventions continued the process of colonization.... Even when professional education programs profess an openness to indigenous models, often only mainstream social work models are taught and First Nations students are left to accommodate traditional methods as best they can.... Social work expounds values and beliefs, such as universalism, professionalism and individualism, to name a few, that run counter to many indigenous beliefs and values (such as interdependence and inclusion).[2]

The authors' focus on differences in values systems is important here, because people from one system who do not understand the other will often judge it harshly. When, for instance, social workers brought up within western nuclear families encounter groups of people who share children among themselves as a community, they may fail to see the level of supervision that communities and extended families provide, and they may judge the nuclear family harshly, interpreting lesser levels of supervision as a lack of caring. In a similar way, the aboriginal preference for not giving explicit instruction to children, but instead providing opportunities for them to learn through watching and trying things on their own, may not be well understood by western social workers trained in the use of explicit instruction. When they don't see what they expect to see, their conclusions are often negative about things like level of care, supervision and instruction. These cross-cultural misinterpretations caused many of the apprehensions of aboriginal children. When coupled with poverty, unemployment and the greater use of alcohol within aboriginal families, assumptions such as these led social workers to conclude that aboriginal families were failing their children, simply because they were not doing what healthy non-aboriginal families would do.

Of course, there were many families that were indeed broken, and many parents (especially the men) who were committing crimes and facing jail. In those instances, the case for apprehending their children would have been stronger. But unfortunately, the use of jail only added to the levels of violence, loneliness, anger and despair in many communities, simply because that is how many incarcerated people react to prison.

THE IMPACT OF JAIL

Aboriginal people are significantly overrepresented as offenders in the Canadian criminal justice system. Incarceration rates of aboriginal people are five to six times higher than the national average. Statistics from Correctional Service Canada show that while aboriginal people represent only 2.8 percent of the Canadian population, they account for 18 percent of those who are incarcerated in federal institutions. In the Prairie provinces (and, I suspect, northern Ontario), 50 percent of all prisoners are aboriginal. Dr. Kirmayer cites a recent survey in which 39 percent of aboriginal adults reported family violence as a problem in their community, with 25 percent reporting sexual abuse and 15 percent reporting rape. My twenty-six years as a prosecutor in those communities suggests to me that those figures are low; I rely, instead, on the leaders in places like Hollow Water who estimate that 80 percent of all people in their community have been involved in sexual abuse, as victim or perpetrator, or both.

We have not, as a society, asked what jailing does to the people already caught up in violent behaviour, nor have we asked what happens when they return to their small, vulnerable communities after serving their time.

I recall once listening to a man who for many years had been a member of an urban aboriginal gang and had served substantial jail time as a result of his illegal activities. He made the startling suggestion that while residential schools may have been the largest destabilizer of First Nations in the past, the new leading force was jail.

When I began to learn about complex PTSD, I thought back to his assertion, and it became immediately clear that jail is the perfect environment to promote this disorder. After all, every inmate is likely to experience, often to an extreme degree, the causes of complex PTSD, including social, psychological and legal subordination; a conviction of powerlessness and helplessness; incidents of racism; an environment of neglect and deprivation; and a sense of repeated interpersonal victimization. In other words, aboriginal inmates of correctional institutions might well be dealing with three forces known to cause complex PTSD: family and community histories of economic, social, political, racial and legal subordination to, and isolation from, the non-aboriginal world; childhoods marred by violence, neglect and addictions at the hands of traumatized adults; and actual imprisonment by the dominant society, with all of the physical, emotional, mental and spiritual deprivation that entails.

Perhaps we should not be surprised that the leaders of many First Nations are expressing a concern that young men sent to jail are coming back worse than when they were taken away.

Instead of learning good lessons, they often return with greater skills of intimidation and criminal activity, and with a frightening criminal arrogance that no one can penetrate. Many families and communities are concerned about the hair-trigger anger and the explosions of extreme violence upon the slightest provocation within their young people, exactly what a complex PTSD diagnosis would predict. I recall one case where a probation officer almost begged me not to recommend a custodial sentence for a young girl whose crimes would normally have demanded exactly that: "If she gets into the hands of some of those other kids in custody," he told me, "they'll use her so badly she'll never get back to a normal life. The community is just going to have to figure out how to deal with her." I agreed entirely, and she was put on probation. Our system being what it is, I have no idea whether that worked or not.

The conclusion, in my mind, is inescapable: with the absence of effective detraumatization or decolonization programs, jails will only do further psychological harm and put communities further at risk. In my view, we should be sending as few people into that environment as we safely can, while helping aboriginal people create rehabilitative programs in both the correctional facilities and the communities themselves. Those programs must recognize the colonial roots of these psychological challenges and offer holistic strategies designed to recover lost psychological ground.

Raymond Corrado and Irwin Cohen, authors of a study on the mental health of British Columbia's survivors of residential school, underline the urgency of the mental health issues facing so many aboriginal Canadians:

> Upon leaving the residential school system at 15 years of age, only a small minority returned to intact families.... Nearly half of the case files that provide information about the subject's criminal history report convictions, mainly for

assault and sexual assault. While there were multiple victims mentioned for many of these criminal incidents, most involve intimate partners and family members.... In only two cases did the subjects not suffer from a mental disorder. The most common mental disorders were post-traumatic stress disorder (64.2 per cent), substance abuse disorder (26.3 per cent) and major depression (21.1 per cent). As expected, half of those diagnosed with PTSD were co-morbid with other mental disorders, including substance abuse disorder (34.8 per cent), major depression (30.4 per cent) and dysthymic disorder (26.1 per cent).[3]

It's not just the relatively small communities where this is an issue. Carol LaPrairie, a sociologist with long-standing interest in aboriginal issues, studied the characteristics of aboriginal people living in the inner cores of four large Canadian cities in 1995. Her research revealed startling data:

- Three-quarters of all persons interviewed had suffered childhood abuse.
- Among these, one-quarter had experienced abuse "of the most severe kind."
- For most of the people interviewed, abuse and violence were facts of childhood and adult life.
- Many were experiencing a high incidence of current instability in home and family life.
- Many were chronically transient, moving around a great deal.
- Many experienced severe or moderate problems in dealing with their own consumption of alcohol.
- Many had few skills and little formal education, and experienced chronic unemployment.

- They were subjected to victimization more than other urban people.
- Many lacked any connection to stable influences.[4]

I hope that, by now, I have given a picture of how these desolate living circumstances came into being. They were caused by a host of factors, especially residential schools and racial denigration, over more than a century. None of today's horrible statistics support Sir John A's negative opinion about aboriginal people. They do indicate, I think, that he and others in his time had no idea what taking generations of children away from their families and communities would do to them.

In my view, however, it no longer matters who intended what result. What does matter is the need to recognize that policies put in place forty or sixty or a hundred years ago remain tragically powerful today, and we all have a responsibility to do whatever it takes to get things back on a respectful path again.

That impact of colonization has not been recognized by the vast majority of non-aboriginal Canadians. It certainly has not been recognized by most governments. No government or church volunteered to fund the Truth and Reconciliation Commission, the Aboriginal Healing Foundation or the individual compensation schemes we have heard so much about. That funding happened only because aboriginal people took those governments and churches to court. Faced with huge liability for their past actions, the churches and government agreed to settle the cases. Many people seem to think the settlements were volunteered out of sympathy and a desire to see justice done, but that's not the case. While some churches were more forthcoming than others, and all of the churches were more forthcoming than the government, they agreed only when they were forced into a legal corner. And, when the five-year mandate of the Aboriginal Healing Fund established in the Settlement Agreement came to an end, so did government support. It has now shut its doors, after a meagre five-year existence.

Before closing this segment on colonization, I want to underline something that is easy to miss but essential to recognize. Despite the astounding assaults on the mental, physical, emotional and spiritual health of so many aboriginal people, the majority are *not* in jail, nor are their lives swamped by addictions, violence and despair. While the rates of suicide, incarceration and addictions are indeed higher than in the non-aboriginal population, and call for concerted attention from everyone, we must keep in mind the remarkable truth that a much higher proportion of aboriginal people have found ways to keep the colonial onslaught from overwhelming them.

That doesn't mean everything is as it should be. I know many professional aboriginal people who tell me that no one in their families ever shared their feelings, and that they still labour under that same impediment with their own families today.

The success of the majority of aboriginals who have come through those astounding challenges, with so much of their faith, hope and humour intact, should tell the rest of us something about the power and validity of traditional Teachings. It should also tell us that it is imperative that we do whatever we can to support their revitalization.

My goal in discussing colonization has been to dispel some myths and paint a clearer picture of the ongoing issues. I hope I have made the case for the following propositions, many of which may be new to most Canadians:

- Residential schools were only one part of the intentional colonization of aboriginal people; the other parts included loss of land, the shunting aside of women, the banning of many ceremonies and the constant denigration of all things aboriginal.

- We should expect huge differences in the experiences people had at residential schools—the positive experience of one does not make the bad experience of another a lie.
- Children didn't have to be physically or sexually abused in those schools to have their adult lives seriously affected by a host of forces, including extreme loneliness, constant racial denigration, loss of social and cultural context, traumatic bonding to school staff, fear of other students, and an almost complete denial of opportunities to develop healthy emotional skill sets.
- All the losses suffered by children in those schools were then passed on to their children and have directly led to today's continuing violence, addictions, despair and social breakdown in many communities.
- In those troubled communities, healing cannot be accomplished in less than a full generation, and in more remote and troubled communities, it will likely take much more than one.

Finally, there is the need to recognize that recovery strategies cannot continue to be instruments of further colonization. Up until now, I have spoken of diagnoses like complex PTSD rather freely, as if they were the perfect way to understand the psychological impact of residential schools and other instruments of colonization. As I have been reminded by my aboriginal friends, these are western diagnoses, western ways of articulating that psychological impact. As such, they would naturally lead us toward western recovery processes as well.

What if aboriginal people articulated the challenge differently? What if we all asked what sorts of healing processes flow out of aboriginal Teachings instead? If well-intentioned non-aboriginals, anxious to help, nevertheless insist on shoving aside aboriginal healing approaches in favour of western-based healing programs, does that not serve as a further denigration of aboriginal capacities—precisely what all the other colonization strategies did?

And wouldn't that be the most grotesque irony of all?

PART THREE

HEALING FROM COLONIZATION

CHAPTER 9

HOW TO BEGIN

Sporadic attempts at aboriginal healing have been made for many decades, some conducted by governments or churches, some by communities themselves, and some by groups of aboriginal people through Canada-wide programs sponsored by governments. Some have involved work within communities, while others have established centralized residential treatment centres. The programs have focused on many issues, from alcohol abuse to family violence, sexual abuse, gambling and gas sniffing.

In this chapter, I want to talk about how so many of these programs are now recognizing that there is one key ingredient to healing all those issues: re-establishing traditional visions of aboriginal life. I quoted the Hollow Water First Nation at the beginning of the book because they said it best when they declared that healing is really "decolonization therapy."

I want to share what two people told Lee Brown about the healing they experienced as part of the talking circles they held during their training to become social workers in British Columbia in the 1980s. One said:

> I learned more of the spiritual teachings of our own people [weeping]. It was something I had been looking for a long

time, and then I realized that it was something probably my father had been looking for his whole life. And I couldn't believe that we been so deprived that they have taken away from us ... [more crying, sobbing]. I guess even now I still have a hard time that the language, all those things that had been taken ... it was like I knew a word [deep sigh], maybe rebirth is a good word the religion uses. For me it was like a rebirth.[1]

A second trainee put it this way:

Learning of our own culture and, you know, all the wonderful things about it, the values of our culture ... was totally inspiring, beautiful and really kinda transforming. I started to really feel good about who I was.... I could walk down the street with my head up and started not really worrying so much about what people think about me if they saw the colour of my skin or any of those other outward things. Because I knew inside I had found something indescribably beautiful.

Now, nearly thirty years after those students held their talking circles, we have Joseph Gone reporting on people's reaction to alcohol treatment at the Pisimweyapiy Counselling Centre in northern Manitoba. While that centre focuses ostensibly on alcohol abuse, most of its attention goes to the damage done by residential schools, to individuals and to aboriginal people generally. It teaches people that they are not alone—that, in fact, there are thousands carrying the same burdens of negative self-definition. Once again we can hear people speak about coming out from under the burden of negativity they had been carrying for so long:

Well, I feel a lot more confident about myself. I don't feel like I'm worthless or anything like that. I don't feel like I'm never going to amount to anything because today is the only day I look at sometimes, and today's the day that I'm doing something positive. And I don't beat myself up if I can't succeed in something ... I'll just say, "Okay, I made that mistake but I can still go on." Pick myself up here. And it's given me that encouragement to just [keep] on going.... Sometimes, I guess, I'm living in the past, where I'm at a point where I start feeling hopeless. But in reality there is hope.[2]

Another graduate from the treatment centre told Joseph Gone about her healing experience there:

And I've always been confrontational against healing and therapy and counselling. Always like, "You don't need that. It's up to the individual himself."... So when it came to counselling, [the court] recommended it. I was like, pfft!... And then one day they said, "Hey, listen, [you can] go to jail or you can do this, plus counselling." Sure, why not? I was like, "Oh, cool. I'm here [in the program] for [the] courts." Whatever. "Give me what you got." And I left there crying that same day. Since that day, man, it's been very uplifting, I guess, to be able to try to understand what you went through, what our ancestors went through, to be able to see what our parents went through.[3]

She learned that she was far from alone in seeing herself in such negative terms, and she learned how much of that negativity was due to residential schools.

I've been exploring aboriginal approaches to healing for nearly thirty years, and I've found myself increasingly frustrated by the failure of western governments to recognize the need for, and the sophistication of, these processes. There are thousands of people who could be having the healing experiences of the people I just quoted, but they are left to struggle on their own. Look around the streets of any northern town and you'll see those who have given up and let themselves sink into alcoholic numbing. Look into our jails and you'll see many aboriginal offenders who were children only ten or fifteen years ago, but who lived in dysfunctional households where anger, violence and addiction were what they saw and learned to copy. In my career, I watched two generations of people coping as best they could with terrible circumstances, and I was a part of the system that sent many of them to jail. I didn't want to see any of them incarcerated, but by that stage of their lives their lapses into violence had made them simply too dangerous to roam freely among the rest of us. Without effective long-term healing, it was the only option that made sense. My frustration came because I knew of healing processes that would have prevented them from ever becoming that dangerous in the first place.

I remember a conversation I had with a member of a band council who had been chosen to coordinate court activities with my office. His community in northwestern Ontario had only about 350 people, and we had worked well together for several years. He asked me if I would come to the community the night before the next court and join them in a sweat lodge that he had just built. I told him that I was honoured to be asked and would be very pleased to join them. After some discussion about where the lodge was and how he had learned to build it, I gave in to my curiosity and asked why I had been invited. He slowly explained that traditions like sweat lodges caused a great deal of concern in his community among the churchgoers, and there was some resistance to bringing them back. In fact, he said that the opposition was strongest among the lay ministers, all of them aboriginal, in the four local churches (he also told me that they each claimed to have a certain number of followers within the community, but if you added them all up, the number of followers was double the community's actual population!). He told me that he hoped that when the children of the community saw the Crown attorney going into their sweat lodge, they might think that it was an okay thing to do, and some of them might decide to take up the tradition later on.

I confess that I found that conversation so sad. There he was, asking a professional white man to demonstrate respect for an aboriginal tradition so that it might be validated in the eyes of his own children. I wondered about the fear put into the hearts of those people by the missionaries, so much that the community's own lay ministers felt the same way and warned their parishioners against such "heathen" practices. I wish I could say that this was an uncommon situation across northern Ontario, but it's not. Aboriginal people are struggling against such warnings to a significant degree—all of them now made by their own people. Many families are split right down the middle, with huge divisions between those who became Christian and those who carry on the traditional ways.

When I went to the sweat lodge a month or so later, I found that it wasn't constructed outdoors as I'd expected, but inside a garage to better resist winter temperatures that could reach minus fifty degrees Celsius. I joined eight or nine other men; there were no women or children. All of them appeared nervous, and I wasn't sure if it was because the ceremony was so new to them or because I was there, or perhaps both of those things together.

That sweat lodge, like most others in my experience, had four "rounds" dedicated to different themes. In between each round, the canvas flap was opened to let in cold, fresh air; after the flap was closed, the next took place. Our first round was dedicated to the

Elders. We asked for the strength to help them and to understand the challenges they faced. The second was dedicated to the children of the community, and it was then that the intensity of the sweat lodge suddenly jumped off the dial. Everyone had a story and a prayer because everyone had been directly touched by one (or more) of the thirteen youth suicides that the community had suffered over the previous two years. We all cried. And we cried hard. I don't know any Cree or Ojibway, but I sang their songs with them, out loud, with all my might. I was no longer the visiting Crown attorney—I was a parent joining other parents in expressing their unspeakable losses. We couldn't see each other in that moist darkness, but we knew each other, felt each other and joined each other in those tears, songs and prayers. The very notion of a court being able to do anything to stop those suicides, or to change the circumstances that had given rise to them, seemed absolutely ridiculous. My tears were not only for their losses, but also for the blindness of my world and its assumptions about what it could do, and what aboriginal people could not do.

I found myself asking, how could we not see what was promising for them, and what only made matters worse? I felt deeply ashamed. And then, because I was with them and one of them in that sacred letting-go, my shame melted away and my hope returned. We carried on, dedicating the last two rounds to Mother Earth and to our opportunities to develop the strength we'd need to live good lives in right relations. Those men were there, in that place and ceremony, because they cared and because they hoped. They were praying for strength to live with their losses and to find ways to bring health back to the young people and to the community. They had asked me to join with them in that, and I did. I've never forgotten them, or that night, or their songs and prayers. Their faith and bravery continue to astound me, and their first, frightened steps back into traditional ways to grieve and ways to re-dedicate themselves cause me immense joy. As long as their present-day churches don't scare everyone away from traditional ceremonies and thoughts, they'll come through. I am so honoured to have shared their first tentative, powerful steps in what I think of as a promising march back home from the cultural wilderness created by residential schools.

I know they are not alone. One of the communities in my region had no sweat lodges fifteen years ago, but now they have six or seven. Elders across the country are coming forward to share the ceremonies and Teachings of the past; while they sometimes find people afraid to listen to the old ways, they continue speaking with anyone who will listen. Powwows are regaining strength and numbers, as are the sun dances of the prairies and the potlatch ceremonies of the West Coast. In perhaps an ironic twist of fate, many of the children taken into non-aboriginal homes in the sixties and seventies are graduating from universities and doing whatever they can to learn about their aboriginal histories and to reassert the strengths of the culture they were denied. When I watched television coverage of the Idle No More marches and demonstrations, I thought I saw many of those once-displaced children now asserting adult dedication to ancient ways. In fact, their voice may be even stronger—and better educated in traditional as well as western ways—than that of their brethren who were left behind in slowly decaying communities.

At the same time, several healing programs using traditional practices are doing inspiring work with the troubled people of those communities. In the next chapter I'll discuss the three programs that I've become familiar with. On the surface, they are not at all similar. The first, Hollow Water's program, was created by a single First Nation to respond to sexual abuse. Its program extends over many years and involves many workers and many sorts of healing activities. The second is the National Native Alcohol and Drug Addiction Program, which offers residential treatment for substance abuse that extends over four or five weeks. The third, called the RedPath Program, is a privately created business that trains workers to present twelve weekly sessions in their home communities on the development of emotional skill sets. What struck me about all three is that, despite the clear differences, they are all built on a common conviction that returning to health demands a return to traditional Teachings. As much as they focus on separate issues such as sexual abuse, addiction and emotional suppression, all three have a common definition of a "healthy aboriginal person" and share a powerful determination to restore that definition to their people. They are all, in a sense, programs of cultural restoration where the word "holistic" starts to show its true meaning.

CHAPTER 10

THREE HEALING PROGRAMS

HOLLOW WATER'S COMMUNITY HOLISTIC CIRCLE HEALING PROGRAM

In my previous book, *Returning to the Teachings*, I wrote rather extensively about the healing program at the Hollow Water First Nation on the eastern shore of Lake Winnipeg. At Hollow Water, they use a great many traditional processes and Teachings, including the talking feather in group discussions, the four directions of the medicine wheel, the mind-body-emotion-spirit dimensions of human beings, and ceremonies like the sweat lodge or vision quests. They also show allegiance to traditional Teachings by insisting on healing instead of punishment, and on the engagement of everyone touched by a particular act, whether victim, offender, family member or close friend. They see their work as community building, and they engage as much of the community as they can. Following notions of embeddedness, they know that a single act touches—and can affect—a wide circle of people, and all of their relationships. A solid healing process must also do the same.

There are, however, two things that are so remarkable about Hollow Water that I want to repeat them here. The first has to do with how they created their healing team. Federal and provincial governments fund many kinds of service providers in First Nations, including grief counsellors, family workers, child care workers, alcohol and drug counsellors, nurses and nurses' aides, teachers and teachers' aides, and suicide prevention workers. In some communities, there are nineteen people on full-time salaries for work related to community healing. Each of them answers to a different outside supervisor, however, and the agencies demand confidentiality. That means, as I have seen, nineteen workers who cannot share information about the families they are working with. They also receive totally separate training, and that training may be based on competing notions of how to best bring about healing. The result is that one troubled family might have six different workers playing active, but totally uncoordinated, roles with them.

What Hollow Water did was as simple as it was revolutionary: the workers told their outside agencies they were going to come together as a healing team to share their information and design common training. Over time, that training began to focus increasingly on recovery from colonization, particularly residential schools. As a result, Hollow Water staff have insisted on establishing their own training programs, as well as their own processes for healing, with special emphasis on holistic family and community healing. It took exceptionally brave and determined people to do that (and a few courageous officials in justice, health, education and other bureaucracies), but they are succeeding.

I do not underestimate the enormity of that challenge, for it is in the very nature of western bureaucracies that each agency has its own rules, its own definition of the job to be done, a fierce determination to maintain control and minimize the risk of program failure, and an inevitable sense of turf that makes it institutionally difficult to become partners in holistic approaches. It's not a question of bad faith or malevolence on the part of such agencies—it's just the way our bureaucracies operate. While it may be appropriate for Toronto to have nineteen agencies working within separate institutions and answerable to different supervisors, it is almost ludicrous to see nineteen healers in a community of five hundred people prohibited from working together. It is even more foolish when the root issue is the common experience of colonization trauma and the central goal of these healers is the same: restoring traditional ways of approaching life.

The second aspect of the program that deserves attention, however, is the importance of group healing in their processes, some of which have lasted five years. I want to share something I saw in one group healing session at Hollow Water. The circle I sat in was held for a woman who had been sexually abused for many years. She came into the circle for the first time and took her chair quietly, not looking anyone in the eye. She sat hunched over, head down, shoulders curved, fingers curled into tight, small fists and her legs and ankles twirled around each other. She didn't move. The topic of that particular circle was how people felt about their own bodies after sexual abuse. Most members of the healing team were themselves survivors of sexual abuse, and each of them was at a different stage of healing. As in all such circles, everyone had an opportunity to speak, in turn, as the feather was passed. They could speak as long as they wished, or not at all, for they were equals with complete freedom to choose their own level of participation. This was the circle where I heard those two women speak about still feeling so dirty after their abuse many years earlier that they turned the mirror to the wall or pushed their grandchildren off their knees.

As I listened to a full circle of women telling personal stories like that, I watched the woman who had suffered the abuse. At the start, she seemed to be barely breathing, but as the others spoke, a gradual transformation took place. It was as if she were exhaling for the first time in decades, slowly breathing out, then in, stretching and straightening the smallest degree. Instead of trying desperately to be as small and invisible as possible, she appeared to be taking the first tentative steps toward joining the others in the room. Her fingers uncurled, her back straightened somewhat, and her shoulders began to fall open. She did not speak about her own abuse in that first circle, but at its conclusion she expressed her thanks for being included, for being able to listen to others speak.

As I have since realized, a host of important healing steps were just beginning to occur with her, and all of them came from the fact that she was in a group of healing people, not sitting alone on a couch with a single therapist nearby.

First, the stories that others told began the essential, but lengthy, process of helping her to believe that she was not a freak for feeling everything she did. They too had once felt all those dirty, lonely, fearful things. She desperately needed to hear that from them, described in words and tones that resonated with all the secret screams and wails inside her. She needed to feel that her responses were normal, as extreme and disturbing as they may have been. Obviously, it would take much more than one circle for her to fully embrace that message, but it was a beginning. A detached western therapist with no similar experience, nor any professional permission to share it if she did, couldn't even begin to send as strong a message.

Second, that circle, comprising those women speaking so openly about their own days of abuse and fear, was a safe place in which she could, when she was ready, say anything she wanted. The sad truth is that many victims—and offenders—have learned to deny the full extent of their pain, even to themselves. Revealing it to others had too often resulted in those people turning against them, using their vulnerability as a weapon. They had never experienced a safe place before, where people could speak openly and safely about their anger, fear and hurt. In relational terms, they had learned to be closed, secretive and suspicious, for those were the lessons of their pain. In the circle, however, they are given the experience of many relationships founded on respect, openness, trust and caring, for that is how the healers relate to one another. Seeing members of the healing team all feeling safe together and sharing their stories has to send a stronger message of safety than even the most understanding, but single, western therapist can.

Third, the stories in the circle stood as a demonstration of the potential of the healing process, for every person there had begun where that victim now sat. Their behaviour in the circle, the kinds of relationships they now manifested between themselves, demonstrated that they had been able to move, however slowly, into new ways of thinking, believing, feeling and relating. If they could do it, it was indeed possible. I suspect that many victims and offenders alike have come to the conclusion that, no matter how other people might live, their world will always be mean, selfish, violent and sad. I also suspect that no one can simply tell them that their lives can be changed for the better. They have to hear it from others who once felt just as trapped and frightened, but have moved to a safer, stronger sense of themselves.

Fourth, every person's story made it clear that they all had found their own way out of their pain, their own helpers and their own pace. It is understood in traditional Teachings that every person is unique and that no one has the wisdom to tell others what they should and shouldn't do. The healers offered their own stories as encouragement and illustration, not instruction. What seemed critical about that message was its implicit statement that each person, whether victim or offender, is competent to reconfigure her own life. It is a message that stands in stark contrast to the central harm done by violence: making the victim feel that she is powerless, worthless and somehow deserving of the abuse. I suspect that a therapist could insist on that competence a thousand times, but it would mean very little compared to hearing the same message from people who had been exactly where you were, and once believed, like you, that they'd be mired there forever.

What seems essential, then, is that the circle be primarily composed of people who have experienced similar harm. Their real, human, emotion-centred words are what convince people that they are not alone in how they feel and that they, too, are capable of moving themselves into healthier ways. As I watched that one woman uncurl her fingers, let her shoulders drop and take the odd glance at others in the circle, I was imagining that same beginning for thousands of others who were similarly disconnected from healthy relations. And it didn't matter whether the law would call them victims or offenders, because all had suffered the same disconnections and were dramatically in need of a similar experience of right relations.

Interestingly, western psychology seems to be on the verge of endorsing such group-based, narrative-centred approaches to treating addictions. In one recent study, talking circles were used in what was called a "relational psychotherapy mothers' group" for heroin-addicted mothers in Connecticut. That study found exactly what aboriginal people have known for centuries: that "the use of a group format helps addicted mothers to develop their interpersonal skills, to perceive the universality of many dilemmas pertaining to their roles as mothers and to benefit from cohesive and mutually supportive interpersonal networks."[1] The researchers also discovered that drug-abusing mothers "are often wary of treatment approaches that seem to focus primarily on their 'deficits' as parents, such as those in which they are 'taught' parenting skills from a strictly didactic standpoint." Finally, group processes were recognized as giving participants the confidence they needed to find their own way forward. The study phrased it this way: "The discovery-based, non-directive approach ... serves to empower the mothers, implicitly acknowledging their motivation to become better parents and their own capacities to foster the positive development of their families."

There is another significant aspect to the program at Hollow Water. Their healing team includes people who have offended in the past but have moved far enough along their healing journey to now render assistance. The healers at Hollow Water clearly live by the aboriginal vision that people are all essentially good, and that although certain forces can propel us to do bad things, everyone, with the right spirit and assistance, can be restored to positions of respect. In this case, ex-offenders are seen as particularly valuable when other offenders come into the circle, not just for the empathy they bring, but for two other attributes as well. First, they are often quicker than everyone else to see how offenders are minimizing their crimes, hiding from their impacts, offering hollow justifications or excuses, or blaming others for their own choices; after all, they once used all those strategies themselves. They are thus able to insist, in ways that others cannot, that those strategies be shed. Second, their experience of the pain involved in having those defensive strategies slowly stripped away gives them extraordinary patience. They know how excruciating it is to finally acknowledge, especially to yourself, that there was no justification for all the pain you brought to others, that the responsibility was solely yours. At the same time, the fact that they once sat where the offender now sits, but have since earned a place as a respected and valued healer in the community, stands as a powerful motivator in itself, for it declares that it is indeed possible to put the crime behind you in the eyes of the community.

I remember once remarking, after an offender's circle had been completed and he'd gone on his way, how full of good feeling the circle seemed to be, even when the offence had been one of serious sexual abuse of a child. Everyone looked at me quizzically, and then opened a discussion that put forward a number of propositions: How can you bring about openness if you are closed yourself? How can you bring about respect if you show disrespect? Caring if you punish? Trust if you ambush? Faith if you condemn? In their view, the values you hope to teach must be the values demonstrated in the process itself. I shudder to think of the values I regularly demonstrated during the course of a criminal trial.

On that same trip to Hollow Water, I saw one other thing that made a lasting impression on me. At coffee break, Burma Bushie, one of the leaders of the healing program, was summoned to the front desk to speak with someone. A member of the healing team looked down the hallway and recognized the person waiting for Burma. I recognized him too. I knew that this man had sexually abused all three of his daughters over many years. I saw that he and Burma were sharing a joke of some kind, and as I watched Burma laughing with him I found myself feeling outraged. I think I was actually muttering comments under my breath, like, "How can she do that! How can she joke with him, knowing everything that he's done?" When the circle resumed, I had to ask the question directly, and I did. Burma chuckled and answered immediately, turning to the other members of the circle. "Remember when we first started working with him? How he tried to manipulate us all with his anger? Now he's trying the same thing with humour—he's *moving*!"

I know that Burma wasn't trying to embarrass me, but I did feel embarrassed. What had I expected from someone who could do those things to his own children—immediate, heartfelt remorse? Anyone who could do what he had done must have developed a warped view of himself and proper relations. It would take a long time to undo that way of thinking and acknowledge the damage done. So of course it would take a long time, and many stages of movement, to turn him around. How could I have pictured anything else? I felt so naive, so unsophisticated. I thought back to all the court cases I'd had where we listened to an accused expressing his "deep and profound remorse," when in fact he hadn't been through any process at all that might take him to that heartfelt position. But we tended to believe him. And we tended to come down even harder on people who didn't express such remorse.

I should add that I remember Burma calling me about three years later, telling me that the three daughters of that man, who had been kept totally separate from him all that time, now wanted to try bringing the family back together. She was so afraid that they hadn't done enough with all of them, and that the offences would resume. There was nothing I could say; it was clear that the healing team had to trust their own judgment. They decided to risk it, and things went well. The family had, in fact, been restored to right relations. When I thought about the fact that it was done with no jail time at all, I was taken back to the words of Elder Mary Anne Anderson, who had suggested, years earlier, that of course they did nothing *to* people who had caused harm; they counselled them instead.

I should point out, however, that the *threat* of jail was important. As Burma explained, a real healing process is extremely painful for people who have done harm, simply because it takes them to an emotional awareness of the pain they have caused others. Because that process would likely take years, their pain would last for years. Having that threat of jail in the background, she insisted, was absolutely necessary to keep offenders honestly participating in their healing program. In Hollow Water, that threat existed either because the accused had not yet been sentenced or because participation in the healing program was made a term of his probation or conditional sentence order. In fact, they had dealt with one man who, before sentencing, gave up on the healing program and asked the court to just send him to jail. Real healing, he said, was just too painful.

The Hollow Water healing team have dealt with many instances of sexual abuse and have had only one other failure. It happened in their early days, when they trusted someone enough to let him return to his home, where he again subjected his victim to a sexual assault. Since that event, they have not had a single recurrence. Their use of traditional Teachings and processes has proven vastly superior to either jail or the combination of jail and western therapy. Whole families have been reunited, in good health, and the community is no longer afraid to bring sexual abuse into the light of day.

Hollow Water was my first exposure to the power of traditional Teachings, especially the power of group work involving people who come into the circle with personal experience of the abuse being disclosed.

THE NATIONAL NATIVE ALCOHOL
AND DRUG ADDICTION PROGRAM (NNADAP)

This program began as the National Native Alcohol Abuse Program in 1974 and evolved into its present form in 1982. It now has forty-nine residential alcohol and drug abuse treatment centres across Canada, more than five hundred and fifty community-based prevention programs and approximately seven hundred full-time workers. In 1995 it added nine residential treatment centres under the National Youth Solvent Abuse Program (NYSAP). In 2007, with the support of the First Nations and Inuit Health Branch of Health Canada, the Assembly of First Nations, and the National Native Addiction Partnership Foundation, a comprehensive national review of services related to aboriginal substance abuse was undertaken. The final report, entitled *Honouring Our Strengths: A Renewed Framework to Address Substance Use Issues Among First Nations People of Canada*, was issued in 2011.[2]

I was invited to work for the First Nations and Inuit Health Branch in 2009, and did so until shortly before the final report was made public in 2011. During that time, I sat in on several of the multi-day regional conferences held across the country and joined many of the smaller policy discussions between those conferences.

The fundamental question that emerged during the review was whether aboriginal addictions treatment should continue using a disease-based model like the one on which Alcoholics Anonymous (AA) is built, or whether it should shift toward a culture-based, decolonization model instead. While NNADAP originally took its inspiration from AA, that was primarily because aboriginal people supported its reliance on group activities, it had a nonhierarchical organization, and it involved the interpersonal sharing of struggles. Its insistence that people confess themselves to be lifetime alcoholics, however, offended aboriginal sensitivities. Because it was also agreed that most aboriginal people who abuse intoxicants are, in fact, using them to manage the trauma in their lives, the real challenge was to find the best ways of defusing that trauma.

Three definitive documents contributed to the process of moving to a decolonization model for aboriginal addictions treatment. The first, called "Indigenous Intelligence,"[3] was a paper presented in 2006 by Elder James Dumont as the inaugural J.W.E. Newbery Lecture, a lecture series created to commemorate the man who established the native studies program at the University of Sudbury. I wrote about it in some detail in the first section of this book, and I will now refer to it as the Dumont paper. The second document was a paper James Dumont put together with Carol Hopkins, a Delaware woman who was by that time the executive director of the National Native Addictions Partnership Foundation, the group that oversaw the NNADAP review process. Called "Cultural Healing Practice within National Native Alcohol and Drug Abuse Program/Youth Solvent Addiction Program Services,"[4] this document became the primary source used in the NNADAP/YSAP renewal process. I will call it the Dumont-Hopkins paper. The third source was the final renewal document (approved by Health Canada) that set out the cultural foundation and the various treatment options to be used within the NNADAP and YSAP programs for years to come.

The review process took many months, but it was ultimately successful in shifting the foundation of addictions treatment from a disease-based model to one centred on the impact of historical trauma, where traditional Teachings were seen as the key to an effective response. The Dumont-Hopkins paper proposed that NNADAP/YSAP treatment must "set a foundation for understanding the vital role culture and cultural practices play in addressing addictions" and was insistent that "Indigenous-specific cultural practices, drawn from an Indigenous world-view, would provide the best route back to wellness."[5] The authors spoke of what they had learned from traditional healers: "Traditional healers place significance on re-establishing a connection with spirit, family, extended family networks and community ... to connect with ancestors, to address grief and promote health and spiritual connection."

Dumont and Hopkins also suggested that the true goal of healing is "coming to know oneself spiritually and in relation to Creation." Their definition of wellness involves "restoring connection to the original pattern of relationships to others, including spiritual family and community." They stress, as well, the mind-body-emotion-spirit essence of people, contrasted with the primary western focus on body and mind. The following statement expresses the founding vision for all healing:

In the Indigenous mind, though humankind is a "special creation event," the human person is of the earth and from the earth. Like all of the created world, the human being is part of the balance of nature. It must find a special yet interconnected place within the created whole. The human person is a relative to all other persons of the Earth, and, along with all creatures, calls the Earth Mother.[6]

The final renewal document set out ten principles to guide treatment, seven of which spoke directly about the importance of such Teachings. I will provide those seven principles here because they underline the degree to which traditional Teachings are considered essential to successful life in the modern aboriginal world:

- *Spirit-Centred:* Culture is understood as the outward expression of spirit, and revitalization of spirit is central to promoting health and well-being among First Nations people. System-wide recognition that ceremony, language and traditions are important in helping to focus on strengths and reconnecting people with themselves, the past, family, community and land.
- *Connected:* Strong connections are the basis for holistic and integrated services and supports. Healthy family, community, and systems are built on strong and lasting relationships. These connections exist between Indigenous people, the land, and their culture, as well as relationships between various sectors and jurisdictions responsible for care delivery.
- *Holistic Supports:* Services and supports that are holistic consider all potential factors contributing to well-being (e.g., physical, spiritual, mental, cultural, emotional, and social) over the lifespan, and seek to achieve balance within and across these areas.
- *Community-Focused:* Adopting a community-focused lens will help to both ensure that diversity within and across communities is respected, and enhance overall system responsiveness to factors that make each community unique.

- *Balanced:* Inclusion of both Indigenous and Western forms of evidence and approaches to all aspects of care (e.g., service delivery, administration, planning and evaluation) demonstrates respect and balance. It is also important to maintain awareness that each is informed by unique assumptions about health and well-being and unique worldviews.

- *Culturally Competent:* Cultural competence requires that service providers, both on- and off-reserve, are aware of their own worldviews and attitudes towards cultural differences; and include both knowledge of, and openness to, the cultural realities and environments of the clients they serve. To achieve this, it is also necessary for indigenous knowledge to be translated into current realities to meaningfully inform and guide direction and delivery of health services and supports on an ongoing basis.

- *Culturally Safe:* Cultural safety extends beyond cultural awareness and sensitivity within services and includes reflecting upon cultural, historical, and structural differences and power relationships within the care that is provided. It involves a process of ongoing self-reflection and organizational growth for service providers and the system as a whole to respond effectively to First Nations people.[7]

This focus on spirit, as we can see, is now becoming central to all NNADAP/YSAP treatment regimes. As a result, they concentrate on things like identifying one's spirit name, clan family and national identity. When you look at everyone's spiritual connection to Creation, you understand that family and community are central to discovering one's role within Creation, and to defining what responsibilities are thus engaged. Many activities help to define and solidify such roles, whether they be talking or healing circles; drum or dance groups; indigenous language learning; or activities with other people like crafts, gardening or hunting. All of these activities are already part of some NNADAP/YSAP treatment programs, and they serve to re-engage people in healthy ways, reversing the disconnection and the despiritualization brought by colonization.

The motivation for change is also centred in traditional Teachings. When people hear about the spirit that unites all aspects of Creation, they are motivated to learn about that spirit, to reach out and become active in spirit-centred ways with all the relationships that surround them. The focus is on the gifts that we were given to participate in that spirit-centred way, not the deficits that have held us back. Prayers, especially in ceremonies like the sweat lodge, first offer thanksgiving for all the blessings bestowed on us, and then only ask for help in developing our gifts so that we can help create stronger relationships, whether with the old people, the youth or the nonhuman aspects of Creation.

Because Dumont and Hopkins see suicide as "a response to not knowing of one's purpose in life,"[8] they pay a great deal of attention to the many ceremonies that set out the stages of progress through life. There are, for instance, the "walking-out ceremony" for babies taking their first steps on Mother Earth; fasting ceremonies for adolescents struggling to find their roles, connections and gifts; ceremonies celebrating the arrival of new life; burial ceremonies and memorial (or ghost) feasts; and ceremonies like the full moon or fire and water rites celebrating gender roles and responsibilities. As the Dumont-Hopkins paper expresses it, "ceremony increases one's knowledge and understanding of self, as well as one's place and belonging in the world."

Recall the response of children in the troubled community to Teachings about women and water, and men and fire, and my expectation that they would resist the notion that they had responsibilities. Recall, as well, how excited they were to hear that they had roles to play, that their lives had meaning. I also suspect that such Teachings are equally important for adults who have become disconnected from everything except their pain and their need for alcohol or drugs. When they go back to their troubled families after the healing program, they often find that their efforts to heal are ridiculed or denied by other people, but the water doesn't turn them away, nor does fire or the sky or all the other nonhuman persons with whom they have begun to build relationships. Even if the human community continues to drag them down, offering tobacco and prayers beside a stream brings increased peace and a sense of belonging. The stories of vulnerable people learning to take comfort in those kinds of nonhuman relationships are commonplace within aboriginal communities.

Finally, NNADAP/YSAP treatment centres create new human communities as people come together, in groups, to learn about aboriginal history, to see all the common disconnections in their separate histories, and to learn about the connectedness that sits at the centre of traditional thought. Most of the activities are conducted in groups, with people sharing their stories and feelings with one another. Here is how one person described her experience within NNADAP treatment to Joseph Gone:

Healing to me, honestly, is understanding your past. Trying to accept the things that you can't change and dealing with things face to face, not ignoring them, not putting them aside, and dealing with them in the wrong way by blaming people, by reacting violently, [or] taking those short-term stimulants, like alcohol and drugs.... To me, healing is just trying to get to know who you really are, who you can be, what it is in life that you are here for, your purpose. And that to me is healing, living a comfortable life, not a perfect life, 'cause it's not perfect. Nobody can be perfect.[9]

While there are many different aboriginal groups in Canada, each demonstrating many cultural differences, all are working to restore their unique Teachings, practices and ceremonies. Even though NNADAP/YSAP residential treatment programs are time limited, they can provide a foundation on which to begin building a lifelong healing journey.

Whether all of the above makes sense to non-aboriginal people is, in my view, entirely irrelevant. This was the aboriginal people's world view, they are determined to restore it, and they are doing so. To be honest, I like everything I've been able to understand thus far, and I can see how the restoration of this set of beliefs would be good for all human beings—as well as all the nonhuman beings in our world!

I think it's also interesting to note that the aboriginal response to issues like addiction demands so much more than just looking at the addiction itself. Instead, the focus is on the deepest questions of human existence: Who are we as we struggle though the Great Mystery? How do we define ourselves? Where should our dreams lie? What goals deserve our best efforts? Are we standing within a balance of our mental, physical, emotional and spiritual dimensions? In other words, all of our challenges come out of the same disconnection from a healthy perception of what we are and what we can be. The addictions portion is almost a tagalong. In my mind, this is part of the concept of a holistic existence: everything boils down to health in the widest sense. This concept is at the heart of traditional healing, and I believe that NNADAP/YSAP programs now have a much better chance of succeeding in their addictions goals, simply because they are built on that fundamental concept.

The third program I wish to discuss also moves from an identifiable sub-issue like addiction into the larger challenge of overall aboriginal health. While its immediate focus is on what westerners call emotional intelligence, its ultimate goal is to restore the possibility of achieving balance between the emotional, physical, mental and spiritual dimensions of every human being. To be frank, it is, in my view, the most perceptive and promising healing program I've encountered—and it holds benefits for all people, not just those aboriginal people who find themselves captives of their own emotional suppression.

THE REDPATH PROGRAM

A few years ago, I received two papers in the mail, though I don't recall who sent the first one. It was a report on the UBC study that found limited emotional skill sets in non-aboriginal men who had been convicted of spousal abuse. The second paper came from a Mohawk woman named Peggy Shaughnessy, whom I have since met and learned from. It was called "Promoting Emotional Intelligence: An Intervention Program for Use with Aboriginal Peoples."[10] The report came out of the Emotion and Health Research Program at Trent University, in Peterborough, Ontario, and it described a healing program the department had run jointly with Peggy, who had graduated from Trent some years earlier. Together, they looked at the emotional competencies of seventy-eight aboriginal men incarcerated in federal prisons. These were men who had either committed serious crimes or such a number of lesser crimes that shorter sentences to provincial jails were considered inadequate. Trent University put them through a standard testing procedure that had been slightly modified to account for aboriginal ways of responding to questions or stating positions. Unsurprisingly, all of the men showed substantial deficits in emotional intelligence (EQ), including

- the ability to identify and express emotional states;
- the ability to link emotions with specific situations and personal behaviours;

- the ability to guide future behaviour using feelings and emotions; and
- the ability to mentally regulate negative or extreme emotional states.

Of those seventy-eight men, twenty-three agreed to go through a twelve-week course of healing designed by Peggy. She called it the RedPath Program because of its reliance on traditional aspects of aboriginal culture. The hope was that her program might break through some of the tough-guy personalities that the inmates had developed and spur an increase in emotional skill sets. The paper didn't give details about her program, noting only that it used traditional concepts like circles, storytelling, ceremonies and traditional Teachings. After the twelve weeks of her program, Trent University administered the same EQ test that they had used at the start and found that the changes were greater than anyone had expected. They reported "a significant increase in various dimensions of emotional intelligence," and they made the following recommendation:

This study indicates that the RedPath Program can enhance emotional and social skills even in the most high risk Aboriginal population. Therefore, it is recommended that this program be used to enhance emotional and social competencies in a variety of Aboriginal groups to deal with the cross-section of problems (addictions, violence, etc.) plaguing North American Aboriginal Communities.[11]

Obviously, I was intrigued. If her program could bring about such dramatic changes in people whom I knew to be among the most hardened group of aboriginal offenders, how powerful would it be if it was undertaken with more general groups? And how much more powerful would the program be if it took place not within prison walls, but in more open settings where aboriginal ties to the natural world could be felt so much more strongly?

I managed to locate Peggy Shaughnessy, and in due course met her in Peterborough. She told me about her life, and about how she began to work with offenders in prisons, learning about them and their lives. She took herself back to school, ultimately earning a master's degree in psychology from Trent University. She then designed her RedPath Program, employing what she had learned from her degree and her awareness of traditional Teachings, and conducted it within the walls of Kingston Penitentiary. When Trent's follow-up testing revealed how beneficial the program was, she formed her own company and started taking it across Canada. She now focuses on group training so that her graduates can go back into their communities and use the program to help people there develop emotional skill sets. Between June 2005 and February 2010, she conducted forty-five such sessions across Canada, training over six hundred people. I asked if I could join one of her three-day training programs, and not long after I did exactly that.

I knew that her work reflected my own interest in the relationship between emotional skill sets and the addictions and violence that plague so many aboriginal communities. What really got my attention, however, was the fact that she saw the restoration (or creation) of emotional competencies as an essential *first* step in helping people heal. Until people developed those skills, she felt it was virtually impossible for them to regain control over any aspect of their lives. She describes that dynamic this way in her program materials:[12]

> Most people will say (that they go through life putting up walls) to protect themselves, that they have been hurt so much that they don't want to get hurt again. Most times,

however, this is an unconscious way of not wanting to deal with the pain and the hurt that they have hidden inside … the only way the walls will ever come down is if participants are willing to begin the journey of introspection in order to first identify the emotions and the effects they have on their lives. If they are fearful of this journey then they are going to have difficulties for the rest of their lives.

Interestingly, she puts a heavy emphasis on the responsibility each person carries to bring himself out of his emotional imprisonment. In her booklet "Living without Violence," she phrases it this way:

Although many things have happened among aboriginal peoples … and it is important that we discuss and see where the problems existed …. we must move forward and take some responsibility for our own actions. Healing can never begin for our self or our communities unless we too take some responsibility for our own actions.

Her focus is on helping people develop an appreciation of *all* the emotions that run through us, not just mad, sad, glad and scared. In fact, she lists 101 separate feelings to be examined during the program. For instance, the column under *mad* contains words like *upset, angry, furious, cold, mortified, outraged, jealous, miserable, deserted, bitter* and *offended*. In her view, people lacking emotional skill sets have never thought about the distinctions between all those "mad" feelings; all that comes out is "mad." This means that they lack the tools to understand the more subtle dimensions of their feelings, and the ability to trace them to particular events or kinds of behaviour. Until they learn that kind of tracing and develop the skills to respond with particularity, they just "get mad." That too often leads to violence, because it is raw emotion that explodes then, generalized anger that isn't tied to particular events and is for that reason unmanageable. It just builds up as "mad" until someone or something causes that accumulated anger to explode.

Over the course of her program, people are presented with various scenarios and asked to imagine what the characters felt. As the group discussions progress, more and more of those 101 feelings are brought out and distinguished from one another. As time passes, people begin to develop the emotional vocabulary that permits them to join in more nuanced understandings and discussions about emotional reactions. Often, when it is expected that certain materials will prompt deep emotional responses, discussion is delayed to allow people to settle down, and they are instead given the chance to do things like beadwork, drawing, singing, dancing or making collages to discharge or articulate whatever they felt.

She places heavy reliance on the traditional Teaching that each of us has four dimensions: the physical, the mental (which she calls the psychological), the emotional and the spiritual, calling them "The Four Rooms" that everyone has. Early in her program, everyone is asked to list on a flip chart the kinds of things that people put in each of those rooms. In the Physical Room, for instance, people will put things like what they look like, whether they look like a "half-breed," and whether they have to explain their identity even to their own people, simply because their hair is too light or their skin colour is a little different from that of the brother or sister sitting beside them. In the Psychological Room, people list things like whether they attended residential school or are a product of residential school, whether child welfare or the Sixties Scoop was part of their life, and the same with other potential sources of conflict, such as youth detention centres, colonization, alcoholism, assimilation, drug addictions, abandonment and both physical and sexual child abuse. The Emotional Room is often described as the place where we hide our negative feelings like low self-esteem, frustration, boredom, anger, hate, confusion, hurt, embarrassment, shame, depression, loneliness, jealousy, anxiety, rage, guilt, lack of trust, and so on. Finally, the Spiritual Room is often described as nearly empty, lacking things like native language abilities, support from aboriginal communities and the Teachings themselves. The purpose is to see the kinds of things that go in each room. People are then instructed as follows:

> We should be aware of what is in each of our own rooms and what needs tidying up. It is also important that these rooms get visited every day and that one room should never be visited longer than another. If we want harmony in our lives we must visit each equally.

A series of questions then follows: What rooms did you find were most cluttered? Were there any rooms you couldn't get into? If you could get in, did you look to see what was hidden? Did you look deep enough? What else did you find? Was it a surprise? Were you honest with yourself? After assessing our rooms, where do you think those things came from? Why are some rooms harder to visit than others? If you found nothing, why do you think that is?

It's not hard to see how such questions get people digging into their own situations and histories, and starting to trace their own development.

People are also given assignments after each day's sessions. These are aimed at getting them to describe what they saw or felt as the session progressed. Here is how the tasks are described:

> Assignments will be given each day where people will be asked to write a poem, draw a picture, tell a story or cut out pictures to create a collage of something for that particular

session. They will then have their creative pictures at the end of the session … participants must learn to look at themselves in order to be able to heal from the past and begin to look at a brighter future not only for themselves but for their community.

For instance, in one part of the program, the topic was violence, and the group was asked to consider the following kinds of questions:

How would you define violence? What do you think are the different types of violence? What kinds of violence do you see (a) in your community and (b) in society in general? How would you describe residential schools? What were some of the outcomes of residential schools? Would someone like to volunteer and tell a story of their personal experience from residential schools? How do you think those things have contributed to violence in aboriginal communities? What stands out most for you in today's session?

Then, at the start of the next session, after people have produced their assignments, the following kinds of questions are asked:

What does violence look like to you? Was this assignment difficult to do? Why or why not? What was the hardest part to do? How did you feel when doing this assignment? What was the main theme of your assignment? Does this affect your life? How?

As I said, Peggy uses many fictional scenarios to prompt emotional reaction and encourage discussion. Some are whimsical traditional stories about animals that strive to make certain points. Others are less metaphorical and very tragic, but describe events likely familiar to most aboriginal people—including a poem about a three-year-old who is ultimately killed by her abusive, drunken father. Some of them are short poems, some are longer stories, and some are newspaper articles about real events in aboriginal communities that cause people to think more deeply about their own lives.

At one point in the program, everyone is instructed to spend the evening, without distractions, watching the powerful movie *Once Were Warriors*, about a deeply troubled Maori family in New Zealand. Because it is expected that the movie will trigger the recollection of similar violence in almost everyone present, there is no discussion at all the next morning; many people are likely to be too upset for safe discussion. Instead, everyone is asked to work on whatever crafts they feel will best let them handle and express what they saw in the movie. Great care is taken to make sure people are not moved too quickly into their own horrors, and no one is required to say anything about their own lives, though most often they do. When people are later asked how they respond to such crisis situations, their responses are listed for everyone to think about. Peggy describes the purpose of making those lists:

What you are trying to do here is (ask) if people drink, hit others (for example their children, their partners, the dog, the police officer, etc.), become emotionally abusive, blame others, emotionally fall apart, etc.... This is the part where you begin creating patterns so that eventually participants will begin recognizing their own patterns and want to change them. There is a difference (between) someone telling you to change and wanting to change yourself.

It is critical to repeat that no one has to say a single word about events in their own lives that may have been brought into consciousness by the fictional scenarios put to them. As Peggy told me, "Their stories are their own. If they choose to share them with us, that's fine, but we won't pressure them at all." The central goal, after all, is to help them find coherent ways to tell their own stories to themselves. One man hardly said a word during the entire program but called Peggy six months later to describe how he now felt so free because of it.

This insistence reflects a bedrock principle of aboriginal life: people must be free to find their own paths through the Great Mystery. The goal of the discussions is to help people move into more particularized awareness of their own emotional lives by helping them develop more nuanced tracings of their own emotional reactions to events. Only then can they begin to control how their emotional stories unfold in the future. They are also given traditional Teachings about how to handle their most deeply felt emotions. For instance, they are given detailed Ojibway Teachings about the six other ways to discharge grief or anger besides talking: singing, dancing, sweating, crying, yelling and praying. Ceremonies that encourage using all paths leading to emotional discharge and rededication to stronger lives are also encouraged.

It is Peggy's hope that everyone will slowly gain the skill sets necessary to understand the life path they have followed thus far. Until they do, Peggy believes it is unlikely they will be able to change its direction.

In their paper "Moving Towards Healing: A Nunavut Case Study," researchers Christopher Fletcher and Aaron Denham see something similar in Inuit healing approaches:

> [Inuit] healing is also a question of organizing life experiences into a coherent and functional sequence; of getting things into "their proper places ... like a puzzle." The fragmentation of self and of one's social relationships is a potential consequence

of a painful or traumatic past experience. The need for healing is often recognized by the identification of such fragmentation.... The separation of one's body, emotions, and spirit ... necessitates unification, a placing of things back into their proper places. For the individual, healing is recognized as occurring with the unification of the separated facets of self and upon being able to properly locate or position misplaced experiences.[13]

As we have seen, that is exactly what Peggy's program attempts to do. As proof of its potential, even for non-aboriginal people, Lampton County Council in southwestern Ontario asked Peggy to work with fifteen people who had been struggling with addiction, abuse, poverty and violence. After her involvement, fourteen of them had become addiction free, eleven returned to school, three found employment and got off social assistance, and one person regained custody of a child. Lampton County reviewed the results and funded a second program for others.

I want to stress something one more time: no one in her program has to name names or tell stories about things that happened in their families. They can if they want, but they don't have to. In my view, this is a substantial benefit, because so many people are carrying secrets of abuse, and they want them to remain secret.

I recall, for instance, a case of spousal abuse in a remote community. After the husband pleaded guilty, I met with him and his wife because they wanted to talk about counselling. I mentioned that their own community had a mental health worker who did that kind of work. They answered that they wouldn't work with her, because they were worried about the things they told her becoming known in the community. I then told them about a psychologist I knew from Sioux Lookout who might be happy to counsel them when he came into the community on his monthly visits. They thought about that and then asked where the records of his visit would be kept. As far as I knew, they would be kept in the community at the nursing station. On hearing that, they said that this also presented too much of a danger. They wanted to discuss the many things in their lives that had driven their relationship into its present state, and that meant talking about relatives on both sides, and about what they had done to them over the years. But they didn't want what they said to ever get out to anyone, much less those particular relatives.

I should have known. As I indicated earlier, many leading members of northern communities estimate that fully 80 percent of all adults in some communities either were sexually abused as children or sexually abused others themselves. Many carried both kinds of secrets, and they wanted them to remain secrets. That couple felt totally trapped, knowing that they needed to honestly deal with events from their past, but knowing, as well, that such discussions had to remain private.

Even when the healing process is going to take place far away, the worry that stories will get back to the home community remains. I remember a shocking illustration of that dynamic. One of the remote communities in my region had fallen prey to regular violence among its young adults, and two outside social workers had been called in to see what they could do. When we flew in to hold court one day, those workers met us at the airport and asked if they could talk to the judge and me before court. When we got together, they told us about sixteen young men they had been working with, all of whom faced a number of serious charges on the docket that day. They had managed to uncover signs of sexual abuse from years before, abuse that the workers felt was behind the youths' explosions of violence. They had then contacted a treatment centre in Alberta that specialized in sexual abuse, and had gotten funding from the community's Chief and council to send all sixteen of them out for the five-week program. They asked us if we would consider adjourning their cases to the next court so the boys could go into counselling in Alberta.

I suspect that the two social workers were a little surprised at how excited their proposal made the judge and me. "Finally someone is really getting at the issues and doing something about them!" we said. In fact, we were so excited that we called all sixteen boys up to the front during court and told the community about the plan and how happy we were to see it taking shape. As I recall, we even brought the two social workers up to the front to congratulate them, and we urged everyone else in the community to join them in their wonderful healing initiative.

Two weeks later the judge called and asked to meet me. He told me he had received a telephone call from the workers, and the news wasn't good. The Chief and council had called them in after the court had left. They asked where the boys were being sent. They were told the name of the healing lodge. The next question was what they were going there for. The answer was to talk about many things in their past that were bothering them. The Chief and council asked what kinds of things. The workers answered that they had begun to talk about sexual abuse, and that the healing specialized in helping people deal with that issue. Shortly after that discussion, the Chief and council withdrew the funding and fired both social workers. The boys would not get into healing.

The judge and I both knew what the Chief and council were worried about. Who knows how many people were involved in the abuse of those sixteen boys? If those boys all started talking, naming names, and that naming got back to the community, the result would be chaos. When the boys came back, there would be hell to pay. Far better just to keep everything quiet.

To be honest, neither the judge nor I could blame them. Past abuse is so widespread in some communities, and the fear of disclosure so deep, that unless the community has built its own plan to handle it, that disclosure might cause untold disruption and violence. Unlike Hollow Water, the community had no plan, and no idea how to start one. All they could do was hunker down. It was so dispiriting.

It is such a common constraint on healing. James Waldram discusses it as follows:

> Confidentiality is also an issue, as sometimes a client will not engage with an Elder who is part of his or her extended family or otherwise known to the client. "But the Elders back in my community," said one client, "I don't want them because I know the Elders and they know me and ... I don't open up as I would if [it was] somebody else."[14]

Dr. Kirmayer points out that the problem goes beyond having faith in confidentiality and extends to the burden such confidentiality puts on the people who must absorb those stories:

> There is little opportunity for the sort of anonymity that protects the practitioners' professional role in large cities. This anonymity has both ethical and practical uses: it provides privacy and safety for clients who wish to talk about embarrassing matters and it allows the helper to have some respite from being constantly "on call." In small communities, helpers are often related to the people they are helping and have no way to step back from their role; this can rapidly lead to "burn out."[15]

Perhaps that's why Peggy Shaughnessy's RedPath Program is so successful: people are taken deeply into their own histories without ever having to reveal them to others. I sense that many of the people

I have dealt with are carrying lengthy histories of abuse at the hands of others, so lengthy and serious that disclosure would have a substantial ripple effect within their families and communities. I know for a fact that the courts could not handle all the charges that would emerge if everyone were to disclose every offence committed against them.

We know that aboriginal healing goals don't require blaming, and perhaps they can do without naming as well. It may just be that creating a detailed and coherent—but privately held—personal life story is the best way in the most troubled communities. I know that Hollow Water insists on bringing all parties touched by each situation of abuse out into the open, often bringing them together to speak of what they've endured and how they'd like things to change, but that complexity may just be too great for many communities. For them, simply getting people in touch with their own hurts and fears, then learning how to manage the emotions that come to the surface, may have to be enough.

Quite apart from its potential to offer healing opportunities to people trapped within their own emotional deadness, Peggy's program must be seen as a critical step in raising children. Their parents may not be able to model such emotional maturity, but it must come from somewhere if the emotional suppression of previous generations is to be avoided by future ones. One small community in British Columbia, the Seabird Island First Nation, has recognized the importance of bringing children into emotional maturity, and has used funding from the national Aboriginal Head Start Program to give children the emotional skill that they will need as they grow into adulthood.

That being said, I have to point out that Peggy Shaughnessy's program suffers from having to spend so much time and energy simply trying to squeeze into the funding criteria of government programs, and it must do so repeatedly as funding is often only for a short time. The RedPath Program has had to offer five "different" programs to satisfy five different government agencies: the Child and Youth Program; the Emotion Management Program; the Addictions Treatment Program; the Living without Violence Program; and the Pre-employment Program. All of those RedPath programs identify the same ultimate causes of problems and use the same healing processes to overcome them; they just have to be named differently to qualify for funding from various government sources.

That issue was identified as a major problem for all healing programs by four researchers, Phil Lane Jr., Michael Bopp, Judie Bopp and Julian Norris. In their paper "Mapping the Healing Journey," they report that the Eskasoni First Nation registered the following complaint:

> There are many small pots of money and we have to act like a chameleon—always changing the appearance of our mandate in order to get funding. These funds include Building Healthy Communities, NNADAP, The Healing Foundation and Brighter Futures. But there is no core funding that supports the essential long-term work of building and maintaining a coherent initiative.[16]

Dr. Kirmayer has identified the same challenge in dealing with government, but takes the impact of that structural failure even further:

> Some of the structural problems faced by communities result from government policies and administrative practices, notably the segmentation of policies, programs and services that aim to address issues of mental health, substance abuse, social services, corrections and other social problems that

are all aspects of the same underlying social problems. This artificial separation of practices and professions, aggravated by conflicts over jurisdictions, has wreaked havoc with Aboriginal communities.[17]

In fact, it might not be unfair to call those government structures another form of colonization. The western determination to consistently break things down into ever-more-specialized areas of expertise means that funding structures follow the same specialist preference. As a result, holistic aboriginal visions must also be broken down into smaller segments, even though it is holistic healing that is seen as essential.

Nevertheless, Peggy has prevailed so far, and seems determined to offer her program wherever she can find a certain number of people interested in taking her training back into their communities. I am inspired by her work and amazed by her success, especially when considering the obstacles before her.

I KNOW THAT I HAVE only briefly described these three programs. I hope, however, that I have made my central point: they are all founded on the belief that healing must engage in bringing back the traditional Teachings. Those Teachings restore the spiritual centre of what colonization took away. I repeat once again the assertion made by the Hollow Water First Nation that appeared at the beginning of this book: "Much of what used to be described as 'healing' is now viewed as 'decolonization therapy' by the Community Holistic Circle Healing Team."

More fundamentally, though, there is the absolute conviction that those Teachings are, in themselves, the best guidelines for how to live a life that is, in all respects, a healthy one. As I said earlier, a healthy aboriginal life is not at all the same as a healthy western life. As a result, aboriginal healing programs will try to take people to different places, and they will use very different processes. In the next chapter, I'll describe what I see as twelve areas of significant variation between aboriginal and western practices. Although I will point to all twelve distinct features of aboriginal healing programs, it is clear that those principles all work together, and they all serve to promote the single, holistic goal of helping people establish right relations. It is my hope that pulling them out for separate discussion will underline just how different aboriginal and western approaches really are.

CHAPTER 11

ABORIGINAL HEALING: TWELVE STRIKING DIFFERENCES

THE SPECIAL FOCUS ON SPIRIT

I hope I have made clear how significant it is that aboriginal Teachings take a holistic view of human beings, insisting that constant attention be paid to their physical, mental, emotional and spiritual dimensions. Non-aboriginal medical specialists seem to agree that there are complex connections between our physical, mental and even emotional dimensions, but I have seldom seen any real discussion among western practitioners of the role of our spiritual dimension.

I suspect that when many non-aboriginal people hear about the spiritual component of healing, they think of either voodoo-like practices or loyalty to a particular religious institution. I had the same impression until my first sweat lodge, where the keeper told me that if I found anything I felt comfortable with, I could "take it home" with me, and if there was anything I was not comfortable with, well, I could just leave it there with him. It was a deliberately nondenominational experience that was open to everyone, no matter whom we prayed to or even *if* we prayed.

One dimension of spirituality involves connecting people to forces larger than themselves and giving them a role within that greater scheme of things. In my first sweat lodge, the themes and songs and prayers took me out of myself and into an emotional sense of connection to the people, patterns, forces and entities surrounding me. This sense of discovery and connection to larger forces seems to be a central part of traditional spiritual practices, whether in naming ceremonies that cement particular relationships and responsibilities, or vision quests that demand putting yourself in the hands of those greater forces and, in the process, learning to see yourself as a humble, grateful participant in a spirit-centred universe.

Traditional spiritual Teachings are critical because they aim specifically at restoring a conviction of meaningful participation in an interconnected and spirit-centred world. Within aboriginal thinking, we are all sacred beings, sharing identical spirit with all other aspects of Creation. With hard work we can manifest that spirit to greater degrees, building stronger, more respectful relationships. It is a strength-based vision that emphasizes the spiritual gifts and responsibilities we were given, and our duty to honour both.

Western therapy often seems, by contrast, weakness based, focusing on what's wrong with us. Instead of offering hope to pull us forward, it too often dwells on the fear of falling even further into illness. The two therapies seem to rely on fundamentally different motivators.

What most non-aboriginal people haven't considered is that the recent history of aboriginal people has been, first and foremost, one of forced disconnection from their families, languages, lands, traditions, social structures and beliefs. Ensuing generations then became mired in poverty, social marginalization and emotional turmoil, becoming further alienated from any conviction of positive significance. Far too many people have been left just where residential school put them, distant from any sense of healthy connection or meaningful contribution. One counsellor in an aboriginal treatment centre captured that need for spiritual reconnection in a discussion with medical anthropologist James Waldram:

> I have discovered that Aboriginal clients look for Aboriginal thinking, feeling, and the Aboriginal spirit in the person they are talking to, and if they don't find it, they close off just as quickly if that person's face is brown or white or green. So, a non-Aboriginal person can work with an Aboriginal client if they have respect for the Aboriginal value system, if they have knowledge of it and respect it. If they don't, the best you can hope for is that they would deal with the mind only and not go into the heart and certainly [not] into the spirit. That kind of therapy, which is based on the mind only, isn't worth very much in my opinion.[1]

This much is clear: spiritual Teachings and experiences form the starting point in aboriginal healing, and they have virtually no present role in western therapies.

THE DEFINITION OF A "HEALTHY PERSON"

Following from that spiritual connection with all aspects of Creation, human beings are recognized as, fundamentally, the sum of all their relationships within Creation, whether with other people, birds, animals, trees, rocks or rivers. A healthy person is thus someone who understands that he is a nested component of that complex web of interconnections, who acknowledges fundamental dependence upon them, who is aware that he has been given significant responsibilities within those responsibilities and who is determined to fulfill them as best he can. His "self" interest is perhaps better understood as his "other" or "all" interest. That vision is deeply embedded in aboriginal languages, practices, ceremonies and psyches. Western therapies promoting individual self-definition, self-assertion and self-promotion will feel improper to aboriginal people, and may be met with pronounced resistance.

Carol Hopkins spoke to that issue at one of the NNADAP renewal forums, stressing that, in aboriginal understandings of healing, "the client is the individual plus his or her family and community." She also identified a treatment goal as seeking "reconnection to family and others." In the same vein, the director of a treatment facility for solvent-sniffing aboriginal youth, Debra Dell, explained that "their wishes for a life post-treatment revolve around connection with family, with other people and the land."

I contrast this with how Judith Herman sees the goal of western therapy:

> The community activists Evan Stark and Anne Flitcraft state as their therapeutic goal with battered women the restoration of autonomy and empowerment. They define autonomy as "a sense of separateness, flexibility, and self-possession sufficient to define one's self-interest ... and make significant choices," while empowerment is "the convergence of mutual support with individual autonomy."[2]

In my view, aboriginal healers would not support "a sense of separateness ... sufficient to define one's self-interest" as a successful healing outcome. In fact, the opposite is more likely. Recall that I mentioned the contrasting hierarchies within Creation, where the western hierarchy puts humans at the top, in place to rule everything else, while the aboriginal hierarchy puts them at the bottom, as the most dependent creature in Creation. As a result, the first responsibility people have is to establish good spiritual relations with everything else, making accommodations at every turn to accomplish the greatest health of everything. But if aboriginal people see life as an interconnected bundle of responsibilities, western psychology sees instead a collection of autonomous rights against all other life forms. It seeks the creation of individual attributes like autonomy, initiative, competence and identity, while aboriginal healers seek relational values like openness, sharing, humility and respect. Aboriginal healing thus helps to establish healthy reconnection to family, community and all of Creation.

Dr. Kirmayer speaks about the impact of that interconnected view on the structure of therapy:

> The cultural concept of the person that underwrites most forms of psychotherapy is based on Euro-American values of individualism. This individualistic and egocentric concept of the person can be contrasted with more sociocentric, ecocentric or cosmocentric views, which understand the person in relation to the social world, the environment, and the cosmos.... Power and status are measured not by the individual's mastery of the environment but by his ability to calmly acquiesce and adjust to a shifting world. Dependency may be viewed as a sign of relatedness and acknowledgement of the importance of others from whom one draws self-worth. The value of the person lies not in his uniqueness or separateness but in his relatedness to a larger social entity.[3]

Western and aboriginal therapies thus have different, if not contradictory, goals. That may explain why western therapies are often met with pronounced resistance. I think it's worth repeating how Joe Couture articulated the difference:

> A traditional native sense-of-self may find a relentless focus on self as alien, disquieting, undesirable or unnecessary. Rather, a general Aboriginal self is one of an "embedded, enfolded

socio-centric self.".... Native mind is therefore a mind-in-relational activity, a mind-in-community.[4]

In my view, it is only natural to expect that a different definition of a healthy person will require different healing approaches built upon different kinds of Teachings.

THE RELIANCE ON GROUP HEALING

It should come as no surprise, then, that most aboriginal healing involves working with groups of people together, not single patients, and aims to return all of them to useful roles within Creation. Nor should we be surprised to discover that different definitions of a healthy person call for different healing environments.

For instance, American psychologists Rachel Goldsmith and Jennifer Freyd explain how western psychology sees the relationship between the western therapist and his or her patient: "Therapeutic relationships that provide safety and validation for a range of emotional experiences contrasts with clients' experiences of abuse and neglect, and can facilitate emotional awareness."[5] With respect to safety, I question whether sitting with a single, impartial, professional therapist would feel safer than sitting with a group of other people who have gone through exactly what you have. At every step they would know how you feel and how they should (and should not) approach you. With respect to validation, I find myself asking who might be in a better position to validate someone's swirling emotions: that single therapist observing strict professional boundaries that prohibit personal engagement, or multiple victims who have lived through similar experiences? In their paper "Moving Towards Healing: A Nunavut Case Study," researchers Christopher Fletcher and Aaron Denham report what an Inuit man involved in group healing told them:

So I can share my own [Inuit] stories, you know. I think that's the thing about healing, the way we have done, is sharing your stories in a way that one person heals. But, by hearing somebody else's story, it may also give other people hope or give them something else to think about, a different way of seeing something. If we all felt very ashamed about being sexual abuse victims and there was nobody else to tell us otherwise, and we would always feel ashamed. So it's very good to hear people's stories as they're healing and going through the different stages of healing.[6]

Then there is the dynamic called *transference* that Judith Herman feels is especially challenging in western therapy. She describes it this way:

The patient enters therapy in need of help and care. By virtue of this fact, she voluntarily submits herself to an unequal relationship in which the therapist has superior status and power. Feelings related to the universal childhood experience of dependence on a parent are inevitably aroused. Those feelings, known as transference, further exaggerate the power imbalance in the therapeutic relationship.[7]

When the therapist is not a single person but a circle of people sharing similar experiences and never assuming superior status or power, I have to wonder whether the issue of transference is simply avoided. When I spent time in healing circles, I never had the impression that one person was directing the show. The circle leader merely set out the themes and then let everyone speak to them as they wished. Nor did the circle leader ever try to sum up what had been said; everyone's words stood on their own. Here is how one man in treatment described the experience to Joseph Gone:

I never really showed anyone in the group the real me. Showed my feelings. I'm always trying to be like, "I'm strong, you can't hurt me, nothing has hurt me." No one knows the kind of guy I was, always trying to keep a straight face, like [I'm] really strong, not to show any emotion or anything like that. But it taught me how to express that, and express how I really felt inside me and bring it out, and that really helped. It took a lot of weight out of my shoulders and I felt lightened after that, when I was finally able to cry in front of people without even being ashamed or stuff like that, without even being shy. It just went to show that I'm human, just like everybody else.[8]

Hearing words such as these makes me ask another question: Does the aboriginal preference for group work not give people a greater experience of being open and honest with others? When people begin to make important self-discoveries, and begin to form new ways of relating to the world around them, would they not find it easier to expose those new dimensions to the world out there after already going through that experience within the healing circle itself? It might be one thing to expose your weaknesses or your tentative, emerging self to a single therapist, but the rest of the world remains outside—and frightening. Who emerges from the healing process with more confidence—the person who has only shared with a single, professional healer or the person who has already shown his true self to a circle of other people?

Judith Herman also speaks to another critical issue, that of trust between the therapist and patient. She seems to feel that it isn't easily won:

Though the traumatized patient feels a desperate need to rely on the competence and integrity of the therapist, she cannot do so, for her capacity to trust has been damaged by the traumatic experience.... She may attribute to the therapist many of the same motives as the perpetrator. She often suspects the therapist of exploitive or voyeuristic intentions.... The dynamics of dominance and submission are re-enacted in all subsequent relationships, including the therapy.[9]

In my experience, the dynamics in aboriginal healing circles are about as far from dominance and submission as you can get, reflecting instead the core values of humility, respect and equality. While members tell their own stories when they are able, there is no issue of control, nor any sense that the storytelling is encouraged for voyeuristic reasons. People are simply doing their best to describe themselves to others, in the hope that all might learn. As one former student told Lee Brown:

I think that a lot of the talking circles that we had [involved] ... being able to share without fear of being judged.... just learning about the emotional being and the psychological being ... of us as human beings. Learning about all of that and how it works, how to start to heal those hurts, was so beneficial.[10]

Storytelling circles encourage group exploration of feelings, struggles, hopes, fears, satisfactions and strategies for recovery. As feelings are discussed, their shades and subtleties are explored and expressed, leading to deeper understandings of how each person has experienced the world. In the process, all are jointly developing the *language* of emotion that they need to capture those nuances, even if only for themselves. As their explorations penetrate more deeply, each person begins to experience what safe relationships feel like, what it's like to trust others to not abuse what you share with them. Long-suppressed pain, fear and anger can be allowed to come to the surface. As they listen to one another, they begin to understand that it is not abnormal to feel the way they do. As they see that others are moving forward on their healing journeys, they begin to develop the critical belief that recovery is possible for them, too. And when they see that others have had to find their own paths to recovery, within their own realities, they begin to plot their own and gain the belief that they can. At every step of the way, the circle says, "You can!" It is clearly a strength-based approach if ever there was one.

There is a further dimension to group work that I have seen on several occasions: putting an offender in a circle with a group of victims who have suffered not from his actions but from the similar acts of others. Offenders seem more willing to participate in groups where none of the participants were involved in his particular crime at all, perhaps because they know that their own acts of violence will not be part of the discussion. As various victims begin to speak, however, a change occurs. As they discuss common kinds of injury, fear, anger, helplessness and so on, you can almost see the offender beginning to realize that his victims would feel the same as these people in the circle. And as the victims also speak of how long they have carried their pain, the offender begins to ask himself if his own victim is still suffering the way they are. As the discussion proceeds, there is a much better chance that he'll let his victim's pain inside him, hearing it through the voices of others. Most offenders don't understand the emotional impact of what they have done. They cling to the belief that everyone is making a mountain out of a molehill. When they hear a group of people speaking in common terms about how deeply they were affected, that begins to change. In many cases, it suddenly hits them: "Oh my God, I really hurt somebody." That won't happen immediately in cases of serious, long-standing abuse, but it will happen eventually, once the stories start to really sink in. This emotional response, in my view, may be less likely when offenders are in the hands of single therapists who have not gone through such victimization, and would not be permitted to speak of it anyway.

Thus far, I have only mentioned aspects of group work that I think would help people from any culture begin to explore their personal emotional burdens and fashion paths back into health. There is, however, a benefit from group work that is specific to aboriginal people coming together as a group: they can begin to explore the full impact of racial oppression in their own lives *as well as* in the lives of their parents and grandparents. By entering into that discussion, they can begin to understand that their fear, hurt and anger are small parts of a much larger dynamic that has touched all aboriginal people, and their sense of personal failure can begin to fade away.

INDIVIDUAL HEALING GROUNDED IN SOCIAL HEALING

In aboriginal healing, there are two reasons to focus on the social aspect. First, the damage was done to the group as a whole. Through all the various colonization forces, the group shares that history. People must be brought to the point where they can begin to recognize that they suffer group trauma, not just individual weakness. Second, communities must join in the healing activities to provide a healthy home. Just as a healthy individual is defined in aboriginal terms as one who understands being interconnected with her relations, family, community and all of Creation, the communities also have a role to play as part of those connections. Researchers Christopher Fletcher and Aaron Denham phrase the relationship this way: "Individual healing is thus a socially situated activity. Framing healing as a social rather than an individual project is an important approach within traditional Inuit social organization where socio-centric renderings of the individual are fundamental to Inuit personhood."[11] While they were discussing Inuit culture, their words certainly apply to other indigenous groups as well. Group discussions are so powerful largely because people begin to recognize how common all of their struggles have been, and how they can, together, start designing a new future. William Mussell, the aboriginal psychologist from British Columbia, emphasizes that point:

> For most learners, the process of discovering or rediscovering their personal and cultural identity was crucial in initiating the journey toward wellness. Developing an understanding of the connections between the historical past and the present was a critical factor in shaping this new sense of identity. The majority of graduates discovered their abilities as critical thinkers, shed negative beliefs about themselves and their cultures, and were empowered as change-agents in both their personal and work lives.[12]

Needless to say, such group discoveries can happen only when the healing is brought not just to individuals, but also to groups of people sharing similar histories. In that sense, group healing may be of much greater importance in an aboriginal context. It may be the only way that self-blame can be minimized and convictions of self-worth can begin to grow. As we have seen, self-worth for aboriginals does not come from a sense of individuality, as it often does in western culture. And, just as self-worth has different roots, so too does emotional health.

Moreover, it is clear that many aboriginal people, especially those who have grown up since the last residential school closed, have almost no idea about all the forces of colonization that have been arrayed against them for the past several centuries. Until that history forms a central part of the Canadian education system, it may have to be presented in healing processes instead, where group consciousness of that history can begin to develop.

And one of the most profound impacts of colonization has to do with forcing children in residential school to bury everything they felt.

RESTORATION OF THE EMOTIONAL REALM

Within western culture, we have separated the mind from the heart, and put the heart in an inferior position. As a child, I remember well being told that I shouldn't let my emotions get in the way of clear thinking, that we are "rational animals" who can control our emotions as we seek truths in whatever we do.

I was therefore interested to see the opposite hierarchy within the aboriginal world, where it is understood that the heart is our primary motivator, and a primary goal ought to be a pure heart. I wrote earlier about Elder Dumont and his assertion that it is the heart that guides the mind's creations by giving them shape, energy and direction. Lee Brown makes a forceful argument for the restoration of traditional Teachings that guided the heart into fullness, and I recall hearing regularly that Elders were powerful speakers because they "spoke from the heart."

When I dug a little deeper into the difference, I discovered that the English word *emotion* comes from the Latin word *emovere*, which translates as "something that sets the mind in motion." That seems to suggest that we once believed, as aboriginal people do today, that the heart takes the leading role. Lee Brown gives another phrasing of the aboriginal understanding of the relationship between the two: "In the medicine wheel philosophy, the mind and the heart are connected. Indeed, the mind and the heart are not only connected, but the heart is the root of the mind."[13]

Lee Brown goes on to suggest that the western determination to stress the mental over the emotional began with the cultural decision, centuries ago, to separate reason from the passions, and to then characterize the passions as dangerous urges that reason must control. Mind became almost the definition of humankind: as Descartes declared, "I think, therefore I am." Interestingly, the current Dalai Lama indicates that in the Tibetan language, there is just one word to capture *both* dimensions, working together, and he had this to say about the western determination to separate one from the other: "My conjecture ... is that, going back to the Enlightenment, even as far back as Aquinas, there is an enormous priority placed upon reason and intelligence. What can impede reason? Emotion. You have two categories that are set in opposition to each other."[14]

Going back a moment to Judith Herman's description of the therapist–patient relationship, she points to the conflict that arises when those two dimensions are set in opposition:

> The therapist's empathic attitude, derived from his emotional understanding of himself and from his transitory identification with, and concern for, the patient, has elements in common with the empathy of the "good-enough mother" with her infant.... There is, however, also a totally rational, cognitive, almost ascetic aspect to the therapist's work with the patient which gives their relationship a completely different quality.[15]

As I read her words, a number of questions occurred to me. How convincing can the "empathic attitude" of the therapist be if he must also maintain that "totally rational, cognitive, almost ascetic aspect" to his work? When he can't join in with his own story? When he can't cry with his patient? Can his "transitory identification with the patient" come close to what is offered in a healing circle by other people sharing their similar experiences of life, and doing so in an emotion-centred context?

I suspect that this greater aboriginal emphasis on the emotional dimension of human beings can be traced to the relational lens. If your eye goes to human relationships, you are examining people's emotional engagement in those relationships. If, by contrast, your eye goes to things and their powers, reason becomes revered as the power that not only sets us apart but also defines us. In their paper "Healing the Generations: Post-Traumatic Stress and the Health Status of Aboriginal Populations in Canada," academic researchers Terry Mitchell and Dawn Maracle write about how this preference plays out in the western medical system:

> Health programs are most often disease-specific, focussing primarily on the physical aspect of an individual rather than the emotional, cultural, mental, and spiritual (holistic) aspects of health. Little or no attention is given to personal and collective histories and related trauma.... A PTSR [post-traumatic stress response] model ... promotes a holistic perspective on health that is consistent with cultural concepts of the Medicine Wheel with its focus on the interaction and balancing of the mind, emotions, spirit, and body.[16]

In the western world, the debate over the roles of the emotional and mental dimensions still puts the mental in a dominant position. It chooses, for instance, to use labels like "emotional *intelligence*" and "*mental* illness," even though the paramount issues are clearly emotional. Central therapies like cognitive-behavioural therapy seem built around the premise that individuals can think their way into different behaviour, rather than experience their way into different relationships. Even the phrases "affective *competencies*," "emotional *literacy*" and "emotional *skill sets*" seem to imply that these can be learned by the mind, when it may be more accurate to suggest that they must be explored first by the heart.

An emphasis on "heart learning" is also reflected in the aboriginal reliance on storytelling. The understanding is that stories about real events first grab the heart, and then the heart sticks them in the mind. Discussion that is restricted to issues or intellectual theorizing, by contrast, tends to bypass the heart altogether. For me, such discussions also stay in my mind for the shortest time, especially when compared to real-life stories like the ones the Elders tell.

It is clear that within aboriginal healing, primary attention is paid not to an intellectual understanding of aboriginal history or the position of individuals within it, but rather to their emotional and spiritual history, and to the emotional skill sets that were seldom developed within that history. Here is what Joseph Gone reports one man telling him about his first smudging ceremony:

> The first time I smudged, it just felt different. My body felt different. All the things in you just went down. You just felt so light. Man, [I] did that and felt better about myself, and I could speak better and say whatever.... You don't think about what you're going to say, you say what you feel. That's what I learned in there too, you don't think from your mind. You just say what you feel, your emotions, how your emotions feel. Your emotion speaks for you.[17]

As the RedPath Program insists, people have little chance of returning to health until they develop coherent emotional pictures of the forces that got them into their present state. And all the goals set out to entice them into healthier decisions rest on their emotional—and spiritual—appeal. The mind seems to consider them "good" only after the heart has made the decision first.

I recall reading a tribute made to a retiring salesman who had "led the pack" during his career. His one piece of advice struck me: "Sell to the heart," he told his followers, "and the heart will seize the mind."

My aboriginal teachers would wonder why that advice was seen as nearly revolutionary!

CEREMONIES AND CATHARSIS

I have already spoken about the grief people carry from all their losses, and the shame that has helped bury it. I have also spoken about how deeply those losses have been buried; the emotional roadblocks to healing are immense. Sometimes those emotional roadblocks just seem to dissolve in group discussions, with a powerful outpouring of emotion. Joseph Gone quotes many people speaking of their first disclosure of past abuse. One of them put it this way:

> I find that pain and that not disclosing is buried inside you. And if you want to keep it there and let it always bother you then that's [your choice]. But if you disclose it, it's your healing. It's your healing, but if you bury it, and don't want to say nothing about it, then it's going to affect your life, I think. It affected mine. The funny thing about mine ... is I had buried it so deep.... And I don't know what happened, but something dug way down inside and triggered for me to just almost bluntly disclose.... I just got very, very emotional, my breathing, everything, shaking all over.... After I had said that [I had been sexually abused], I could have jumped on the fence and flew over the building.[18]

Another person speaking of personal disclosure told him this:

I failed, because I wasn't on the healing journey 'cause I still had unresolved issues. I still had something blocking. Then I started disclosing and I learned [about] myself. [I'd] say the hardest thing I had to disclose was when I was sexually abused by the priest. That was the hardest. I cried. Today when I tell it, I can speak it. Before, I used to cry. So angry ...[19]

Other people seem to find that various ceremonies help them break down those roadblocks. Lee Brown reports what one woman told him about how the smudging ceremony worked for her:

I remember that the first time we burnt sage I cried. I cried and I cried. I remember I was thinking ... that I hadn't cried in a long time ... an overwhelming feeling of tears came and I just wept and I have no idea what happened. During that time I wept for probably two weeks straight. Not constantly, but I used to drive from Merritt to Kamloops. I remember driving and I would be crying, crying going home and crying coming back. I just cried buckets, it was incredible but after it all was over I was ready to learn.[20]

I mentioned earlier the Ojibway Teaching that there are six ways to release grief apart from talking about it: crying, yelling, sweating, singing, dancing and praying. In that one sweat lodge I mentioned where people cried about the suicides of children in their community, all those cathartic ways to release came into play, except for dancing, and they made a powerful combination. In a conversation with Joseph Gone, one man explains the power of the sweat lodge:

Only our cleansing ceremonies, which oftentimes are commonly known as the sweat lodge ceremonies, it's a sacred ceremony, and it addresses all four areas of our being. It cleanses physically, mentally, and emotionally and spiritually. Because in our cleansing ceremonies, as we know them, we have that opportunity to share with one another whatever it is that's bothering us, whatever it is that's not right in our lives, that's hanging over our shoulders, so to speak, or the dark cloud above our heads. It gives us that opportunity to release that there. It gives us the opportunity to share with one another whatever teachings we've acquired in that time of our lives, the teachings that we have that have been passed down to us from our Elders. Oftentimes, if we're sincere about the ceremony itself, we come out of there feeling refreshed in all areas.[21]

The sweat lodge is only one ceremony. There are many others specifically created to permit this discharge of raw emotion. Once again, many of them are done as a group, with anguish being shared. Lee Brown reports on the simple ceremony of opening every day's discussion with a circle in which people describe how they feel as they begin:

There was the opening circle every morning.... People would talk about their lives. That ... never happened before in the schools that I went to. Sometimes people would, it would be their turn to speak and sometimes they would just sit there and cry for fifteen or twenty minutes, half an hour, forty five minutes and nobody would say a word. We would all sit there and be with that person while they discharged.[22]

The aboriginal need to unburden is huge in Canada, but the ceremonies can absorb it. What is needed is support for the spread of the Teachings that can bring those ceremonies properly back to life. Those Teachings cannot be put in books; they are complex, they must be experienced to be understood, and they demand many years of dedicated learning and experience. In my view, learning them is even more demanding than the years of education to become a psychologist. It is the experience of going through those Teachings and ceremonies that really counts.

To be truly learned, the ceremonies also demand mastery of the languages that articulate their fullness. And like any formal education, that too will take time and money. It strikes me as odd that we invest a great deal of money and effort to protect the French language in Canada, but few people ever consider doing the same to preserve indigenous languages. In the simplest terms, don't we owe it to them?

THE UNIQUENESS OF ABORIGINAL HEALERS

Building A Nation (BAN) is a healing program located in downtown Saskatoon, Saskatchewan. The program uses aboriginal ceremonies, cultural traditions and life-skills teaching to help people facing addictions or legal issues, facilitated by counsellors who speak aboriginal languages and are familiar with aboriginal culture. In "Building A Nation: Healing in an Urban Context," James Waldram describes one aspect of that program:

> BAN therapists often begin their work with clients by explaining who they are, not simply as trained individuals, but as individuals who are part of families and communities, who have histories. Frequently, they narrate the stories of their own lives as a means of demonstrating that healing is possible.... Trust, an integral component in the therapeutic encounter, is thus established in part by the therapist

detailing his or her own struggles, providing a model for disclosure.[23]

Joe Couture, the Métis-Cree psychologist, notes the primary difference between the western world's therapist–patient relationship and the aboriginal preference for tradition-based healer–patient relationships:

> There is a level of intimacy and emotional involvement that is deemed necessary and salutary to the eliciting of a positive response. A peculiarity of this ultimate interaction is that the Healer seeks not to "direct," but rather to "facilitate" a process of empowering. [The] healer function is predominantly instrumental and plays out at once on the physical, emotional, mental and spiritual dimensions.[24]

Elders listen in a way that is nonjudgmental, something that is highly valued by people needing their help. In speaking with Joseph Gone, one person defined "a perfect healer": "Ideally, it would be an elderly person who is very personable, who is both an [elder] and a healer, who is very people-oriented, very in-tune with their own culture and their own identity, who is not judgmental."[25] An aboriginal man in NNADAP treatment told James Waldram almost exactly the same thing:

> A good therapist is an individual who has a lot of compassion and empathy. Someone who, I guess, is open-minded … [who] doesn't say you should do this, you should do that, do it this way, do it that way, you know. And it redeems you. It leaves you to think about the issues at hand and how you're going to deal with it. And listening. If you ask them something, they can only sit there and they don't want to

make suggestions. They don't, you know, direct you, say "do this, do that way."[26]

Dr. Judith Herman, the American psychologist who created the complex PTSD diagnosis, appears at first to be in emphatic agreement with the idea that each person must find her own way back to health:

> The first principle of recovery is the empowerment of the survivor. She must be the author and arbiter of her own recovery. Others may offer advice, assistance, affection and care, but not cure. Many benevolent and well-intentioned attempts to assist the survivor founder because this fundamental principle of empowerment is not observed. No intervention that takes power away from the survivor can possibly foster her recovery, no matter how much it appears to be in her immediate best interest.[27]

She goes on to say, however, "Therapy requires a collaborative working relationship in which both partners act on the basis of their implicit confidence in the value and efficacy of persuasion rather than coercion, ideas rather than force, mutuality rather than authoritarian control."

As I read those words, I found myself asking how the therapist's offering of "advice" and "persuasion" fits with achieving the necessary autonomy and empowerment of the survivor. The difference is made clear by the words of another man in addictions treatment talking to Joseph Gone:

> An Elder wouldn't say, "Do this."... He or she will tell you a story, and in that story you have to pick up what it is he's trying to tell you.... So they don't give advice, but they will

just tell you a story and you got to listen. But in a Western style, you listen when they give you suggestions. They suggest in the Western style…. Whereas in the Aboriginal style, they tell a story, and from that story you've got to [figure out] what he's trying to tell you. You've got to pick up words he's trying [to convey], and it's usually done in Cree because it's more meaningful.[28]

As I've said before, there are many paths through the Great Mystery, and it is seen as presumptuous to tell others what paths they should take or what lessons they should draw from any experience. I once thought that Elders were egotistical because they talked only about their own lives and choices, and they refused to give their "objective" opinions about the issues being considered. I now see that, in their view, only an immature person would suggest that he has identified the real issues, has formulated the appropriate theories, and is ready to tell you what you should do.

Aboriginal people also express a preference for healers who are experienced in local culture, history and ceremony so they can bring that awareness and those healing resources to bear. They also speak out against our western insistence on having therapists who will not bring their own lives into the discussion. Christopher Fletcher and Aaron Denham report this about the Inuit healing experience:

The healing model adopted by the community members did not employ strict distinctions between healers/counsellors and those being healed. Instead, a continuum of role and practice was acknowledged. Healers were also individuals on their own healing journey … perhaps the most significant difference emanates from the relative lack of distinction between healer and sufferer in this program.[29]

The uniqueness of aboriginal history may explain part of it, but it is clear that aboriginal people want to work with healers who have had almost identical experiences. A BAN client explained to James Waldram, "The reason why I could never go see a non-Aboriginal therapist is because they could never walk in my shoes. They never experienced that, so how can they relate to what I'm talking about if they haven't experienced it? And that's a big thing."[30]

Finally, aboriginal people would simply prefer to work with other aboriginal people because of an overall difference in the life experiences each group has known. One person told Joseph Gone about her session with a non-aboriginal counsellor:

> But she was white. I wasn't comfortable talking to her. It's not that I'm prejudiced or anything, it's just that I know that she can't understand what [life is like for me]. I know she's a counsellor. I know she's educated and whatnot. I know she been going to school. She should know [how best to] diagnose me, but deep down, I figure she doesn't know how we are. She's white, I'm Native. I talked to her about three times, and I cancelled all the rest of my appointments with her because I wasn't really compatible with her.[31]

It is not the case, however, that non-aboriginal therapists and psychologists are automatically excluded from the healing role. I know of several who have immersed themselves in traditional Teachings, and many of them have quietly expressed a preference for aboriginal approaches. Some have taken themselves into traditional ceremonies and emerged from them convinced of the wisdom of those ancient ways. They are welcomed into aboriginal healing processes and are forming wonderful partnerships.

In short, aboriginal healing is primarily nonhierarchical, with little to distinguish the healer from the person being healed. There are no professional boundaries that require exclusion of the healer's private life. Healers are free to share as they wish, and they do. Because many have travelled exactly the road their clients find themselves on, their sympathies are not synthetic or kept at a distance. They are real and present. When their clients speak with hesitation, they recall that feeling and know how to respond. They have a visceral, experiential knowledge that gives them understanding, patience and, when needed, exactly the right words to move things forward. The notion of a healer who is only professionally involved is seen as a barrier to the task of reconnection. The two therapies aim at different healer–client relationships, with the aboriginal version based on mutual respect for common experience in life. It seems clear to me which approach works best, at least for aboriginals, and perhaps for everyone else, too.

I should also point out that Health Canada has helped create a group of about five hundred aboriginal people from across Canada who are well versed in colonization, especially the residential school component, and in traditional ways of healing. They were required to help survivors who came before the Truth and Reconciliation Commission to tell their residential school stories, and they have demonstrated admirable knowledge, sensitivity and determination. There are clearly not enough formally trained psychologists to assist in First Nations healing. Even if there were, their lack of familiarity with aboriginal philosophy and healing would disentitle them from acting. However, these aboriginal healers are ready, able and willing. If they were pulled together after the TRC completes its work and reassigned to permanent healing roles in their communities, the results would, in my view, be amazing. I met perhaps fifty of them, and each experience was wonderful. To fail to use their gifts in their communities would be a terrible waste.

RESPECT FOR THE WORTH OF EVERYONE

The aboriginal vision of human beings suggests that with hard work we can nurture our spirit, learn to recognize our gifts and begin to honour our responsibilities. The healer's wish is to emphasize what we can become, because it is within us already. In many ways, it is a vision that is similar to that expressed by a Buddhist monk who often travels with, and translates for, the Dalai Lama: "Since the potential for actualizing Buddhahood is present in every sentient being, the Buddhist approach is therefore closer to the idea of original goodness than that of original sin."[32]

I suggest that a similar perspective, the idea of "original goodness," is evident within aboriginal thought. On many occasions I have been reminded by aboriginal people that it is always necessary to separate a person from his acts. Those acts may be harmful, and in that sense they will be judged as contributing or not contributing to harmony, but the person is an entirely separate issue. It is assumed that we are all good, and we were all put on Mother Earth to contribute to Creator's grand design. Some of us may be able to contribute greatly, but some of us may have been burdened by forces too powerful to resist at particular times. We must all help those people overcome the forces arrayed against them, and help them move toward fulfilling their implicit promise of contribution. As I sense it, that is why it is understood that everyone, each one of us, is on the same healing path, with all of us moving forward into greater manifestation of the goodness that we were born into. It's just that some of us face greater challenges than others, and need more help than others. So it is that the expression "original goodness" seems to fit aboriginal notions of who we really are and what we can become: we are all gifted with the potential to be strong creators of harmony in our relations with all of Creation, though few of us will ever achieve anything close to full relational harmonies.

I don't sense that same strength-based focus in western therapy, although that may be changing. At the moment, we seem to focus most of our attention on our deficits, faults and failures, not our potential. The western premise seems to be that all of us must be on constant guard against our own weaknesses, to make sure they don't catch us and drag us further down. In *Dancing with a Ghost*, I wondered if this emphasis came out of the churches and their doctrine of the original sin, a vision in which we begin our life as sinners and spend the rest of it trying to resist "natural" urges toward more sinful behaviour. If so, the contrast with aboriginal visions of being born into sacredness, goodness and kindness is striking—and it shows in how healers work with their clients. They use all their Teachings to convince people that they carry Creator's promise and are capable of many wonderful contributions to Creator's world. They just need to unburden themselves of negatives and learn how to bring out the positives that are within them.

For that reason, everyone resists making negative characterizations of other people. It is almost a rule: do not label people in negative terms. In Hollow Water, for instance, there is no such person as "the offender"; instead, there is the person who has caused harm. Similarly, there is no such person as "the victim"; there is, instead, the person who suffered harm. I recall an Elder once asking the court, "How can you call someone 'bad' and then expect them to be good?" One man in addictions treatment told Joseph Gone, "Labelling myself as an alcoholic, as a drug addict, to me, honestly, was uncomfortable. In Pisimweyapiy Counselling Centre you don't have to label yourself. You come in here and you learn from what they have to teach you."[33]

A therapist in an aboriginal treatment centre made the same distinction between western and aboriginal healing processes in conversation with James Waldram:

We get a lot of people that come here and tell us that they have been to a non-Aboriginal therapist and this is what they told him and it breaks their heart to hear the non-Aboriginal assessment of their mentality, of the type of individual that they are. It really, really hurts them to get judged and to be told that this is what they are. And a lot of times what happens is those people find their way over here and they tell us, and they cry and they hurt because they are told they are a bad parent or this assessment that they got told them that they are crazy.... We have the Medicine Wheel to help us stabilize our way of thinking and ... using sage or sweetgrass to smudge and to calm us down so that we are seeking with the proper memory in regards to the individual feeling that they ... don't know who they are, they are crazy people.[34]

As I mentioned, people's acts are carefully separated from their being, so that their identities remain grounded in the potential for growth and contribution. This choice is even reflected in aboriginal languages, because they refrain from creating long lists of judgmental nouns like *criminal, psychopath, fool, freak* or *failure*. In fact, I don't recall ever hearing anyone in a healing circle offer a diagnosis of any kind. There was no description of people being obsessive-compulsive or a manic-depressive or a psychopath. What they will say, instead, is that he is working his way through such-and-such events, or that he is rebuilding his self-esteem, or he is facing the results of his violence toward others. The description always goes either to acts and events or goals to be sought. It does not go toward negative characterization of the person himself.

As I suggested earlier, people who cause harm are understood to have somehow learned to see relationships as being based on values like power, secrecy, manipulation, fear and control. The healing challenge, therefore, involves not trying to change *the person*, but helping that person change her way of relating so that it rests instead on values like openness, generosity, caring and respect. In other words, it is the way of relating that is assessed and judged, not the person. Given the driving presumption that everyone is capable of learning new ways of relating, it is critical that people not be defined by a particular act.

Many offenders, I suspect, have been pushed into a sense of isolation from the meaningful world, and being negatively labelled helps cement that perception. They often develop a deep-seated conviction that they are, in themselves, wholly without worth. Many see no role for themselves except for being used at the whim of others. While the western world refers to this as a lack of *self*-esteem, I suspect that the aboriginal phrasing would instead somehow describe a lack of belief that they have any healthy role within Creation.

It is precisely that healthy role that the medicine man gave to the disconnected children in their school that day when he taught about connections between women and water, and men and fire. I have already discussed the kinds of positive lessons that can come from the sweat lodge, or from immersion in the Teachings of the medicine wheel. All of them are positive experiences of coming together, of sharing and of rededicating oneself to healthy relationships.

Finally, there is the traditional Teaching of being thankful, at all times, for everything that we are given. This, too, is part of the strength-based nature of traditional Teachings. Their focus on the positive is intended to always bring us forward, out of the negatives in our lives. No matter how far down we have fallen, we remain surrounded by all the blessings of Creation. Recall Elder Dumont's Teaching that Creator placed us on Mother Earth so we could reflect back the majesty of his Creation. There are a growing number of aboriginal people, including many who live in urban environments, who come into each day that way, observing their own sunrise ceremony, thanking the sun for coming once again, re-dedicating their lives to the creation of right relations in everything they do.

Here is what Rod McCormick, a Mohawk professor at UBC, wrote about the expression of thankfulness at the opening of any aboriginal gathering:

> The expression "all my relations" ... in many ways encompasses an Aboriginal worldview and a pan-Aboriginal definition of interconnectedness that we as Aboriginal Peoples have with family, community, nation and creation. It is a clear declaration that we are all in relationship with one another in this world. In using an example of this teaching from my own culture (Haudenosaunee, also known as the Iroquois Confederacy and the People of the Longhouse), the proper way to open any gathering is to recite a thanksgiving address in which our world is thanked as relatives. Those relatives may include mother earth, sky father, grandmother moon and our brothers and sisters in the plant and animal regions. "All my relations" also encompasses the spirit people—those who came before us and those not yet born. It is an affirmation of our interconnectedness to all of creation.[35]

I find myself asking which approach is likely to bring people more quickly out of their problems and guide them into better ways of relating: the western approach, with its focus on problems, or the strength-based approach, which connects people to the magic and balance in the universe and convinces them that they have significant roles within it. Everything is seen as possessing strength and worth, just as everything can contribute to the strength and worth of everything else. The more we work on creating strong relations, the more we will feel that strength and worth grow within us, and the more blessed we will find our own lives.

THE BELIEF THAT IT'S NOT ALWAYS NECESSARY TO *TALK* YOUR WAY BACK TO HEALTH

The stories, poems, movies and articles shown to people in the RedPath Program aren't chosen just because they are evocative. They are carefully selected to slowly take people into deeper personal layers, allowing them to develop new tools of emotional discernment and management. Knowing that everyone coming into healing carries different vulnerabilities, skills and challenges, close attention is paramount, and one central rule prevails: no one has to contribute stories about their own lives unless they choose to do so. As the feather is passed, it merely provides an opportunity to speak, not an obligation, and it never dictates the kinds of things you should speak about.

I suspect that this point of "not talking" reflects more than a respect for privacy or sensitivity to an individual's lack of confidence, or even the difficulty of finding the right words. Recall that people are encouraged to express their feelings in any way they choose, whether through drawing, beadwork, making a collage, singing a song, doing a carving or anything else that feels right. Nadia Ferrara is an adjunct professor of anthropology at McGill University and a senior policy manager at Indian and Northern Affairs Canada who has worked with the Cree and Naskapi people of northern Quebec. She makes this observation:

In 1895, Freud's doctrine was that a patient must talk, remember and verbally express important, emotionally-filled early childhood experiences. From this point on, expressive verbal psychotherapies became the dominant treatment modality in our Western-cosmopolitan society. Expressive psychotherapies have not been widely adopted by cultures outside of the Western world.... Every culture provides a creative forum in which people can express their thoughts, feelings, fantasies, or dreams. The Cree and Naskapi Indians, for instance, are encouraged to engage in the art-making, creative process after receiving a vision or experiencing a dream ... in Native American societies, "art is not viewed as marginal, unessential or extracurricular. Instead art is viewed as a way of seeing the world, and a way of being in the world."[36]

Deborah Chansonneuve sees this in terms of the aboriginal preference for what is known as *experiential learning*:

Another core belief shared by Inuit, Métis, and First Nation cultures is the value and importance of experiential learning. In an Aboriginal belief system, knowledge is considered a reflection not of what people say but of how people live.... Examples of culturally relevant experiential learning include storytelling, art therapy, talking circles, or performance art where participants have the opportunity to express powerful feelings indirectly through stories. Sharing their own stories, and having those stories validated by others who have lived through similar experience, is a powerful form of affirmation and healing. Treatment models based on creative self-expression have proven to be more effective with Aboriginal clients than talk therapy and instructional learning.[37]

Researchers Christopher Fletcher and Aaron Denham report seeing much the same approach within Inuit circles:

For [Inuit] men, going out on the land, often alone, is a primary and preferred method of healing. When compared to group or individual talk therapy, men find it easier to go out on the land and engage in activities, rather than to sit and share in a group.... Talk itself is not a prerequisite to healing in these instances.... While not foreign to Inuit social practice in the past, people said that the concept of voicing pain was not conceptualized as a healing act as it is now.... The experiential model offered within the [Inuit] workshop paradigm was preferred to "sitting there and being lectured." In other words, doing was favoured over more abstract forms of learning.[38]

As a side note, it is interesting that among the Inuit, talking about problems was seen as "abstract," while doing apparently unrelated things like trapping or berry picking was seen as a more direct way to approach healing challenges. In western culture, we seem to have the opposite view, where talking is seen as the more direct and much less abstract response. If anything, that should warn us against making the assumption that aboriginal people share our therapeutic preference for talking things out. Many do not ever wish to speak openly about what has happened in their lives. But, they still need healing processes that give them a coherent personal picture of their lives, as well as a spirit-based picture of how they can change their ways of relating in the future.

THE IMPORTANCE OF LAND
IN THE HEALING JOURNEY

In an earlier section, I spoke about the importance of being on the land for maintaining or establishing the health of aboriginal people. In my view, experiences on the land can bring about positive changes in all of us, aboriginal or non-aboriginal. Perhaps no lesson is more immediate and powerful than learning how futile it is to believe that you can dominate the landscape. Instead, the lesson involves learning to accommodate yourself to its realities.

It is common to arrange canoe expeditions for troubled urban youth who carry heavy loads of anger or hostility. I've seen it work many times: it doesn't take long before they learn that no matter how hard you try to change or defy it, the weather will be what it is. Thunderstorms don't fade away just because you swear at them. If you don't ready yourself for their arrival, you'll at least get wet and cold. Groups learn to work together to accommodate themselves to the realities of not only weather, but also currents, rapids, mosquitoes, the need to find firewood and the like. People learn that they can't easily paddle a canoe on their own, or carry out all their other duties. They must find ways to put their own desires into the context of other people having different desires. The art of compromise begins to develop. No one has to talk about the things in their lives that have disturbed them, but they are unlearning the habits of defiance, anger and selfishness that developed in their wake. At the same time, they are learning about the rewards that come from cooperation and working with mutual respect.

With aboriginal people, the benefits to health and well-being of being out on the land expand dramatically. Whether the activity involves collecting medicinal plants, hunting, trapping or just travelling, the lessons are clear: humans are small, unskilled, dependent *and* blessed with everything they'll ever need. Where the land is traditional to the person experiencing it, it will be full of the stories of his people, and full of spiritual ties that provide nourishment and comfort. For people venturing out into their traditional landscapes, the benefits will be both deeply felt and of lasting significance. I have often heard it said that "healthy land heals," and I can only guess at the power of healthy *traditional* land to take people even further.

Herman Michell, a Cree-speaker of Inuit, Dene and Swedish ancestry who is now associate professor and vice-president of academics at First Nations University of Canada, has his own way of expressing his sense of connection to the land and the way it makes him feel:

> For me, it wasn't just the physical aesthetic beauty of it all nor the momentary awe experienced when one is walking through a forest. It is a deep sense of spiritual connectedness that is hard to describe in human words and most likely would be misunderstood and perhaps even discarded by a person who thinks from a secular and positivist Western science perspective. Being out on the land allowed me to become aware that I was connected to something much greater than myself.[39]

Researchers Christopher Fletcher and Aaron Denham describe the healing connection this way:

> While interacting with the land, a person is not simply a distinct or independent entity; rather, one travels through a landscape imbued with historical, collective, and cultural significance. To experience or travel through the land is to connect with something that is greater than oneself.… Being on the land should not be viewed as supplemental to good counselling; rather, for this Inuit community, it is an essential element of the healing process.[40]

As I've said many times before, regaining a sense of connection is indeed an essential element of the aboriginal healing process. And when that connection is to something greater and grander than oneself, the sensation of being a part of it helps bring people out of their sense of futility and worthlessness, and rejoins them to their better instincts and their more positive sense of self. The land is its own cathedral, full of life, promise, openness and blessedness.

It is indeed a wonderful place to celebrate our participation in the richness of all life on Mother Earth.

THE ADOPTION OF COMPLEMENTARY WESTERN THERAPIES

Aboriginal healing programs routinely explore western approaches, freely incorporating elements of concepts such as cognitive-behavioural theory, resilience theory, emotional intelligence theory, motivational counselling and developmental psychology, not to mention more New Age approaches. The healing challenge for aboriginal people demands the best approaches from all sources.

Genograms have been adopted in some programs. They involve mapping the various generations that preceded you, noting what has happened to all the people along the way. Where family dysfunctions have persisted through several generations, genograms are far from easy to complete, but they reveal the extent of the trauma that has passed from generation to generation. Jo-Anne Fiske, writing in *Aboriginal Healing in Canada*, describes them as follows:

> The genogram identifies the legacies of trauma through generations and shows how pain is passed from one generation to another. As the clients chart a three-generational genealogy, they name the suffering, addictions, and other behaviours associated with individual family members and come to see both the causes and results of multi-generational trauma. They list family losses through death, removal of children to foster care, divorce, and breaks in family relations. They mark history of abuses and traumas such as survivors of acts of violence.[41]

She then offers the following report from one woman who was willing to share her genogram after she completed it:

And the one thing that came up was that my mother, when she was born, her mom put her in the river two times ... because she couldn't afford her, to look after her, she was put in the river to drown, but she got saved both times. And I think that was hard for me to look at, in that there was nine of us children and four of them got adopted ... all younger ones, and the oldest brother got given away, and then I always remembered that when the oldest brother was little my dad used to beat him, and he'd zoom under the porch to sleep because he pooped himself because my dad beat him. And he said it wasn't his son. So I just didn't feel like thinking about all of those things. And the sexual abuse that happened to my brothers. And yeah, the alcohol and the drug [long pause]. It was really hard. I guess because I'm getting deeper to my core, or you know, the onion peelings are coming away, and it's like oh, I didn't want to face it.[42]

Jo-Anne Fiske also mentions the use of both catharsis and cognitive analysis when doing what is commonly called *inner-child therapy*:

Two intertwining approaches are taken to address the inner child: a cognitive understanding and a cathartic release through psychodrama.... The former provides understanding of how the trauma came to be within the social experiences of family and community, the latter is a reliving of the initial trauma. The goal of both approaches is to teach the clients that they are not to blame for the abuse and trauma they have suffered and to find new ways to love themselves. The overall goal of healing the inner child is to release the client from the past while presenting new tools to live in the present.[43]

Psychodrama is a related western technique that is being used in aboriginal healing where people are willing to participate. It asks people to act out the portions of their lives they have identified as most traumatic. Jo-Anne Fiske describes it as follows:

> In psychodrama, clients move from the mental understanding of their trauma and life patterns to the emotional expression, that is, from the thinking about themselves to the feeling of their trauma.... Through the carefully staged re-enactment of a selected traumatic experience, the client is enabled to imagine a different outcome that is empowering. Through recreation of the trauma, clients can create a dialogue and "say what was never said." The therapist may also lead the client to an empathetic understanding of individuals who have caused the trauma. This is particularly relevant as clients come to recognize and resolve the impact of colonial violence suffered by parents and grandparents. Through these new insights, clients can set aside feelings of anger and grievance.[44]

That is clearly neither an easy nor a simple process. But, as we can see here from one woman's description of what she went through during her psychodrama exercise, the process can be transformative:

> That was very hard and difficult. That was a rough week, very rough, rough week. But I lived through it … that's one thing … I lived through that. It was very emotional … very emotional, the stuff that came up with me. My psychodrama was about how I was abused as a child and how much I grew

to hate my brother, as I said, fairly early.... I didn't even want him near me when I was a kid. Just seeing all of that ... I didn't see the people playing as me. I didn't see the people playing as him ... it came to reality for me, that I seen me and I seen him, and it was just too real, and I freaked out and I lost it and I cried and they all said it was awesome, the screaming and yelling and the power of how much I hated him. And I could've did another week, really ... a week of that kind of group was very helpful for me, 'cause I packed around that pain and that shame inside me and the dirty feeling always needing to have a bath because of my sexual abuse. I got rid of it ... it's not my fault anymore. I learned that it's not my fault. This is awesome. That was very awesome for me. And very helpful to my spirit, to my body.[45]

Many other western approaches have been adopted within aboriginal healing processes, but a word of caution is needed. Colonization has truly splintered the culture of aboriginal people, leaving many as Christians, many hanging on to traditional views, and many simply lost in the void. When that splintering is put together with the fact that many traditional cultures existed, each with their own ceremonies and customs, the result is clear: no single cultural foundation for healing could ever be adopted.

One of the advantages of community-centred healing is that it avoids pan-Indianism—the erroneous assumption that all aboriginal cultures and traditions are essentially the same. Community-centred healing permits unique cultures to express themselves in the design of locally appropriate healing approaches. Gregory Brass, a Saulteaux (Plains Ojibway) who was coordinator of the Aboriginal Mental Health Research Team at Montreal's Jewish General Hospital from 1999 to 2000, looked at how challenging it can be for aboriginal people of one unique culture to find adequate self-definition. He interviewed one young man from the Stó:lo Nation of British Columbia's Lower Mainland who was unhappy with his heritage being lumped in with customs such as the sweat lodge, smudging and powwow dancing that had never been part of it:

> When I was going to high school I wasn't taught about my own history. I wasn't taught anything about place names, or villages, wasn't taught anything about *sxwey'xwey* masks, wasn't taught anything about winter dancing. But I was taught that there were Prairie Indians, and that to be Indian you lived in a tipi and had a long flowing headdress, and you're proud and you're noble, and you hunted buffalo, things like that. I wasn't taught about local Native culture. And of course watching TV, and watching movies, and everything that was to be Indian was exactly what we were taught in school. Pan-Indianism … you take that one culture and one people and apply it to everyone.[46]

Joseph Gone notes what one administrator at a healing lodge told him about the dangers of pan-Indianism:

> I think another significant challenge is that of pan-Indianism. It's a major threat, I think, to the unfolding of what can be a very significant and powerful healing process that could unfold in our communities. But it's a set of beliefs and practices that are dangerous in their appearance as being Indigenous, but are, in fact, a hybrid of too many Indigenous practices that could spell disaster.[47]

He also points out, however, that the same administrator didn't seem as concerned about using New Age approaches:

Interestingly, while this hybridity of Indigenous practices was viewed with some alarm by this administrator, the combining of Western therapeutic approaches and Cree tradition within the Pisimweyapiy Counselling Centre activities did not seem to trouble him at all. Moreover, the gravitation of some PCC staff toward alternative and New Age therapeutic approaches—including the principles of stillness, space, and gravity espoused by Tulshi Sen—seemed to elicit understanding rather than condemnation from this administrator: "Our people, as lost as we are, will gravitate to anything that they see as being even remotely Indigenous."[48]

As should be clear by now, it would be a mistake to assume that all aboriginal people adhere to traditional beliefs that once defined their culture. The fact is that many have taken up Christianity and feel threatened by those traditional beliefs. Recall the councillor who asked me to come into his newly built sweat lodge as a way to encourage the youth to set aside the fear and denunciation of traditional practices created by the Christian leadership of his community. Medical anthropologist Naomi Adelson writes about that same dynamic becoming even more threatening in northern Quebec:

There seems to be an almost palpable line dividing two particular camps of opinion in one very small community: those who are ardent (Anglican) church adherents and those who are actively and avidly turning to Native Spirituality. It seemed as though the debate was growing more fractious with each passing year. Indeed, with rumours of a Biblical rationale to kill one of the guest spiritual elders a few years ago, the vocal and sometimes bitter debate had reached new heights.... While others are somewhat less intransigent about the degree to which Native Spirituality can be incorporated into other local belief systems, there remains a sense among these elders that it is still coming from outside of the community itself and not necessarily an essential ingredient in the local efforts of cultural recuperation.[49]

As she also reports, there are even battles between the various Christian denominations *within* some aboriginal communities:

Healing thus often connotes a recuperation of Aboriginal awareness, which is increasingly becoming synonymous with Native Spirituality. For others, however, this form of spirituality is not only abhorrent, but anathema to their fundamental Christian beliefs. Indeed, fundamentalist (Pentecostal) Christianity is on the rise in some Cree communities, while others continue to adhere to the older, more established churches (Church of England, Catholicism)—regardless of their origins. Yet others are attempting new forms of syncretic religious practices, readily incorporating both Christian and Native spirituality.

In other words, the result is what you might expect after several centuries of heavy colonization, especially by the western churches: much confusion, discord and outright animosity. Where those feelings have not yet been resolved, it is unlikely that healing will be achieved. So, while western practices have been successfully adopted to complement aboriginal healing methods in some communities, a danger remains: the discord between aboriginal and western approaches may in some cases be heightened by the discord between competing western practices, and heightened further still by the wide variety of traditional aboriginal cultures that exist across North America. There are likely to be as many different visions of "appropriate" healing approaches as there are culturally different people espousing them, both aboriginal and non-aboriginal. Some will want to jealously protect and revive only traditions that prevailed within their original cultural landscape, while others will be simply looking for anything that makes people feel better about themselves. Some will face intense pressure not to give in to nontraditional approaches, while others will sail ahead without opposition, trying out various techniques that come to their attention.

In short, it seems to me that the search for a single preferred way of healing is unlikely to succeed. There are too many aboriginal cultures, each with their own ceremonies and ways of getting at hidden pain. They need to be able to breathe life into those approaches once again. At the same time, they need to be free to strike their own balance with western ways. In my view, having a wide variety of approaches may yield promising results for everyone, regardless of racial or cultural background. At the very least, it would be entirely counterproductive for central governments to try to dictate single therapy plans to all First Nations people. *Just* as they took divergent paths before contact, they are apt to choose divergent therapeutic paths today.

Aboriginal healing, however, remains aboriginal healing, no matter how many western therapeutic techniques it absorbs, primarily because it begins with its own distinct definition of a healthy person. Whatever western processes are incorporated, they are wrapped into that different starting point, especially within the focus on group work. Because aboriginal healing reconnects people in aboriginal ways, with special attention to the emotional and spiritual dimensions, it does what no non-aboriginal therapy can do: it puts the lie to centuries of denigration. It says, "You were wrong about us," the most important decolonizing declaration of all.

And then, finally, there is the understanding that no one is ever healed, simply because there are always things we can do to move toward greater mental, emotional, physical and spiritual health, and into better balance.

HEALING AS A LIFELONG EFFORT

Without question, aboriginal people have many more healing challenges than the general population. From that perspective alone, many will spend their full lifetimes coming to terms with the destructive forces that have surrounded them. One woman explained this to a research team led by James Waldram, and her words convey the enormity of it all:

> I'm going to deal with my healing for the rest of my life, there's no doubt about it. Because there's always going to be something that's going to trigger … something from my past. And how to deal with that? And being able to come here and talk to other people about my own experiences and about how to deal with it, some of that negativity and all this stuff that happened to me, you know, at the residential school and what went on in foster care. You know, how it had shaped my well-being.… No, there's no way [that a person is ever completely healed], not with the psychological damage, emotional damage, the physical damage, and with any spiritual damage that's done to you. Because it's still there. And no matter where you go in your life, it's going to be always something there that's going to have an impact, that's going to hit you, that's going to hit you and remind you, take you back to that place where you don't want to go. It's knowing these things, I think … you're aware of them and you talk about it and you start dealing with it. Then I think

[you] become a strong person. But it doesn't mean that you necessarily are really totally healed, because it's impossible.[50]

Within aboriginal traditions, there is something else at work, something that flows from the recognition that no one can ever claim to be meeting their responsibilities perfectly or to be perfectly healthy. The belief is that we can always think, say, do and be better than we are now. In that sense, we are all engaged in healing, which is to say that we are all on the same road, together, trying to move closer to Creator's spirit in everything that we do.

As I said earlier, some of us start that journey with many blessings, and others begin while facing great threat and suffering immense injury. But we all undertake essentially the same journey, and it lasts throughout our lives. Gene Thin Elk, a Lakota Sioux spiritual leader who has spent twenty-two years with the University of South Dakota working in both cross-cultural training and drug and alcohol rehabilitation, offers the following vision:

The Red Road is a holistic approach to mental, physical, spiritual and emotional wellness based on Native American healing concepts and traditions, having prayer as the basis of all healing. Native American psychology is essential in reaching the inner person (spirit) using specific sound, movement, and color. All these essences are present in the Medicine Wheel.... Healing is a way of life for the Native American who understands and lives the cultural traditions and values.[51]

In other words, healing is seen not simply as a response to injury but as a life goal to be sought. I don't see this as just a semantic difference—it is fundamental. While we are all born into Creator's magnificent spirit, we can never come close to Creator's splendid manifestation of true-spiritedness. The wisest Elder grows into ever-deeper humility as he recognizes how distant he is, and will always be. Healing stands primarily for moving-toward, not just recovery-from. It involves always trying to manifest that which is within us but is so difficult to reveal.

Christopher Fletcher and Aaron Denham suggest that the Inuit share the same vision:

> The colloquial definition of healing, which suggests a repair or joining of separated parts within a specific bounded temporal space, does not correspond to how the term was used by [Inuit] study participants. For this community, healing is not something that has a particular beginning and conclusion nor is it an activity that one frames outside of the mundane dimensions of life. The common perception of healing is that it remains a long-term, lifelong process or journey.[52]

That presents a real problem for governments funding such programs: how can they be realistically evaluated? How, for instance, do you evaluate alcohol treatment, when the aboriginal approach is to work on all the colonization horrors that gave rise to that particular addiction in the first place?

In 2002, Phil Lane Jr., Michael Bopp, Judie Bopp and Julian Norris put together a paper called *Mapping the Healing Journey* for Corrections Canada. In it, they took an in-depth look at six of the leading healing programs in Canada, including Hollow Water in Manitoba, Mnjikaning (Rama) in Ontario and Eskasoni in Nova Scotia. In their report, they recognized that drug and alcohol dependencies were merely consequences of the much broader challenge posed by five hundred years of colonization, stating, "Given the experience with NNADAP, there would appear to be inherent challenges in evaluating the effectiveness of healing programs, especially with the complex constellation of issues that healing/post treatment programs address."[53]

Jo-Anne Fiske came to a similar conclusion:

> Working with clients during their treatment cannot provide retrospective measures of effective practices. While this suggests that quantitative studies are needed to generate measures of success, it also indicates that measures frozen in time may not generate the answers sought. If accepting the principle that healing is a life journey, how can one find the right moment in clients' lives to measure their position within this journey?… Measures of treatment effectiveness that focus on individual change and coping skills cannot address this socio-political context and the ongoing barriers to Aboriginal health that are embedded in it.[54]

How, then, do we evaluate healing practices such as ceremonies and their capacity to facilitate long-term changes in how people live their lives? How can we do that when these approaches are part of lifelong and holistic healing?

It may just be that we can't. It may just be that western governments will have to display something that has been in short supply thus far: trust. In my view, governments will have to fund experimentation as communities and/or treatment centres try different approaches and combinations. That is what the Aboriginal Healing Foundation was starting to do before the federal government decided not to renew their funding. Just as the process of colonization involved many forces combining in unexpected ways to produce the disastrous results we see in some communities today, the process of undoing those colonization injuries will be equally complex and long-lasting. Supporting traditional healing practices means committing for the long haul, and trusting that the use of taxpayers' money will, ultimately, lead injured people back to health. That is what indigenous people want, and that is what the vast majority of them will work hard to accomplish.

Conclusion

I know that I told the following story when *Dancing with a Ghost* was reissued in 2006, but that means it was missed by people who had only the original 1992 edition. It is a story that keeps coming back to me as I wrestle my way along between the aboriginal and non-aboriginal worlds, so I'll repeat it here. It has to do with my discomfort working in this cross-cultural space.

I was sitting at my desk in the Kenora Crown attorney's office working on a file one day when my secretary buzzed me and said there was someone on the line whose name she didn't get, but who insisted on speaking with me. She thought the call was from somewhere in the Northwest Territories, but she didn't understand the woman's name or the place she was calling from. When I lifted the receiver and said, "Hello, Rupert Ross here," I didn't know what to expect. I then heard the voice of an older aboriginal woman crackling across the line. "Is this Ross? The Ross that wrote that *Dancing* book?" she asked. I admitted that I was, not knowing whether she was angry or pleased with me. She continued, "I don't read English. I live up here in Rae Lakes. You know where that is? Anyway, I've been promising myself I'd do this for four years now, call you. My son-in-law, he read that *Dancing* book to me. And I had to tell you. Whatever time Creator's got left for me, that book, it made me decide to walk the Red Road. Whatever time I got left, that's what I'm gonna do. So I needed to thank you for that." As I heard her scratchy voice over the phone, I had goosebumps all over.

I had two reactions to the fact that *Dancing* had made such an impact on her life. The first was joy that I had contributed to her decision to re-engage her indigenous self, to walk the Red Road with pride. And the second was just as powerful: sadness. How could the world have turned against her so powerfully that it took away so much of who she really was? How could she have lived so much of her life so afraid and ashamed of her indigenous self that she hid it from herself and from the world? It was the same kind of reaction as the one I had when I was invited into the sweat lodge way up north so that the kids might think it was okay to go back to the tradition: a combination of joy at being of use and sadness that it had come to this.

I was very conscious of being a white guy who was inserting himself into her life and the history of her people. It was not a comfortable place, being a member of the race that had put her down so deeply. I found myself close to tears thinking about what she had suffered at our hands. Then the joy took over again: if I could help in her re-emergence, and if I could touch others the same way, then it would be okay. I still go back and forth between those two feelings. I've been told by many indigenous people, however, that this is the role that was given to me, and that I must share my experiences as widely as I can.

I'm still not sure what will bring aboriginal and non-aboriginal Canadians into a respectful relationship. In fact, apart from some early fur traders like David Thompson, who seem to have understood the sophistication of traditional societies, I don't think many non-aboriginal Canadians have ever had such a respectful relationship with aboriginal people. I certainly do not see much evidence of respect for traditional societies in European writings at the time of contact, and little seems to have changed. Despite my privileged education, no one ever told me about the variety and sophistication of traditional approaches to governance, psychology, family raising, metaphysics, pharmacology, spirituality, holistic thinking, or a host of other foundational structures that existed within aboriginal societies at the time of contact. Just as important, no one ever told me about residential schools. As a result, none of us ever came to suspect that something of value was *taken away* by those residential schools.

Perversely, all the tragedies we see today make it easy for many to believe that it has always been this way. If truly respectful relationships are ever to emerge, non-aboriginal Canadians must come to understand that there were healthy, vibrant and sophisticated human societies on this continent at the time of contact. When European settlers arrived and saw a comparative dearth of technological sophistication, it may be understandable that they assumed an absence of social and cultural sophistication as well. But surely the time has come to admit how wrong that judgment was. Ironically, the very absence of preoccupation with technology may have given traditional peoples substantially more time, especially during the long winter months, to dedicate their creativity to social, psychological and spiritual dimensions instead, helping them achieve certain sophistications that, in my view, continue to elude the rest of us.

In short, I want to suggest that we need to replace the myth of cultural inferiority with the truth of cultural richness and diversity. We must also understand that, while severely damaged by every strategy of colonization, traditional Teachings remain valid in today's world. If we all absorb that truth and make it part of our daily consciousness, perhaps we can start building a relationship centred on the most important value of all: mutual respect.

It was not there in the past, and there is not nearly enough of it today, but it could be there in the future if enough people take up the challenge. I hope this book helps more of us to understand where the particular challenges lie and the kinds of responses that might best meet them. I hope, as well, that the *urgency* of effective responses is clear, because far too many aboriginal children are now harming themselves and each other, sometimes fatally. As communities like Hollow Water have proven, we are not without the knowledge of how to turn things around. What is needed, from everyone, is the will.

The Dalai Lama has said that Buddhism will come to the west not as religion but as psychology. Could we not approach traditional aboriginal Teachings in the same way? After all, they too are centred on helping people create balanced and healthy mental, emotional, physical and spiritual connections—and they have stood an even longer test of time. What might we learn if all of us, including those aboriginal people who adopted Christianity, approached traditional practices as nondenominational ways of promoting health rather than as religious ceremonies proclaiming adherence to particular beliefs? Would that make it easier to accord them the same respect and curiosity we show the Dalai Lama and Buddhist teachings?

And isn't that a good question to ask, about the difference in the way we listen to the Dalai Lama and the way we listen to aboriginal people?

I ALSO WANT TO repeat something I've said many times before: no matter how many ways I have experienced the indigenous world, I have discovered that I cannot move calmly and naturally within it. It is not, after all, my world, but a very different one, from fundamental principles right down to small behavioural patterns. And, to illustrate how true this is, there's a (funny!) story I just have to tell.

Back in the winter of 1992, I spent a week at the Eskasoni First Nation on Cape Breton Island as the guest of Alex Denny, then Grand Captain of all Mi'kmaq. Sadly, he has since passed on, but he lives vividly in my heart and my memory. One morning he brought me a bright-orange survival suit and told me we were going eel-spearing out on the river ice. The eels, he told me, spent a portion of the winter buried in the silt on the river bottom, just out of sight. Getting them involved chopping a hole in the ice almost a metre wide and then driving a long, trident-ended, wooden spear into the silt, over and over, methodically probing as wide an area as possible. When you felt it hit some resistance, you assumed you'd found an eel and drove it down hard, then angled it quickly upwards and pulled the eel (if there was one) out onto the ice before it struggled free.

We went down to the river and joined five or six other men out on the ice, all of them methodically probing the bottom through the eel grass that waved gently in the current beneath us. After spearing a few eels, Alex took his axe and started chopping a new hole a little further downstream. Even though the ice was only about fifteen centimetres thick, cutting a hole that wide took considerable effort. Wanting to help, I took over the chopping and finally cut free a manhole-size piece of ice. I then stuck the axe under it, trying to lever it up onto the ice so we could resume the spearing. Try as I might, however, I couldn't do more than get one edge of the slab up on top; as soon as I tried to lever the other side upwards, the first side slid back in. I was getting wet and frustrated. On my hands and knees, I looked up to see Alex's legs approaching from our first holes. He stood quietly beside my new hole for a moment, then he put one rubber boot on top of my slab and gently pressed down, submerging it in the water. He then slid that slab sideways, *under* the ice, leaving the hole entirely clear.

I looked around at all the holes by the other men. Not one slab was on top of the ice. I began to laugh at myself, out loud. In *Dancing with a Ghost*, I had written about the traditional modelling approach to education, where children were expected to learn by observing and copying, not by getting verbal instruction. Despite having known that, I had not practised it. Had I looked around,

I'd have seen that everyone else must have slipped their slabs of ice down and sideways, out of the way. I felt like such a fool for not having done what I had already written about. I said exactly that to Alex. He just smiled and handed me the spear.

In the years since, I've had so many similar experiences that my little failures no longer surprise me. I've come to understand that there is a uniformity within the traditional world view that makes a million individual ways of behaving seem entirely natural to them, just as each of those ways of behaving seem out of the ordinary to non-indigenous people like me. If you note a difference and ask for an explanation, you often get a quizzical look that seems to say, "Why do you ask? Isn't that just an ordinary way to behave?"

On that same trip to Eskasoni, Alex Denny also tried to clue me in to the issue of asking questions across the cultural divide. We were driving from one house to another when he said, almost as if it was an announcement of some sort, "I think your visit is working out okay." After a pause, he completed his thought: "You've been here three days already, and I haven't heard you ask a single question." Of course, after hearing that, I simply couldn't ask him what he meant! But I've thought long and hard about it ever since, and I think part of what he was saying was that he appreciated that I just came to be with them, rather than to study them. I recall that he later got into an uproarious discussion with other community members about a non-aboriginal university student who camped out on their beach for an entire summer and spent every day going from house to house with his clipboard, asking a zillion questions and dutifully writing down all the answers. It appears that people started making things up, and then got together to compare their stories and laugh about what they had each told him. "We can't wait to see his thesis," one person exclaimed, "because it ought to be totally confusing!"

I have come to see Alex's comment about not asking questions as containing a further suggestion as well: if I live in one vision of life, I can only ask questions that make sense within that vision. When I am speaking with someone who truly occupies another one, the question itself will often be entirely meaningless and nothing will be learned. It is far better to simply be with the other person and slowly absorb how he relates to the world, learning what kinds of questions have meaning within that other vision. It is only after intense engagement with healthy indigenous people over thirty years that I think I've gained some understanding not only of what they are saying or doing, but also of the vision that makes those words and actions sensible. That does not for an instant mean that I truly understand, or that I can naturally say and do the same myself. I am still trying to lever that ice slab up and out of the hole more frequently than I should probably admit—and I still chuckle about it. That's just the way it is.

I'VE THOUGHT LONG and hard about how to bring this book to a close. Following the course usually chosen by all the Elders whom I've come to know and respect, it must close with a story, something personal, something meaningful to me. In that way, I hope it might also have some meaning to the people who happen to hear it.

And I think I've got one.

It has to do with a letting-go circle I took part in some years ago in Banff. About twenty of us from all over North America had gathered for several days at the Banff School of Management to conduct what we called our "science dialogues," exploring similarities and differences between quantum physics and indigenous metaphysics. I think only one or two of us were non-aboriginal. One of the members of the group, an aboriginal man from California, got a telephone call one night advising him that his elderly father was dying, and suggesting that he should make his way home as quickly as possible. Also in the group was an Anishinaabe spiritual leader.

He told us that the traditional Anishinaabe letting-go ceremony was usually done only after death, but he suggested that it might help the man make his journey back to California with the knowledge that his father may have already passed on. All of us were invited to participate, and we all did.

The focus, then, was on death in our lives, especially of our parents. We all came together in a circle. During the ceremony, we held tobacco in our left hands, closest to our hearts. That tobacco became saturated with our sweat and tears as the circle progressed. It is not my place to speak of what happened in the circle; let me just say that the tears that flowed told me that I was not alone in still carrying a great deal of grief about the loss of my own dad. At the end of the ceremony, the tobacco was collected into a white cloth called a *tie*, and it was explained that someone would be chosen to take the tobacco—and all our sweat and tears—to a place where it would go back into Mother Earth. For reasons I still don't understand, I was selected to be that person.

And I knew instantly where it had to go.

The Banff School of Management is on the lower west side of what local aboriginal people call Sleeping Buffalo Mountain. I had often climbed the zigzag path to the long, skinny ridge at the top. Up there, off the path and on the east side of the ridge, I had found the stump of a huge tree that years earlier had been hit by lightning and knocked burning down the steep cliff. That blackened stump stayed in my heart because when I looked inside its charred circle, I saw beautiful green mosses clinging to the black sides. They led me to contemplate renewal, and that seemed appropriate at the eastern doorway, where new life is understood to originate.

I knew that our sweat and tears had to be placed in that particular spot.

The first challenge was that it was now mid-winter. The winding path would be covered in snow and ice. So would the ridge on top.

The short few steps off that path and down to the tree stump sloped a bit steeply toward the edge of the cliff. I admit to being more than a little nervous as I pulled on my winter boots, toque, mitts and heavy coat and headed out the door, carrying the tie.

Then, as I began my climb, I realized another challenge: it was quickly getting dark. From my location on the west side of Sleeping Buffalo Mountain, I was looking down over the town of Banff, and I could see that the western sky didn't have much light left. As I wound my way higher up the mountain, it was getting darker. I began to ask myself if I might be carrying things too far, whether I was just a little too caught up in the ceremony for my own good. But I kept walking. As I approached the top, there was no light at all in the western sky. I kept wondering what I was doing, with a wife and children at home, climbing this mountain to go to an extremely dangerous spot, just to fulfill some fanciful notion of a ceremony that I had never been a part of before.

Nearly to the top, the path took me south, climbing the last little bit to the ridge. Then I would turn 180 degrees and follow the ridge path north toward my tree. In my last few steps going up, I saw some light in the sky, much further south, and for a moment I wondered what it was. Then, as I hit the very top and stopped, I understood its source. It was Grandmother, the Moon, and she was absolutely full in the clear winter sky. I stood there as she rose, watching everything around me emerge from darkness into her incredible silver light. I stood, laughing, all by myself on top of that little mountain. I think I watched her rise for fifteen minutes or so.

Then I slowly turned north, toward my tree, and saw that Grandmother was casting my shadow a long way in front of me. She lit up everything else, all along the path, with that snow brightness you can't believe until you've experienced it. Grandmother Moon guided me down the path, lit my way to the eastern edge and the cliff, and there was my tree stump, standing out against the clear sky. I slowly went down to it, through two feet of feathery snow, and placed the white tie and wet tobacco deep inside, praying with my eyes wide open that it would take the sweat and tears of the twenty of us, and relieve us of some of the grief we had all been carrying. As I made my way back down the mountain, I thought of the death of my own father, and sent him warmth.

One circle, one ceremony, and it did so many things for all of us together. There are hundreds of ceremonies within aboriginal Canada, all of them created to answer the normal stresses—and nurture the dreams—that all people share, aboriginal or otherwise.

I am very grateful to have come to know some of those ceremonies, the Teachings behind them and many of the people determined to bring them back to life.

And I'm happy to have shared them with you. *Megwetch!*

Appendix

Below are short descriptions of many of the authors I have quoted in writing this book. Their important work and long involvement in aboriginal issues was invaluable and has helped me to frame my own thoughts. I am grateful for permission many have given to quote from them at length.

Janice Acoose is a Nehiowè-Métis Nahkawé educator whose roots stem from the Sakimay (Saulteaux) First Nation and her mother's Ninankawe Marival Métis community. Born in Saskatchewan, she attended the Cowesis Indian Residential School in the early 1960s, and was raised culturally in both the Saulteaux and Métis cultures. She received her B.A. Hon., M.A. and Ph.D. at the University of Saskatchewan, and was an associate professor of English at First Nations University of Canada in Regina. She is also a writer, scholar and producer who has used print, video, radio and television to enlighten mainstream society about the beauty, strength and power of First Nations and Métis peoples.

Naomi Adelson is associate professor and chair of the Department of Anthropology at York University in Toronto. She is a medical anthropologist who works and publishes primarily in the area of First Nations health. Her book *Being Alive Well: Health and the Politics of Cree Well-Being* (2000) documents the social, cultural and political factors that both impinge upon and define physiological health for the Cree of Great Whale in northern Quebec. Over the last five years, she has conducted research on the growth of traditional First Nations therapies in relation to community cultural renewal projects, and she is currently working on issues of stress among remote-living First Nations women.

John Amagoalik was born in a hunting camp near Inukjuak, Nunavik (northern Quebec) and grew up in Resolute Bay in the High Arctic. After attending high school in Churchill, Manitoba, and Iqaluit, Nunavut, he worked as regional information officer for the Government of the Northwest Territories and then as executive director of the Inuit Claims Commission. In 1979 he was elected vice-president of Inuit Tapirisat of Canada (now Inuit Tapiriit Kanatami), and he served two terms as president during the 1980s. Throughout the 1990s, as chief commissioner of the Nunavut Implementation Commission, he worked passionately on the detailed planning for the new territory. He lobbied actively for the creation of an electoral process that would guarantee gender parity in the new legislature; however, the proposal did not gain enough support to be implemented when Nunavut was created in 1999. John has been recognized with a National Aboriginal Achievement Award, an Award of Excellence from the Canadian Public Service Agency, an honorary Ph.D. from St. Mary's University, and a Special Recognition Award from the Qikiqtani Inuit Association (QIA). In 1999, John was named a chevalier of the French Legion of Honour.

Betty Bastien is a member of the Piikani First Nation, and her traditional knowledge is located in the Brave Dogs Society and Thunder Pipe Holder of the Blackfoot. She is an associate professor in the Faculty of Social Work, University of Calgary, with primary responsibility for the development and delivery of the Learning Circle curriculum in rural, remote and Aboriginal communities, as well as the coordination and delivery of a graduate program in social work on the Blood Reserve. Dr. Bastien has over thirty years' experience working in provincial and federal governments, First Nation organizations, native studies and international indigenous studies, and has been a consultant in the areas of social development, education, services and evaluation. She is the author of *Blackfoot Ways of Knowing: The Worldview of the Siksikaitsitapi* (2004).

Marie Battiste is a Mi'kmaq educator from Potlo'tek First Nations of Cape Breton (Unama'kik), Nova Scotia. She is a full professor in the College of Education and director of the Aboriginal Education Research Centre (AERC) at the University of Saskatchewan. A graduate of Harvard University (M.Ed.) and Stanford University (Ed.D.), she has written on the topics of literacy, cognitive imperialism, linguistic and cultural integrity, indigenous knowledge and humanities, and the decolonization of aboriginal education. She co-authored *Protecting Indigenous Knowledge and Heritage: A Global Challenge* with James (Sákéj) Youngblood Henderson (2000), which received a Saskatchewan Book Award in 2000; edited *Reclaiming Indigenous Voice and Vision* (2000); co-edited a special edition of the *Australian Journal of Indigenous Education* (May 2005) on the theme "Thinking Place: Animating the Indigenous Humanities"; and was senior editor, with Jean Barman, of *First Nations Education in Canada: The Circle Unfolds* (1995). She has received honorary doctorate degrees from St. Mary's University and the University of Maine Farmington, an Alumni Achievement Award at the University of Maine Farmington, and the National Aboriginal Achievement Award in education from the National Aboriginal Achievement Foundation.

Judie Bopp is a co-founder of Four Worlds International and holds a Ph.D. from the Department of Educational Research, University of Calgary. As a partner in Four Worlds Development Inc., she has done work for the Aboriginal Healing Foundation, the Assembly of

First Nations and the Aboriginal Policy Unit of the Solicitor General (Government of Canada). Her specialty involves community-based program design, implementation, monitoring and evaluation.

Michael Bopp is a co-founder of Four Worlds International and is currently a director of the Four Worlds Centre for Development Learning. He has a Ph.D. in development education and a master's degree in community development. He and Judie have worked in Southeast Asia, the South Pacific, Africa, the former Soviet Union, Latin America, the Caribbean and indigenous North America as specialists in participatory change and development processes.

Marlene Brant Castellano is a Mohawk of the Bay of Quinte Band and professor emeritus at Trent University in Peterborough, Ontario. She held a faculty appointment in Trent's Native Studies Department from 1973 to 1996. She then served as co-director of research with the Royal Commission on Aboriginal Peoples (RCAP). She facilitated the work of the aboriginal subcommittee that drafted RCAP's "Ethical Guidelines for Research," now widely used as a reference for ethical research in aboriginal contexts. She is renowned for promoting community-based research that respects native traditions and maintains a strong involvement with health and educational initiatives for aboriginal Canadians.

Gregory M. Brass is Saulteaux (Plains Ojibway) of the Keeseekoose Band, Saskatchewan. He completed his master's degree in cultural anthropology at McGill University, Montreal. His ethnographic fieldwork focused on a community residential treatment centre for men of aboriginal ancestry. His work examines the construction of an aboriginal identity as an intersection of discursive practices, narratives of self and negotiations of the meaning of symbolic space.

He served as coordinator of the Aboriginal Mental Health Research Team at the Jewish General Hospital, Montreal, from 1999 to 2000.

Lee Brown is a member of the Cherokee Nation and the Wolf Clan, is presently director of the Institute of Emotional Health in Vancouver and was formerly both the director of the UBC Institute of Aboriginal Health and coordinator of the Indigenous Doctoral Program in the Department of Educational Studies at UBC. He was the former coordinator of the Indigenous Doctoral Program in the Department of Educational Studies at the University of British Columbia. He is the co-author of *The Sacred Tree* (1989), an educational curriculum based on aboriginal values and epistemology. He has also been clinical supervisor and a cultural resource to the Round Lake Native Healing Centre in Vernon, British Columbia, and has shared his knowledge of traditional culture and healing in over five hundred indigenous communities in North America.

Gregory A. Cajete is a Tewa author and professor from Santa Clara Pueblo, New Mexico. He has served as a New Mexico Humanities scholar of ethnobotany of northern New Mexico and as a member of the New Mexico Arts Commission. In addition, he has lectured at colleges and universities in the United States, Canada, Mexico, New Zealand, Italy, Japan and Russia. He worked at the Institute of American Indian Arts in Santa Fe, New Mexico, for twenty-five years. While at the institute, he served as dean of the Center for Research and Cultural Exchange, chair of Native American studies and professor of ethnoscience. He organized and directed the first and second annual National Native American Very Special Arts Festival, held in Santa Fe in 1991 and in Albuquerque in 1992. Currently, he is director of Native American studies and an associate professor in the Division of Language, Literacy and Sociocultural Studies in the College of Education at the University of New Mexico. He has pioneered reconciling indigenous perspectives in sciences with a western academic setting, and teaching culturally based science, with an emphasis on health and wellness. He has published four books: *Look to the Mountain: An Ecology of Indigenous Education* (1994); *Ignite the Sparkle: An Indigenous Science Education Curriculum Model* (1999); *A People's Ecology: Explorations in Sustainable Living* (1999) and *Native Science: Natural Laws of Interdependence* (2000).

Joe Couture, a Cree-Métis from Wetaskiwin, Alberta, was a respected Elder, cultural adviser, educator, academic and psychologist who died in 2007. He was the first aboriginal person in Canada to receive a Ph.D. in psychology. At the age of twenty-seven, he was ordained a priest by Oblates of Mary Immaculate in Edmonton, but after twelve years, he left the priesthood and went to the Elders to learn, to fast and to make personal sacrifices to gain traditional knowledge and pursue his vision. His postgraduate work was in the areas of clinical psychology, with a focus on culturally formed cognitive and identity development, and native rehabilitation. Dr. Couture built the native studies program at Trent University in Peterborough, Ontario, the first of its kind in Canada, and served as its chair. He also led the cultural, academic and administrative development of the Nechi Institute, which has become a world-renowned indigenous-based training program for addictions and recovery. He received a National Aboriginal Achievement Award honouring his lifetime accomplishments. Throughout his life, he helped many students, friends and clients in conflict with the law to understand the deep concepts of holistic wellness in two worlds: the modern scientific world and the world of traditional Teachings.

Deborah Chansonneuve is the author of *Reclaiming Connections: Understanding Residential School Trauma Among Aboriginal People*

(2005) and is a consultant on aboriginal culture and gender equality. She has over twenty-five years' experience in gender equality and human rights issues. She has focused her work on aboriginal women and children, and has developed conflict resolution training programs that approach relationships constructively and creatively.

Vine Deloria Jr., of Standing Rock Sioux origin, was born near the Pine Ridge Oglala Sioux Indian Reservation in South Dakota. He was educated at reservation schools, graduated from Iowa State University in 1958, received a master's degree in theology in 1963 from the Lutheran School of Theology in Illinois, and earned a law degree at the University of Colorado in 1970. He soon became a spokesperson for native identity and social change, while working at the National Conference of American Indians in Washington from 1964 to 1967. In 1969 he published the first of more than twenty books, *Custer Died for Your Sins: An Indian Manifesto*, shattering native stereotypes and challenging white audiences to take a hard look at the brutal history of American expansionism across the west. His prose and ideas were charged with biting wit ("When asked by an anthropologist what the Indians called America before the white man came, an Indian said simply, 'Ours.'"). Among his other books are *We Talk, You Listen* (1970), *Behind the Trail of Broken Treaties: An Indian Declaration of Independence* (1974), *God Is Red: A Native View of Religion* (1994) and a variety of works on history, theology and contemporary Indian life. He taught at the University of Arizona from 1978 to 1990, and then at the University of Colorado at Boulder. He retired in 2000 but continued to write and lecture until his death in 2005.

Madeleine Dion Stout is a Cree speaker who was born and raised on the Kehewin First Nation in Alberta. Trained as a nurse, she has addressed aboriginal issues through such roles as president of the

Aboriginal Nurses Association of Canada. She was a member of the influential National Forum on Health and founding director of the Centre for Aboriginal Culture and Education at Carleton University. She spent twenty years with the Medical Services Branch of Health Canada focusing on First Nations and Inuit health. Madeleine is currently vice-chair of the board of the Mental Health Commission of Canada.

James Dumont, whose Anishinaabe name is Onaubinisay (Walks Above the Ground), is Ojibway-Anishinaabe of the Waubezhayshee (Marten) Clan, originally from the Shawanaga First Nation on Eastern Georgian Bay. Since 1974, he has pursued the exploration, participation and learning of the Ojibway-Anishinaabe Midewiwin tradition, achieving fourth-degree Midewiwin the Three Fires Midewiwin Lodge (a contemporary movement of the sacred society), sweat-lodge rites, ceremonial leadership and traditional teacher responsibility. James was "raised up" as Chief at the eastern doorway of the Three Fires Midewiwin Lodge, and as such, is the keeper of the sacred waterdrum and leader in the eastern part of Anishinaabe Midewiwin territory. From 1976 to 2000, he was professor of native studies at the University of Sudbury, teaching courses in tradition and culture, native psychology, native ways of seeing, native education, and issues of indigenous peoples in the international context. He is one of the founders of the department and served for four years as its chair. He retired in 2000 and now teaches in the indigenous master's program with the Seven Generations Institute. In October 2006, he delivered the first lecture, "Indigenous Intelligence," in a series named after J.W.E. Newbery, who started the Native Studies Program at the University of Sudbury.

Nadia Ferrara is a senior policy manager in the Sustainable Development Division at Indian and Northern Affairs Canada.

As a medical anthropologist, she remains on faculty at McGill University, in Montreal, as adjunct professor in the Department of Anthropology. Dr. Ferrara worked for sixteen years as an art therapist, specializing in cross-cultural psychotherapy with aboriginal people in Quebec and Ontario. Her education includes a master of arts in art therapy, a master of science in transcultural psychiatry, and a doctorate in medical anthropology.

Jo-Anne Fiske earned her doctorate in anthropology from the University of British Columbia and is currently dean of graduate studies and professor of women's studies at the University of Lethbridge, Alberta. A commitment to interdisciplinary research led her to take positions in First Nations studies, women's studies and anthropology. Her work lies at the intersection of legal and medical anthropology and addresses questions of policy and social justice.

Joseph P. Gone is a member of the Gros Ventre tribe of Montana, and is associate professor in the Department of Psychology (Clinical Area) and the Program in American Culture (Native American Studies) at the University of Michigan in Ann Arbor. As a cultural psychologist, Joseph engages in his research the key dilemma confronting mental health professionals who serve Native American communities—namely, how to provide culturally appropriate helping services that avoid the neo-colonial subversion of local thought and practice.

Iris HeavyRunner is a member of the Blackfeet Tribe in Browning, Montana. She gained her Ph.D. from the University of Minnesota School of Social Work in April 2005, and serves as co-director of ROSNA (Research Opportunities in Science for Native Americans) at the University of Montana in Missoula. She works primarily with tribal families, tribal colleges and communities regarding the issues of prevention, advocacy and student retention. Previously, she was adjunct professor in social work at the University of Montana and adjunct faculty at Fort Peck Community College. She was a Bush Fellow in Advanced Studies in Child Welfare, a 1996 Department of Education Experienced Faculty Fellow, a 1999 Bush Leadership Fellow, and a training fellow for the National Institute for Native Leadership in Higher Education. Most recently, she was selected as the 2004 Andrew Mellon Faculty Enhancement Fellow by the American Indian College Fund (AICF).

James (Sákéj) Youngblood Henderson was born to the Bear Clan of the Chickasaw Nation and Cheyenne Tribe in Oklahoma. He is now research director, Native Law Centre of Canada, College of Law, University of Saskatchewan. He received a juris doctorate in law from Harvard Law School and became a law professor, creating litigation strategies to restore aboriginal culture, institutions and rights. He has co-authored several books, including *The Road: Indian Tribes and Political Liberty* and *Continuing Poundmaker and Reil's Quest*, as well as many law review articles on aboriginal issues. During the constitutional process in Canada, from 1978 to 1993, he served as a constitutional adviser for the Mi'kmaq Nation and the Assembly of First Nations. His latest books are *Aboriginal Tenure in the Constitution of Canada* (2000) and *Protecting Indigenous Knowledge and Heritage* (2000).

Maggie Hodgson is a member of the Carrier Nation who has worked in the justice arena for sixteen years, and in education and healing for seventeen years. She was the chief lobbyist for the first Healing Our Spirit Worldwide Gathering held in Edmonton, Alberta, in 1992, with 3200 people participating from across the world. She has presented on community healing at many conferences across Canada, the United States, Australia, New Zealand, France, Germany and Norway. She has been a community developer, church and government policy lobbyist, and co-author of four books, and has managed an aboriginal education research and health promotions institute for eighteen years. Maggie has received many awards for her work in community development from various organizations, and has been given honorary doctorates by the University of Alberta and St. Paul's University in Ottawa.

Carol Hopkins, Nozhem ("Mother Wolf") of the Wolf Clan, is from the Delaware First Nation of Moraviantown, Ontario, and has a master's degree in social work. She is the executive director of the National Native Addictions Partnership Foundation, an organization whose mandate is to support Canada's First Nations addictions programs. Carol came to this position from Nimkee NupiGawagan Healing Centre, a youth solvent abuse treatment centre that is founded on indigenous culture and life ways, where she was the founding director for thirteen years. As co-chair of the First Nations Addictions Advisory Panel, she helped develop a renewal framework for the National Native Alcohol and Drug Abuse and the Youth Solvent Abuse programs, and she now co-chairs the leadership team whose mandate is to implement the renewal framework.

John H. Hylton has served as a chief executive, university educator, senior public servant and consultant on many commissions and inquiries, including the Royal Commission on Aboriginal Peoples and the Ipperwash Inquiry. He was the editor of the first two editions of *Aboriginal Self-Government in Canada* (1994, 1999).

Basil H. Johnston is Anishinaabe, born on the Parry Island Indian Reserve in Ontario, and is a member of the Cape Croker First Nation

(Neyaashiinigmiing). Educated in reserve schools at Cape Croker and Spanish, Ontario, he earned a B.A. with honours from Loyola College in Montreal and a secondary-school teaching certificate at the Ontario College of Education. He taught high school in North York, Ontario, from 1962 to 1969, then took a position in the Ethnology Department of the Royal Ontario Museum (ROM) in Toronto. He remained at the ROM until 1994, to initiate a native approach to teaching at the museum, and to record and celebrate Ojibway (Anishinaabe) heritage. He has lectured at a number of universities, including the University of Saskatchewan and Trent University. He has been a highly respected writer, storyteller, language teacher and scholar since his writings were first published in 1970. He has written several books, including *Ojibway Heritage* (1976), *Moose Meat and Wild Rice* (1978), *Ojibway Ceremonies* (1982) and *Indian School Days* (1988), which humorously and heartbreakingly recounts his time as a student at Indian residential school. He also wrote about Ojibwa spirits in *The Manitous* (1995). For his efforts in giving voice to the Ojibway people, he has received the Order of Ontario; honorary doctorates from the University of Toronto, Laurentian University and Brandon University; an Aboriginal Achievement Award for Heritage and Spirituality; and a Lifetime Achievement Award at the 2007 Anskohk Aboriginal Literary Awards.

Angayuqaq Oscar Kawagley was born in Mamterilleq (Bethel), Alaska, and raised by his grandmother from the age of two. Yupiaq was his first language. He earned bachelor's and master's degrees in education at the University of Alaska Fairbanks, then a Ph.D. in social and educational studies at the University of British Columbia. He became a professor of education in the College of Liberal Arts at the University of Alaska Fairbanks, specializing in the integration of indigenous and western knowledge. He wrote on the ethos of assimilation, especially in the boarding schools, and focused on differences between European and Yupiaq world views with regard to ownership of land. Oscar believed that the two world views would merge when global societies evolved from consumerism and materialism and became oriented toward conservation and regeneration. He was the author of *A Yupiaq Worldview: A Pathway to Ecology and Spirit* (1995). Oscar died in 2011 at the age of seventy-six.

Fred Kelly is from the Ojibways of Onigaming, Ontario, and is a citizen of the Anishinaabe Nation in Treaty Number Three. He is a member of Midewiwin, the sacred law and medicine society of the Anishinaabe. He is a custodian of sacred law and has been called upon to conduct ceremonies across Canada and in the United States, Mexico, Japan, Argentina and Israel. He is head of Nimishomis-Nokomis Healing Group Inc., a consortium of spiritual healers and Elders that provides therapy to victims of the trauma and the horrific legacy of the residential school system. Fred is a survivor of St. Mary's Residential School in Kenora, Ontario, and St. Paul's High School in Lebret, Saskatchewan. He was a member of the Assembly of First Nations team that negotiated the historic Indian Residential Schools Settlement Agreement and continues to advise on its implementation. He has served as Chief of his own community, Grand Chief of the Anishinaabe Nation in Treaty Number Three, and Ontario regional director of Indian and Northern Affairs Canada. Fred is fluent in the Anishinaabe and English languages and is a personal adviser to numerous First Nation leaders.

Laurence J. Kirmayer is a psychiatrist and the James McGill Professor and director, Division of Social and Transcultural Psychiatry, Department of Psychiatry, McGill University; director of the Culture and Mental Health Research Unit, Institute of Community and Family Psychiatry, Sir Mortimer B. Davis Jewish General Hospital, Montreal; and editor-in-chief of the scholarly journal *Transcultural Psychiatry*. The author of numerous scholarly articles and co-editor of several books, he has done clinical work and field research on many indigenous issues, including studies of the Inuit of Nunavik (northern Quebec).

Phil Lane Jr. is a member of the Yankton Dakota and Chickasaw tribes and is a traditionally recognized hereditary Chief. He has worked with indigenous people in North, Central and South America, Micronesia, Thailand, India, Hawaii and Africa. He served sixteen years as associate professor, founder and coordinator of the Four Worlds Development Project at the University of Lethbridge, Alberta. His film credits include the National Public Television series *Images of Indians, Walking with Grandfather, The Honor of All: The Story of Alkali Lake* and *Healing the Hurts*. He was the first North or South American person to receive the Year 2000 Award from the Foundation for Freedom and Human Rights in Berne, Switzerland (previous winners include the Dalai Lama of Tibet; Dr. Boutros Boutros-Ghali, former secretary-general of the United Nations; and British Lord Yehudi Menuhin, musician and philosopher).

Phil Lane Sr. was born to a long lineage of hereditary Chiefs and spiritual leaders of the White Swan Band of the Yankton Sioux Tribe on the Standing Rock Sioux Reservation. In 1982 he was a founding member of the Four Worlds International Elders Council. While earning a bachelor of science in forestry at Oregon State University, he began boxing, and collected over 250 amateur and professional fights over eighteen years. He worked designing fish ladders and vertical locks on the Columbia River dams, for which he earned two Presidential Citations from Lyndon B. Johnson. In

1969, he and his son Phil established the first Native American prison group in North America at Washington State Penitentiary, for which he received the Governor's Distinguished Volunteer Award and the State of Washington Certificate of Appreciation. He also received the Baha'i Human Rights Award and the Eli S. Parker Award from the American Indian Science and Engineering Society. Phil died in March of 2004.

Leroy Little Bear is a member of the Small Robes Band of the Blood Indian Tribe of the Blackfoot Confederacy. He received his B.A. from the University of Lethbridge, Alberta, and his juris doctor degree from the College of Law, University of Utah. He was a professor of Native American studies at the University of Lethbridge from 1975 to 1996, and in 1998 became the director of the Harvard University Native American Program. He has served in a legal and consultant capacity to many aboriginal tribes and organizations, including the Blood Tribe, Indian Association of Alberta, and the Assembly of First Nations of Canada. His research interests include the study and comparison of indigenous and western sciences as pathways to knowledge. Leroy was also a member of Alberta's Task Force on the Criminal Justice System and Its Impact on the Indian and Metis People of Alberta, better known as the Cawsey Commission.

Leona Makokis is a member of Kehewin Cree Nation and president of the Blue Quills First Nations College in St. Paul, Alberta, a post-secondary education institution owned and operated by the people of seven First Nations in northeast Alberta. She received a master's degree in educational leadership from San Diego State University and a doctoral degree from the University of San Diego, earning both degrees while working full time as president of the Blue Quills First Nations College, where she continues to teach.

She has received several awards for her commitment to advancing indigenous education.

Stan McKay, a member of the Fisher River Cree Nation in Manitoba, is a spiritual leader, teacher and activist. In 1971 he was ordained by the United Church, and from 1992 to 1994, he served as its first aboriginal moderator. Stan is the recipient of numerous awards, including a National Aboriginal Achievement Award, and he has honorary doctorates conferred by the University of Waterloo, the University of Winnipeg and United Theological College of McGill University. He was director of the Dr. Jessie Saulteaux Resource Centre in Beausejour, Manitoba, a theological school that respects both Christian and aboriginal spiritual traditions. Along with fellow members of the National Native Council of the United Church, Stan successfully advocated for the church's apology, issued in 1986, for its role in the cultural oppression of First Nations peoples.

Herman Michell is originally from the small fishing and trapping community of Kinoosao in northern Saskatchewan. He is an associate professor at First Nations University of Canada and its vice-president of academics. He speaks fluent Cree ("th" dialect) and also has Inuit, Dene and Swedish ancestry. His Ph.D. in education from the University of Regina focused on the inclusion of Cree culture in science education. He has published widely and travelled internationally (South Africa, Netherlands, England, South America, West Indies and Barbados).

William J. Mussell is a member of the Skwah First Nation and is of Stō:lo heritage. He has been chair of the Native Mental Health Association of Canada since 1993. In 2004, he was named one of the leaders in mental health by the Canadian Alliance of Mental Illness and Mental Health, and he is chair of the First Nations, Inuit, and Métis Advisory Committee of the Mental Health Commission of Canada. He is the principal educator and manager of the Sal'i'shan Institute, a private, post-secondary institute founded in 1988 that specializes in First Nations programming. Bill has served on the executive of the North American Indian Brotherhood, and he was among the pioneers of band governance and aboriginal justice matters. Since 1980, most of his professional work has focused on First Nations and aboriginal issues and aspirations in the fields of education, social development and mental health.

Joann Sebastian Morris is from the Sault Ste. Marie Tribe of Chippewa Indians on her father's side and the Cayuga Nation of the Six Nations of the Grand River Reserve of Canada on her mother's side. She holds a master's degree in anthropology from the University of California–Los Angeles (UCLA). She served for several years as the director of the Office of Indian Education Programs of the Bureau of Indian Affairs, U.S. Department of the Interior.

James B. Waldram is a medical anthropologist and a professor in the Department of Psychology at the University of Saskatchewan. His research program focuses on the anthropology of therapeutic intervention, and he has worked in both Canada and Belize. His books include *The Way of the Pipe: Aboriginal Spirituality and Symbolic Healing in Canadian Prisons* (1997), *Revenge of the Windigo: The Construction of the Mind and Mental Health of North American Aboriginal Peoples* (2004).

Cynthia C. Wesley-Esquimaux is a member of the Chippewa of Georgina Island First Nation in Lake Simcoe, and was an assistant professor of aboriginal studies and a member of the Faculty of Social

Work at the University of Toronto. She is also an advisory member of the Mental Health Commission of Canada, and holder of the Nexen Chair for Aboriginal Leadership out of the Banff Centre. In 2013 she took an appointment as the vice-provost for Aboriginal Initiatives at Lakehead University in Thunder Bay, Ontario.

Maria Yellow Horse Brave Heart is Hunkpapa, Oglala Lakota, and is currently associate professor of social work at Columbia University School of Social Work. She received her Ph.D. in clinical social work from Smith College. Previously, she was a faculty member at the University of Denver Graduate School of Social Work, where she served as the coordinator of Native People's Curriculum Project. Dr. Brave Heart developed historical-trauma and historical-unresolved-grief theory. Her interventions for Native Americans have become internationally recognized. In 1992, she founded the Takini Network, a nonprofit organization devoted to community healing from intergenerational massive group trauma among native peoples. Dr. Brave Heart published *Historical Trauma and Unresolved Grief Intervention* and directed the conference Models for Healing Indigenous Survivors of Historical Trauma: A Multicultural Dialogue Among Allies from 2001 to 2004. She also served on the board of directors for the Council on Social Work Education and as a consultant to the National Indian Country Child Trauma Center.

Notes

Chapter 3: Moving into Right Relations

1. Jennie Leading Cloud, quoted in *American Indian Myths and Legends*, ed. R. Ordoe and A. Ortiz (New York: Pantheon Books, 1984), 5.
2. Joe Couture, *A Metaphoric Mind: Selected Writings of Joe Couture*, ed. Ruth Couture and Virginia McGowan (Edmonton, AB: AU Press, 2013), 229.
3. Marlene Brant Castellano, "A Holistic Approach to Reconciliation: Insights from Research of the Aboriginal Healing Foundation," in *From Truth to Reconciliation: Transforming the Legacy of Residential Schools*, ed. Marlene Brant Castellano, Linda Archibald and Mike DeGagne (Ottawa: Aboriginal Healing Foundation, 2008), 387.
4. Carol Hopkins and James Dumont, "Cultural Healing Practice within National Native Alcohol and Drug Abuse Program/Youth Solvent Addiction Program Services" (discussion paper prepared for the Mental Health and Addictions Division, Community Programs Directorate, First Nations and Inuit Health Branch, Health Canada, February 2010), 10.
5. Ibid., 12.
6. Betty Bastien, *Blackfoot Ways of Knowing: The Worldview of the Siksikaitsitapi* (Calgary, AB: University of Calgary Press, 2004), 80.
7. James (Sákéj) Youngblood Henderson, *First Nations Conceptual Frameworks and Applied Models on Ethics, Privacy, and Consent in Health Research and Information* (Native Law Centre of Canada with the First Nations Centre at the National Aboriginal Health Organization, March 2006), 5.
8. Vine Deloria Jr., *The Metaphysics of Modern Existence* (San Francisco: Harper & Row, 1979), 2.
9. James Dumont, "Indigenous Intelligence" (inaugural J.W.E Newbery Lecture, University of Sudbury, ON, October 18, 2006), 5–9.

10. Laurence J. Kirmayer, "Psychotherapy and the Cultural Concept of the Person," *Journal of Transcultural Psychiatry* (June 2007): 235.

11. Leroy Little Bear, *Naturalizing Indigenous Knowledge: A Synthesis Paper* (Saskatoon, SK: University of Saskatchewan, Aboriginal Education Research Centre, and Calgary, AB: First Nations and Adult Higher Education Consortium, 2009), 22.

12. Bastien, *Blackfoot Ways of Knowing*, 132.

13. Angayuqaq Oscar Kawagley, *A Yupiaq Worldview: A Pathway to Ecology and Spirit* (Prospect Heights, IL: Waveland Press, 1995), 14.

14. Leona Makokis, "Our Language Guides Us in Our Relationships" (unpublished manuscript), cited in Little Bear, *Naturalizing Indigenous Knowledge*, 9.

15. Couture, *A Metaphoric Mind*, 10.

16. Jo-Anne Fiske, "Making the Intangible Manifest: Healing Practices of the *Qul-Aun* Trauma Program (*Tsow tun Le Lum*)," in *Aboriginal Healing in Canada: Studies in Therapeutic Meaning and Practice*, Aboriginal Healing Foundation Research Series, ed. James B. Waldram (Ottawa: Aboriginal Healing Foundation, 2008), 47.

17. Rupert Ross, *Returning to the Teachings* (Toronto: Penguin Canada, 2006), 126–127.

18. Little Bear, *Naturalizing Indigenous Knowledge*, 8.

19. Marie Battiste and James Sa'kej Youngblood Henderson, "Naturalizing Indigenous Knowledge in Education: A Synthesis Paper" (unpublished manuscript, 2008).

20. Naomi Adelson, *Being Alive Well: Health and the Politics of Cree Well-Being* (Toronto: University of Toronto Press, 2000), 29.

21. Herman Michell, Yvonne Vizina, Camie Augustus and Jason Sawyer, *Learning Indigenous Science from Place: Research Study Examining Indigenous-Based Science Perspectives in Saskatchewan First Nations and Métis Community Contexts* (Saskatoon: University of Saskatchewan, Aboriginal Education Research Centre, November 2008), 27.

22. Gregory A. Cajete, *Native Science: Natural Laws of Interdependence* (Santa Fe, NM: Clear Light, 2000), 183.

23. Virginia Morell, "The Unexpected Canyon," *National Geographic*, January 2006, http://ngm.nationalgeographic.com/ngm/0601/feature3/.

24. Deborah Chansonneuve, *Reclaiming Connections: Understanding Residential School Trauma Among Aboriginal People* (Ottawa: Aboriginal Healing Foundation, 2005), 44.

25. Judie Bopp, Michael Bopp, Lee Brown and Phil Lane Jr., *The Sacred Tree: Reflections on Native American Spirituality* (Lethbridge, AB: Four Worlds Development Press, 1984), 42–43.

26. James B. Waldram, Rob Innes, Marusia Kaweski and Calvin Redman, "Building A Nation: Healing in an Urban Context," in Waldram, *Aboriginal Healing in Canada*, 222.

27. Quoted in J. Brown, *The Spiritual Legacy of the American Indian* (New York: Crossroads, 1988), 35.

28. Chansonneuve, *Reclaiming Connections*, 24.

29. Charlie Fisher, "Anishinabe People: Indian Bands and the Treaty#3/ Ontario Trapping Agreement: A Path to Success" (unpublished manuscript, 1996).

30. Basil H. Johnston, foreword to *Dancing with a Ghost: Exploring Aboriginal Reality*, by Rupert Ross (Toronto: Penguin Canada, 1992), xiii.

31. Iris HeavyRunner and Joann Sebastian Morris, "Traditional Native Culture and Resilience," *University of Minnesota Research/Practice Newsletter* 5, no. 1 (1997): 1.

32. Mary Lee, "Tipi Ceremony," Four Directions Teachings.com audio narrative, 2006–2012, http://www.fourdirectionsteachings.com.

33. Bastien, *Blackfoot Ways of Knowing*, 48.

34. Kawagley, *A Yupiaq Worldview*, 23.

35. Little Bear, *Naturalizing Indigenous Knowledge*, 7.

36. Couture, *Metaphoric Mind*, 8.

Chapter 4: The Many Sources of Harm

1. Library and Archives Canada, Harold Daly fonds, C-006513.

2. Cynthia C. Wesley-Esquimaux and Magdalena Smolewski, *Historic Trauma and Aboriginal Healing*, Aboriginal Healing Foundation Research Series (Ottawa: Aboriginal Healing Foundation, 2004), 45–46.

3. Ibid., 77.

4. Ibid., 47.

5. Janice Acoose, *Iskwewak: Neither Indian Princesses Nor Easy Squaws* (Toronto: Women's Press, 1995), 47.

6. Joseph P. Gone, "The Pisimweyapiy Counselling Centre: Paving the Red Road to Wellness in Northern Manitoba," in Waldram, *Aboriginal Healing in Canada*, 147.

7. Kristiann Allen, "Negotiating Health: Meanings of Building a Healthy Community in Igloolik," in *The Mental Health of Indigenous Peoples*, ed. Laurence J. Kirmayer, Mary Ellen Macdonald and Gregory M. Brass (Montreal: Division of Social and Transcultural Psychiatry, McGill University, 2001), 71.

Chapter 5: The Residential School System

1. John H. Hylton, Murray Bird, Nicole Eddy, Heather Sinclair and Heather Stenerson, *Aboriginal Sexual Offending in Canada*, Aboriginal Healing Foundation Research Series (Ottawa: Aboriginal Healing Foundation, 2002, 2006), 15.

2. J. Leslie and R. Maguire, eds., *The Historical Development of the Indian Act*, 2nd ed. (Ottawa: Treaties and Historical Research Centre, Indian Affairs and Northern Development, 1978), 115.

3. Rosemary Barnes and Nina Josefowitz, "First Nations Residential School Experience: Factors Related to Stress and Resilience" (unpublished paper presented to the Convention of the Canadian Psychological Association, St. John's, NF, June 2004).

4. Quoted in Linda Jaine, ed., *Residential Schools: The Stolen Years* (Saskatoon, SK: University Extension Press, 1993), 8–9.

5. Waldram, "Building A Nation," 212.

6. Fred Kelly, "Confessions of a Born Again Pagan," in Castellano, Archibald and DeGagne, *From Truth to Reconciliation*, 24.

7. Gone, "Pisimweyapiy Counselling Centre," 142.

8. Maggie Hodgson, "Reconciliation: A Spiritual Process," in Castellano, Archibald and DeGagne, *From Truth to Reconciliation*, 366.

9. Acoose, *Iskwewak*, 25.

10. Quoted in David King, "The History of the Federal Residential Schools for the Inuit Located in Chesterfield Inlet, Yellowknife, Inuvik and Churchill" (unpublished master's thesis, Trent University, 1998), 236.

11. Madeleine Dion Stout and Gregory Kipling, *Aboriginal People, Resilience and the Residential School Legacy*, Aboriginal Healing Foundation Research Series (Ottawa: Aboriginal Healing Foundation, 2003), 40.

12. Quoted in Lee Brown, "Making the Classroom a Healthy Place: The Development of Affective Competency in Aboriginal Pedagogy" (unpublished Ph.D. thesis, University of British Columbia, 2004).

13. Chansonneuve, *Reclaiming Connections*, 11.

14. Raymond R. Corrado and Irwin M. Cohen, *Mental Health Profiles for a Sample of British Columbia's Aboriginal Survivors of the Canadian Residential School System*, Aboriginal Healing Foundation Research Series (Ottawa: Aboriginal Healing Foundation, 2003).

15. John Amagoalik, "Reconciliation or Conciliation? An Inuit Perspective," in Castellano, Archibald and DeGagne, *From Truth to Reconciliation*, 93–94.

16. Waldram, *Aboriginal Healing in Canada*, 212.

17. Wesley-Esquimaux and Smolewski, *Historic Trauma and Aboriginal Healing*, 41.

18. Erica-Irene Daes, "The Experience of Colonization Around the World," prologue to *Reclaiming Indigenous Voice and Vision*, ed. Marie Battiste (Vancouver: UBC Press, 2009), 7.

19. Dion Stout and Kipling, *Aboriginal People, Resilience*, 40.

20. Kelly, "Confessions of a Born Again Pagan," 24.

21. King, "History of the Federal Residential Schools," 225.

22. Janice Acoose, "Deconstructing Five Generations of White, Christian, Patriarchal Rule," in Jaine, *Residential Schools*, 5.

23. Gwen Reimer, Amy Bombay, Lena Ellsworth, Sara Fryer and Tricia Logan, *The Indian Residential Schools Settlement Agreement's Common Experience Payment and Healing: A Qualitative Study Exploring Impacts on Recipients*, Aboriginal Healing Foundation Research Series (Ottawa: Aboriginal Healing Foundation, 2010).

24. Fiske, "Making the Intangible Manifest," 46.

25. Dion Stout and Kipling, *Aboriginal People, Resilience*, 44.

26. Gone, "Pisimweyapiy Counselling Centre," 142.

Chapter 6: Exploring the Psychological Damage

1. Gone, "Pisimweyapiy Counselling Centre," 143.
2. Ibid., 188.
3. Ibid., 144.
4. Acoose, *Iskwewak*, 27.
5. Garnet Angeconeb with Kateri Akiwenzie-Damm, "Speaking My Truth: The Journey to Reconciliation," in Castellano, Archibald and DeGagne, *From Truth to Reconciliation*, 307.
6. Rachel E. Goldsmith and Jennifer J. Freyd, "Effects of Emotional Abuse in Family and Work Environments: Awareness for Emotional Abuse," *Journal of Emotional Abuse* 5, no. 1 (2005): 100.
7. Quoted in Jaine, *Residential Schools*, 124.
8. Corrado and Cohen, *Mental Health Profiles*, 12.
9. Stan McKay, "Expanding the Dialogue on Truth and Reconciliation: In a Good Way," in Castellano, Archibald and DeGagne, *From Truth to Reconciliation*, 111.
10. Judith Herman, *Trauma and Recovery: The Aftermath of Violence— from Domestic Abuse to Political Terror* (New York: Basic Books, 1992), 52.
11. William J. Mussell, "Decolonizing Education: A Building Block for Reconciliation," in Castellano, Archibald and DeGagne, *From Truth to Reconciliation*, 329.
12. Wesley-Esquimaux and Smolewski, *Historic Trauma and Aboriginal Healing*, 66.
13. Herman, *Trauma and Recovery*, 119.
14. Ibid., 52.
15. Gone, "Pisimweyapiy Counselling Centre," 189.
16. Herman, *Trauma and Recovery*, 242.
17. Ibid., 77.
18. Dion Stout and Kipling, *Aboriginal People, Resilience*, 30–31.
19. Herman, *Trauma and Recovery*, 115.
20. Lori Haskell and Melanie Randall, "Disrupted Attachment: A Social Context Complex Trauma Framework and the Lives of Aboriginal Peoples in Canada," *Journal of Aboriginal Health* (November 2009): 60.
21. Castellano, "A Holistic Approach to Reconciliation," 390.

22. Wesley-Esquimaux and Smolewski, *Historic Trauma and Aboriginal Healing*, 1.

23. Cynthia C. Wesley-Esquimaux, "Inside Looking Out, Outside Looking In," *First Peoples Child and Family Review* 3, no. 4 (2007): 68.

24. Maria Yellow Horse Brave Heart, "From Intergenerational Trauma to Intergenerational Healing," *Wellbriety! White Bison's Online Magazine*, May 2005, http://www.whitebison.org/magazine/2005/volume6/wellbriety!vol6no6.pdf.

25. Jason Winters, Robert J.W. Clift and Donald G. Dutton, "An Exploratory Study of Emotional Intelligence and Domestic Abuse," *Journal of Family Violence* 19, no. 5 (October 2004).

26. Brown, "Making the Classroom a Healthy Place."

27. Kimberley L. Shipman and Janice Zeman, "Socialization of Children's Emotion Regulation in Mother–Child Dyads," *Development of Psychopathology* 13, no. 2 (2001): 318.

28. Goldsmith and Freyd, "Effects of Emotional Abuse," 100.

29. Chansonneuve, *Reclaiming Connections*, 45.

30. Paul A. Frewen, Claire Pain, David J.A. Dozois and Ruth A. Lanius, "Alexithymia in PTSD: Psychometric and FMRI Studies," *Annals of the New York Academy of Sciences* 1071 (2006): 398.

31. Dion Stout and Kipling, *Aboriginal People, Resilience*, 42.

32. Waldram et al., "Building A Nation," 212.

33. Chansonneuve, *Reclaiming Connections*, 16.

34. Donald L. Nathanson, interview by Gilbert Levin, 1995, *Behaviour OnLine*, http://www.tomkins.org/pressroom/conversation.aspx (URL no longer active).

35. Haskell and Randall, "Disrupted Attachment," 80.

36. Gone, "Pisimweyapiy Counselling Centre," 188.

37. Wesley-Esquimaux and Smolewski, *Historic Trauma and Aboriginal Healing*, 36.

38. Haskell and Randall, "Disrupted Attachment," 79.

39. Gone, "Pisimweyapiy Counselling Centre," 190.

40. Aldo Santin, Bruce Owen and Nick Martin, "Drugs Dealing Violence, Death" *Winnipeg Free Press*, January 22, 2013, A3.

41. Haskell and Randall, "Disrupted Attachment," 78.

42. Gone, "Pisimweyapiy Counselling Centre," 189.
43. Dion Stout and Kipling, *Aboriginal People, Resilience*, 32.
44. Brown, *Making the Classroom a Healthy Place*.

Chapter 7: Going Home

1. Dion Stout and Kipling, *Aboriginal People, Resilience*, 33.
2. Corrado and Cohen, *Mental Health Profiles*, 11–12.
3. Barnes and Josefowitz, "First Nations Residential School Experience," 21.
4. Mussell, "Decolonizing Education," 49.
5. Dion Stout and Kipling, *Aboriginal People, Resilience*, 33.
6. Fiske, "Making the Intangible Manifest," 45.
7. Ibid., 46.
8. Ibid.
9. Maria Yellow Horse Brave Heart, "*Oyate Ptayela*: Rebuilding the Lakota Nation Through Addressing Historical Trauma Among Lakota Parents," *Journal of Human Behavior in the Social Environment* 2, no. 1–2 (1999): 112.
10. Jaine, *Residential Schools*, 31–32.
11. Wesley-Esquimaux and Smolewski, *Historic Trauma and Aboriginal Healing*, 51.

Chapter 8: Continuing Disconnection

1. Laurence J. Kirmayer, Gregory M. Brass, Tara Holton, Ken Paul, Cori Simpson and Caroline Tait, *Suicide Among Aboriginal People in Canada*, Aboriginal Healing Foundation Research Series (Ottawa: Aboriginal Healing Foundation, 2007), 73.
2. John Coates, Mel Gray and Tiani Hetherington, "An 'Ecospiritual' Perspective: Finally, a Place for Indigenous Approaches," *British Journal of Social Work* 36 (2006): 2.
3. Corrado and Cohen, *Mental Health Profiles*, ii.
4. Carol LaPrairie, *Dimensions of Aboriginal Over-Representation in Correctional Institutions and Implications for Crime Prevention* (Ottawa: Solicitor General of Canada, 1992).

Chapter 9: How to Begin

1. Lee Brown, "Making the Classroom a Healthy Place."
2. Gone, "Pisimweyapiy Counselling Centre," 151.
3. Gone, "Pisimweyapiy Counselling Centre," 150.

Chapter 10: Three Healing Programs

1. Suniya S. Luthar and Nancy E. Suchman, "Relational Psychotherapy Mothers' Group: A Developmentally Informed Intervention for At-Risk Mothers," *Development and Psychopathology* 12, no. 2 (2000), 237, 238, 247.
2. Assembly of First Nations, National Native Addictions Partnership Foundation, and Health Canada, *Honouring Our Strengths: A Renewed Framework to Address Substance Use Issues Among First Nations People in Canada* (Ottawa: Ministry of Health, 2011).
3. Dumont, "Indigenous Intelligence."
4. Hopkins and Dumont, "Cultural Healing Practice."
5. Hopkins and Dumont, "Cultural Healing Practice," 50.
6. Ibid., 11.
7. Assembly of First Nations, National Native Addictions Partnership Foundation, and Health Canada, *Honouring Our Strengths*, 7–8.
8. Hopkins and Dumont, "Cultural Healing Practice," 20.
9. Gone, "Pisimweyapiy Counselling Centre," 185.
10. Peggy Shaughnessy, Laura M. Wood and James D.A. Parker, "Promoting Emotional Intelligence: Intervention Program for Use with Aboriginal Peoples," Emotion and Health Research Library, Trent University Research Report Series, no. 27, n.d.
11. Ibid., 4.
12. Peggy Shaughnessy, RedPath information package (unpublished), produced by Whitepath Consulting, n.d. See www.whitepath consultinginc.com/brochures/Living_Without_Violence_Final.pdf.
13. Christopher Fletcher and Aaron Denham, "Moving Towards Healing: A Nunavut Case Study," in Waldram, *Aboriginal Healing in Canada*, 101–102.
14. Waldram et al., "Building A Nation," 233.
15. Kirmayer, Brass and Tait, "The Mental Health of Aboriginal Peoples," 103.

16. Phil Lane Jr., Michael Bopp, Judie Bopp and Julian Norris, *Mapping the Healing Journey: The Final Report of a First Nation Research Project on Healing in Canadian Aboriginal Communities* (Ottawa: Aboriginal Corrections Policy Unit, Solicitor General of Canada, 2002), 49.

17. Kirmayer, Brass and Tait, "The Mental Health of Aboriginal Peoples," 102.

Chapter 11: Aboriginal Healing: Twelve Striking Differences

1. Waldram et al., "Building A Nation," 240.
2. Herman, *Trauma and Recovery*, 134.
3. Kirmayer, "Psychotherapy," 232.
4. Couture, *Metaphoric Mind*, 229.
5. Goldsmith and Freyd, "Effects of Emotional Abuse," 117.
6. Fletcher and Denham, "Moving Towards Healing," 109.
7. Herman, *Trauma and Recovery*, 134–135.
8. Gone, "Pisimweyapiy Counselling Centre," 193.
9. Herman, *Trauma and Recovery*, 138.
10. Brown, "Making the Classroom a Healthy Place."
11. Fletcher and Denham, "Moving Towards Healing," 104.
12. Mussell, "Decolonizing Education," 336.
13. Brown, "Making the Classroom a Healthy Place."
14. Daniel Goleman, narrator, *Destructive Emotions: How Can We Overcome Them? A Scientific Dialogue with the Dalai Lama* (New York: Bantam Books, 2003), 75.
15. Herman, *Trauma and Recovery*, 136.
16. Terry L. Mitchell and Dawn T. Maracle, "Healing the Generations: Post-Traumatic Stress and the Health Status of Aboriginal Populations in Canada," *Journal of Aboriginal Health* (March 2005): 19.
17. Gone, "Pisimweyapiy Counselling Centre," 190.
18. Ibid.
19. Ibid., 150.
20. Brown, "Making the Classroom a Healthy Place."
21. Gone, "Pisimweyapiy Counselling Centre," 164.
22. Brown, "Making the Classroom a Healthy Place."
23. Waldram et al., "Building A Nation," 227.
24. Couture, *Metaphoric Mind*, 215.
25. Gone, "Pisimweyapiy Counselling Centre," 161.

26. Waldram et al., "Building A Nation," 241.
27. Herman, *Trauma and Recovery*, 133.
28. Gone, "Pisimweyapiy Counselling Centre," 179.
29. Fletcher and Denham, "Moving Towards Healing," 99.
30. Waldram et al., "Building A Nation," 239.
31. Gone, "Pisimweyapiy Counselling Centre," 172.
32. Goleman, *Destructive Emotions*, 153.
33. Gone, "Pisimweyapiy Counselling Centre," 182.
34. Waldram et al., "Building A Nation," 225.
35. Rod McCormick, "All My Relations," in *Mentally Healthy Communities: Aboriginal Perspectives,* ed. Canadian Institute for Health Information (Ottawa: CIHI, 2009), 1.
36. Nadia Ferrara, "The Role of Pictorial Representations in the Assessment of Psychological Mindedness: A Cross-Cultural Perspective" (unpublished master's thesis, Department of Psychiatry, McGill University, 1996), 9.
37. Chansonneuve, *Reclaiming Connections*, 37–38.
38. Fletcher and Denham, "Moving Towards Healing," 122.
39. Herman Michell, "*Nîhîthawâk Ithîniwak, Nîhîthawâtîsîwin* and Science Education: An Exploratory Narrative Study Examining Indigenous-Based Science Education in K–12 Classrooms from the Perspectives of Teachers in Woodlands Cree Community Contexts" (unpublished Ph.D. dissertation, University of Regina, 2007), 17.
40. Fletcher and Denham, "Moving Towards Healing," 123.
41. Fiske, "Making the Intangible Manifest," 63.
42. Ibid.
43. Ibid., 59.
44. Ibid., 58.
45. Ibid., 59.
46. Gregory Brass, "Transformations of Identity and Community Healing of the Aboriginal Offender: Identity Construction Through Therapeutic Practice," in Kirmayer, Macdonald and Brass, *Mental Health of Indigenous Peoples*, 117.
47. Gone, "Pisimweyapiy Counselling Centre," 170.
48. Ibid.
49. Naomi Adelson, "Towards a Recuperation of Souls and Bodies: Community Healing and the Complex Interplay of Faith and

History," in Kirmayer, Macdonald and Brass, *Mental Health of Indigenous Peoples*, 125.

50. Waldram et al., "Building A Nation," 253.
51. HeavyRunner and Morris, "Traditional Native Culture," 2.
52. Fletcher and Denham, "Moving Towards Healing," 101.
53. Lane et al., *Mapping the Healing Journey*, 28.
54. Fiske, "Making the Intangible Manifest," 89.

Acknowledgments

From the aboriginal community, I have had the good fortune to learn so much from the patience, wisdom and humour of the following people: Charlie Fisher, who first got me started on cultural differences; Clare Brant and Marlene Brant Castellano; Basil Johnston; Maggie Hodgson; Leroy Little Bear and Amethyst First Rider; Sákéj Henderson and Marie Battiste; Albert and Murdena Marshall and Alex Denny, from Eskasoni; Joe Couture; Angayuqaq Oscar Kawagley; Dan Moonhawk Alford; Burma Bushie, Valdie Seymour and Marcel Hardisty from Hollow Water; Alex Skead; Cathy and Mide Migwun Bird; Tobasonikwut Kinew; Lee Brown; Carol Hopkins; Cynthia Wesley-Esquimaux; Madeleine Dion Stout; William J. Mussell; Walter and Marie Linklater; Rod McCormick; John Borrows; Ed Buller; Ed Connors; Gaye Hanson; Renee Linklater; Rose Sones; Louise SkyDancer Halfe; Leanne Douglas and Christine Douglas of Rama; Eber Hampton; Peggy Shaughnessy—and all the Grandmothers who appeared beside me at just the right time.

From the legal community, I want to acknowledge the support and help of the following people: Richard Cummine, who was Crown Attorney in the Kenora office and so thoroughly supported my exploration of indigenous cultures that he quietly covered for me in court for over twenty years; Don Avison, who invited me to join the Aboriginal Justice Directorate for three years from 1992 to 1995 and inspired many wonderful adventures; Trevor Jukes, assistant Crown Attorney in Thunder Bay, who was a driving force behind Ontario's aboriginal justice summer school program for Crown Attorneys, and remains a friend and confidant; Barry Stuart and Heino Lilles, former judges from the Yukon; Murray Sinclair of the Manitoba Justice Inquiry and the Truth and Reconciliation Commission, along with co-commissioner Marie Wilson; and long-time friend and former inspector Jim Potts.

From the non-aboriginal medical community: Laurence Kirmayer; Lori Haskell; Nadia Ferrara; Marlene Levene; Rosemary Barnes; Hugo Foss; and my long-time guide through "compassion fatigue," Lawrence Ellerby.

Just writing down their names has brought back so many wonderful times together!

About the Cover Artist

All three of my books now have cover art created by Randy Charboneau, a man who remains special to me.

A friend arranged our first meeting at a restaurant in Toronto. He just told me to be on the lookout for a strong aboriginal man with long black hair and two shopping bags. When I saw him come into the restaurant, I called to him. He came over, put down his bags, shook my hand and said something like, "I have wanted to meet you for years." He proceeded to tell me some of his story, explaining that he had been in and out of prison ever since he was a young teenager. "In fact," he said, "I think I'm the only man who has ever assaulted the warden of Kingston Pen." He was wearing a long-sleeved T-shirt, and I saw that both arms were heavily tattooed. He reached into one shopping bag and pulled out a collection of photographs of himself, most of them taken in jail or prison, and I found myself looking at one of the scariest, most dead-eyed men I'd ever seen. "Then," he explained, "I picked up your first book in the pen library—and it changed my life." He couldn't explain why, except that it got him interested in who he was as an *aboriginal* person. From that point on, he read everything he could about his culture, and it began to grow inside him. Eager to express how he felt about that reconnection, he taught himself to paint, using many Anishinaabe Creation stories as his material. He then opened his second shopping bag and showed me an album of photos of his paintings; I thought they were absolutely splendid, and not only because they came from a man who was finding himself. When he was finally released from prison, he continued painting aboriginal themes, and he created a large wall mural at a jail for young people. We joked about going on tour across Canada, me with my books and him with his paintings. We decided we would call our tour "The Con and the Crown" and use it to talk about what traditional Teachings meant to each of us at our very different stations in life.

Shortly after that first meeting, when Penguin decided to reissue both of my books with new covers, I asked him if he had any paintings that might work. He immediately dashed home and began to work, later presenting us with two paintings, both of which we used.

I am sad to report that, several years later, Randy took his own life. I have no idea if there was a particular cause, or whether he was simply carrying too many burdens from his earlier life. I just hope he has found both peace and a continuance of the joy that I saw in him during that first encounter.

We have found another of Randy's paintings to use as the cover for this book. If anyone can identify who now owns it, Penguin would be happy to compensate them appropriately. I hope Randy is glad that our relationship continues.

Anecdotal Index